A New View of the Irish Language

Editors: Caoilfhionn Nic Pháidín & Seán Ó Cearnaigh

Cois Life • Dublin • 2008

© The Authors 2008

Published by Cois Life Teoranta

ISBN 978-1-901176-82-7

Cois Life acknowledges the assistance of Bord na Leabhar Gaeilge for its Irish-language publications and the Arts Council for its literary programme.

This publication is not grant-aided.

Cover design: Alan Keogh

Printer: Betaprint

www.coislife.ie

A NEW VIEW OF THE IRISH LANGUAGE

Contents

LANGUAGE

Foreword

This book is the most substantive, dispassionate overview of the Irish language by practitioners and scholars, in almost forty years. Its twenty essays include contributions on the historical and present-day development of the language itself, its place in society in general and its contemporary literature. Works in English on this topic are few, and can unfortunately veer between the apocryphal and the apocalyptic.

The Irish language is of obvious relevance and specific interest to Irish people, but increasingly, it is also a point of reference for a growing international body of work which addresses language decline and survival globally. While this volume is primarily intended to inform and enlighten readers about the language and its current position at home, the Irish experience in efforts to reverse language decline is of growing relevance internationally. This is not immediately obvious to English speakers, cushioned by a superpower language, but the issue of language decline is increasingly of concern to policy-makers in many European countries.

We adopted the title of *A New View* in honour of the ground-breaking *View of the Irish Language* (1969), a series of twelve Thomas Davis Lectures edited by Brian Ó Cuív. This book became a central reference work for generations of students of both Irish and Irish studies across the globe. An update has been long overdue, and it is timely to present the story of Irish to new generations.

We were encouraged by the overwhelmingly enthusiastic response of contributors to the invitation from Cois Life to participate in this project. We are deeply appreciative of the wholehearted cooperation and dedication of the team in ensuring delivery of all the essays, and speedy resolution of editorial queries, thus enabling the volume to appear on schedule. Contributors were specifically requested to adopt a communicative style and to keep academic references to a minimum. This has been achieved throughout, wherever possible, and the essays are generally both informative and accessible.

This publication is aimed at a broad public: all those who live, have lived, or will live in Ireland, and the worldwide community who speak or learn Irish, or follow its fortunes with interest. Despite its troubled past and its near consignment to extinction over a century ago, Irish has maintained its precarious existence and is ultimately a story of survival, adaptation and hope in an inhospitable environment.

The Irish language is an inclusive expression of identity for a broad spectrum of people. It has been spoken in the Gaeltacht for millenia and by learner bilinguals for over a century. It has been cast away and reclaimed by generations of the Irish diaspora and is now learned increasingly by foreign nationals residing in Ireland and abroad who take an interest in it. It is this broadly based public support that has enabled, and sustained politically, various government initiatives on its behalf since the foundation of the Irish state. Despite the negative experience for many, of a language badly taught on occasion and unsuccessfully learned, surveys consistently show political and social support for maintaining it and developing its use. The goodwill of this largely English-speaking population is essential for its promotion, and this support must be sought and maintained primarily in English.

Official status and state support, although denigrated persistently by both supporters and detractors of the language, as either too little or too much, depending on the perspective, have provided and sustained the basis of revival policy. The vision for the future needs to be grounded in reality and articulated in a clear strategic policy. In this context, it is vitally important that the Irish state resumes the requisite programme of sociolinguistic research and development, as a vacuum has developed in recent years since the abolition of Institiúid Teangeolaíochta Éireann / Irish Linguistics Institute.

The contributors tell the story as it is, a glass both half-empty and half-full. Some cross-cutting themes emerge in the process: the capacity of the language to adapt and re-invent itself; the immense status value of language legislation but the limitations and dangers inherent in a purely rights-based, demand-led agenda; the urgency of formulating and delivering meaningful educational objectives and relevant curricula in Irish from pre-school to fourth-level; and the challenges facing literacy in Irish and consequent implications for a sustainable literature. Irish is continually in transition and translation, rebalancing its relationships on the island, in Europe, and globally.

A redefinition of revival has so far eluded us and is not offered here. Provision of demand-led services only, is however, a limiting strategy. The place of Irish in education in future decades is crucial. This calls for mature debate and an abandonment of the traditional confrontational lines of battle. Pragmatic and creative solutions can be found which will enable future generations to continue to learn Irish in school as of right. Recruitment of new speakers is essential for its survival and this depends on teaching and learning it well in school at both primary and post-primary levels. Without this, its fate could rapidly become that of Latin, post-Vatican Council. Although this prospect is hardly an adequate reason for teaching and learning a language, it may assist us in determining why the majority of Irish people favour it being taught in school, as the debate regarding how and to whom it is taught is played out in the coming decade.

The revival project which inspired the movement for political independence has left us a legacy of unrealisable expectations. Success or failure have never been defined. Painful as it may feel, the future belongs to those who adapt and move on, a capacity which the language itself, if not its followers, has consistently demonstrated. This volume has twenty Irish contributors. All of these speak and write the language fluently and the vast majority use it daily in their professional lives. Approximately a third of the contributors are native speakers who were reared speaking Irish at home. The majority acquired the language in school as part of the general curriculum on offer, and have clearly benefited from this experience.

The future of Irish is uncertain. It requires us to look in many directions at once, but never backwards or inwards. Raising the ghetto walls, in the Gaeltacht or elsewhere, is no solution. The new compass must include points both real and virtual, from geographical communities to cyber-based networks, from the Aran Islands classroom to the google-user of *focal.ie* inside the Arctic Circle. Looking 'west', however, must remain a source of inspiration and linguistic renewal for speakers of Irish looking in, while preserving and developing a living west is an urgent necessity for maintaining Irish-speaking communities in the heartland. Catastrophic predictions of the demise of the Gaeltacht must be converted from negative energy into inspiration and action. Looking north, the language must develop across the political spectrum, and this vitality sustained in future decades against the threat of waning enthusiasm.

Looking east to the European Union brings major opportunities and responsibilities in terms of status and employment and in ensuring the commitment of the Irish government to provision of linguistic infrastructure for delivery of services. The international context is hugely significant in providing frameworks for management and progress. As English increasingly encroaches as the language of delivery in higher education right across Europe, particularly in postgraduate studies, research and publications, many other languages in the EU will soon face to varying degrees the challenges currently confronting Irish. With over a century of experience of regeneration, there is immense value in applying the expertise garnered in Irish to other more newly threatened languages. Thus Irish-language models can make new and valuable academic contributions internationally.

A crucial new ingredient is the relationship which may or may not develop between the Irish language and the immigrant population in Ireland, several of whom have embraced it with unprecedented enthusiasm. The only major feature ever run by the *Evening Herald* on a Cois Life publication was a prominent feature in the *Polski Herald* on the quadrilingual collection of proverbs – *500 Seanfhocal, Proverbs, Refranes, Przysłów* (2007). As if Irish can only feature in the *Herald* via translation into Polish! However convoluted these permutations may appear, they are positive manifestations which contrast sharply with the traditional grinding decimation of the language through centuries of emigration.

The Irish language is entering a phase of unprecedented challenge and change. The results may be as startling as those which occurred at other historical watersheds like the Flight of the Earls or the revival movement of the late nineteenth and early twentieth centuries. The catastrophists among us may well see it as the end of everything, just as their bardic forebears did four hundred years ago. Hopefully the metamorphosis will herald yet another new beginning, and a future for a language not yet lost in translation.

Is mian linn buíochas ó chroí a ghabháil le gach duine a chuidigh go fial leis an tionscadal seo.

Caoilfhionn Nic Pháidín
Seán Ó Cearnaigh
Feabhra 2008

Contributors

BREANDÁN DELAP

Programme Editor with Nuacht RTÉ TG4. Founding editor of the Irish-language weekly, *Foinse,* in 1996 where he remained until 2003. Was named 'Journalist of the Year' in the ESB National Media Awards in 2003 for investigation of sexual assaults in summer colleges over a forty-year period. His documentary, *Mad Dog Coll,* won an IFTA award in 2000, and he won first prize for print journalism in the Oireachtas competitions 1998. His latest book about the Irish-language media, *Ar an Taifead* (2007), has also won an Oireachtas award.

AIDAN DOYLE

A graduate of the National University of Ireland. Spent many years lecturing in Poland on the Irish language and linguistics before returning to Ireland in 2002. Currently a lecturer in the Department of Modern Irish, University College Cork. Main academic interest is the grammatical structure of modern Irish, particularly its morpho-syntax. Has also published on language contact, historical linguistics, and derivational morphology. His two latest books are *Covert and overt pronominals in Irish* (2002), and, co-edited with Siobhán Ní Laoire, *Aistí ar an Nua-Ghaeilge in ómós do Bhreandán Ó Buachalla* (2006).

JOHN HARRIS

Senior Lecturer in Psycholinguistics in the Centre for Language and Communications Studies and Director of Research in the School of Linguistics, Speech and Communication Sciences in Trinity College Dublin. Has carried out many national studies of the teaching and learning of Irish and modern European languages. Recently edited a special double issue of the *International Journal of Bilingual Education and Bilingualism* devoted to the Irish language North and South.

SEOSAMH MAC DONNACHA

Academic Co-ordinator of Acadamh na hOllscolaíochta Gaeilge, National University of Ireland, Galway. Has published widely on issues relating to language planning in the Gaeltacht, among them the baseline language survey of Gaeltacht schools: *Staid Reatha na Scoileanna Gaeltachta* (2005). Co-authored the 'Comprehensive Linguistic Study of the Use of Irish in the Gaeltacht', published by the Department of Community, Rural and Gaeltacht Affairs (2007).

DÓNALL MAC GIOLLA EASPAIG

Born in Inishowen, Co. Donegal. Educated at St. Columb's College, Derry, and University College, Dublin, where he attained a BA in Celtic Studies and MA in Early and Medieval Irish. Currently Chief Placenames Officer in the Placenames Branch, where he has worked since 1972, and Secretary of An Coimisiún Logainmneacha. Has been Ireland's Representative on the United Nations Group of Experts on Geographical Names since 1998 and has served on that body as both Rapporteur and Convenor of its Working Group on Pronunciation.

LIAM MAC MATHÚNA

Read Celtic Studies at University College Dublin and studied historical linguistics at Innsbruck University. Taught Celtic languages at Uppsala University before lecturing in Irish at St Patrick's College, Drumcondra, where he was Registrar 1995-2006. Currently Professor and Head of the School of Irish, Celtic Studies, Irish Folklore and Linguistics in University College Dublin. Has published widely on vocabulary and literature of Early and Modern Irish. A study of Irish/English code-mixing from 1600 to 1900, *Béarla sa Ghaeilge*, was published by An Clóchomhar (2008).

CIARÁN MAC MURCHAIDH

Senior Lecturer in the Department of Irish at St Patrick's College, Drumcondra. Has published widely on aspects of Irish language and literature. Recent publications include: *Who Needs Irish?: Reflections on the Importance of the Irish Language Today* (2004), *Lón Anama: Poems for Prayer from the Irish Tradition* (2005) and his grammar of the Irish language, *Cruinnscríobh na Gaeilge* (2002) is now in its 3rd edition (2006).

MÁIRÍN NIC EOIN

Head of the Irish Department in St. Patrick's College, Drumcondra, in Dublin. Has published widely on various aspects of literarure in Irish. Her latest book is *Trén bhFearann Breac: An Díláithriú Cultúir agus Nualitríocht na Gaeilge* (2005).

ANNA NÍ GHALLACHAIR

A native speaker of Irish and English. Director of the Language Centre, National University of Ireland, Maynooth. Has taught English at the universities of Bordeaux and Rennes, and Irish and English at the university of Brest. Has also taught Irish, French and German at third level in Ireland. Former president of the Irish Association for Applied Linguistics (2004-2007). Sits on a number of committees dealing with issues around multilingualism, and is a member of Comhairle Raidió na Gaeltachta.

Brian Ó Conchubhair

Assistant Professor in the Department of Irish Language and Literature and a Fellow of the Keough-Naughton Institute for Irish Studies at the University of Notre Dame. Has published essay articles on various aspects of nineteenth- and twentieth-century Irish literature and culture. Currently completing a monograph on the Irish language and the European Fin de Siècle, he previously edited *Gearrscéalta Ár Linne* (2006).

Conchúr Ó Giollagáin

Director of the Language Planning Unit in Acadamh na hOllscolaíochta Gaeilge, National University of Ireland, Galway. Co-author with colleagues in the Acadamh and in the National Institute for Regional and Spatial Analysis, NUI Maynooth, of the *Comprehensive Linguistic Study of the Use of Irish in the Gaeltacht* (2007), commissioned by the government.

Ruairí Ó hUiginn

Born in Dublin and attended Coláiste Mhuire. Completed BA and MA at the National University of Ireland, Dublin. Conferred with PhD in Queen's University, Belfast in 1989. Has lectured in Celtic departments in Uppsala, Galway and Belfast and was appointed Professor of Modern Irish in the National University of Ireland, Maynooth, in 1993. Has published extensively on the Irish language and literature.

Pádraig Ó Laighin

Research Associate at the Social Science Research Centre, University College Dublin. Was Professor of Sociology and Head of the Social Science Department at Vanier College, Montréal, before returning to Ireland in 1996. Played a leading role in the campaign to have Irish designated an official language of the EU, and is now monitoring the implementation of that status. Holds an MA in Psychology from McGill University, and a PhD in Sociology from UCD.

Lillis Ó Laoire

A native of Gort a' Choirce, Co. Donegal. Teaches courses in Irish Folklore and related areas in the School of Irish, National University of Ireland, Galway. Has published a major study of songs and singing on Tory Island and is also a widely travelled performer and teacher of Gaelic song. Currently co-researching the song repertoire of the late Joe Heaney with Professor Sean Williams of Evergreen State College, Washington.

Liam Ó Muirthile

Liam Ó Muirthile is a poet and writer. His latest collection is *Sanas* (Cois Life, 2007). Member of Aosdána.

PÁDRAIG Ó RIAGÁIN

Associate Professor of Sociology of Language at Trinity College Dublin. Previously Research Professor at Institiúid Teangeolaíochta Éireann. Has directed numerous sociolinguistic surveys at national, regional and local levels over the past forty years and has published research reports and papers on topics arising from this research.

AIDAN PUNCH

Born Cork City. Educated Coláiste Chríost Rí, UCC and UCD. Career civil servant who joined the Central Statistics Office as a Statistician in 1972. Worked in price statistics, national accounts and population statistics. Currently Director of Census. Secretary to National Statistics Board on its foundation in 1986. Chair of European Population Committee 2002 and 2003. President of Statistical and Social Inquiry Society of Ireland 2004-2007.

SUZANNE ROMAINE

Merton Professor of English Language at the University of Oxford since 1984. Research interests lie primarily in historical linguistics and sociolinguistics, especially in global patterns of linguistic diversity, language change, language acquisition, and language contact. Has conducted extensive fieldwork in the UK, Papua New Guinea and Hawai'i. Her most recent book, *Vanishing Voices: The Extinction of the World's Languages* (co-authored with Daniel Nettle), won the British Association of Applied Linguistics Prize for best book in 2001. Further details: http://users.ox.ac.uk/~romaine

GEARÓID Ó TUATHAIGH

Professor of History in the National University of Ireland, Galway. Has spent periods as Visiting Professor in North American universities and in Britain. His published work deals mainly with the history of Ireland and Britain in the nineteenth and twentieth centuries and with the cultural history of this period. His work on Irish Studies exhibits a strong inter-disciplinary approach.

IARFHLAITH WATSON

Lecturer in sociology at University College Dublin. His publications include *Broadcasting in Irish*, Four Courts Press (2003). In recent years he has been President of the Sociological Association of Ireland, a visiting scholar at the Sociology Institute in Freiburg University, Germany and a member of the Board of the International Visual Sociology Association.

The Irish Language

Ruairí Ó hUiginn

Irish is normally referred to as a Celtic language. While the term 'Celtic' has a wide variety of ill-defined meanings in the modern world, its use in a linguistic sense is more precise. Here it refers to a group of languages that have close affinity with each other through their descent from a common parent language. 'Celtic' in this strictly linguistic sense was brought to prominence by the scientist and linguist Edward Lhuyd, in his *Archaeologica Britannica* (1707).

All living languages change in space and time. The variety of English spoken, say, in Belfast differs from that spoken in Dublin which in turn differs from that spoken in Cork, and from that spoken in Limerick, in Galway, in different regions of Britain and elsewhere in the Anglophone world. Even within these areas sub-dialects of English can be distinguished, dialects that sometimes are determined by social class. While the mass-media and to a degree education, have served nowadays to weaken regional accents among many speakers, in general the greater the distance between areas, the greater the differences are likely to be between the dialects spoken in each area.

Just as languages change from place to place, so also do they change from age to age. Varieties of English spoken by teenagers of today will differ slightly from that spoken by their parents. Their parents' speech in turn is slightly different from that of the preceding generation. The further we go back in time the more pronounced these differences become. The writings of Shakespeare, for instance, contain very many words and phrases not now in common usage. Earlier works, such as Chaucer's *Canterbury Tales* can be read only with some difficulty by modern readers unfamiliar with earlier forms of the language, and by the time we consider a work such as *Beowulf*, written all of 1,300 years ago, we are confronted with a form of English that is quite unintelligible to all but scholars of Old English.

Changes that affect the sound system or the forms of words in living languages do not normally occur in a haphazard way but are governed by certain laws. On this basis historical linguists are able to trace not only the changes that have taken place within English but can show that English itself belongs to a larger family of languages to which German, Dutch and the Scandinavian languages also belong. These all derive from a prehistoric parent language we call Proto-Germanic. As with all other languages, Germanic changed and evolved, splitting into dialects which in turn became the early forerunners of English, German, Dutch and the other languages of the Germanic group.

We can observe the same process in the case of Latin, the language of the Roman Empire which extended throughout most of Western Europe. In the course of time, however, the Latin spoken in various parts of the empire began to change and diverge from each other. Such divergences may initially have been slight, but in the course of time they became more marked. Different dialects of Latin arose and as these dialects themselves changed and evolved they came to be considered as languages in their own right. Thus Latin evolved into early Italian, French, Spanish, Catalan, Portuguese, Romanian and other Romance languages, and these in turn continued to evolve down to their descendants spoken today. Here we can say that Latin was the parent language from which the Romance group of languages evolved. Even if we had no knowledge of Latin, the similarities between these languages is such that we would have to conclude that they descended from a common parent.

IRISH AND CELTIC

This is what confronts us when we consider the Celtic group of languages. 'Celtic' or 'Proto-Celtic' is the term linguists apply to the parent-language from which Irish and its sibling languages evolved; its closest relatives are Scottish Gaelic and Manx, but it is also related to Welsh and Breton. The Cornish language, of which the last native speakers died in the eighteenth century, also belonged to the Celtic group. At an earlier stage we know that Celtic languages were spoken throughout Britain and in much of Western and Central Europe. Unlike Latin, which was a written language, however, speakers of early Celtic dialects did not commit their literature or traditions to writing. Theirs

was an oral culture and it is only when they came into contact with
the civilizations of Greece and Rome that they learned to write. We do
not have a vast body of literature written in the parent language, but
the similarities between the attested Celtic languages are such that we
can safely assume a common ancestor. This language, as all others,
developed and evolved into separate subgroups and in all probability
there were many different Celtic languages spoken throughout Western
and Central Europe most of which have vanished leaving little or no
trace.

On the other hand, if we try to trace the roots of Celtic, we find that it
belonged at an earlier stage to a language we call Proto Indo-European
spoken perhaps as early as 5,000 BC in the Caucuses. Indo-European
is the parent-language not only of Celtic, but also of Germanic, Latin,
Slavic and most European dialect groups as well as several in Asia.

Within Insular Celtic, i.e. the languages spoken in Britain and Ireland,
two principal subgroups are distinguished. These are frequently
referred to as Q-Celtic and P-Celtic. These designations derive from the
fact that the sound represented by Q was retained in the former group
as Q or as C, whereas in the latter it evolved to P. We can compare Irish
ceann 'head', *ceathair* 'four' with Welsh *pen* 'head', *pedwar* 'four'.
While this is but one of many regular sound changes that distinguish
the two main branches of Celtic it has been found to be a convenient
designation and is therefore commonly used.

We do not know when the first speakers of Irish came to Ireland, but
given that we witness a certain amount of expansion by different Celtic-
speaking tribes in Europe in the millennium before Christ, it has been
postulated that the first speakers of Celtic language came to Ireland
around 500 BC although some place their arrival earlier than that. These
were certainly not the first inhabitants of the island, for the evidence of
archaeology indicates human settlement in Ireland for many millennia
prior to that. What happened to the people or peoples who were here
prior to this point or to the language(s) they spoke is unclear. There
does not appear to be any evidence of a significant invasion so it is
assumed that the country was taken over gradually by Celtic-speaking
people. These may have arrived as separate tribes at different periods
and may have come directly from the continent or through Britain.
The variety of Celtic the first settlers spoke is also a matter of debate,

but there is some evidence that a form of P-Celtic was spoken here in prehistoric times.

Irish history proper begins in the fifth century AD with the arrival of Christianity, Latin and literacy. The introduction of literacy gives us written records. These show Irish to be the language of the country and give no firm evidence of any other indigenous language being spoken here at that time. Rather intriguingly, however, the term the Irish had for their own language, *Góidelg* (mod. Gaeilge) is not in origin an Irish word but is a word borrowed from Welsh.

In its earliest phases writing in Irish is associated with Christianity and with Christian centres of learning. This is borne out by the simple fact that the majority of terms for writing derive from Latin, thus: *scríobh* < *scribere, peann* < *penna, leabhar* < *liber,* etc. While the first records transmitted to us are in Latin, the Latin alphabet was soon adapted for the purposes of writing Irish and from about the late sixth century onwards we have copious written material in the native vernacular. The adaptation of the Latin alphabet for writing Irish involved using a form of Latin then current in Britain from which the first missionaries came. In this orthography the consonants *c, p,* and *t,* when in the middle or end of a word may have the value of *g, b,* and *d* respectively. Changes such as lenition (aspiration) or nasalization (eclipsis) whether at the beginning or the end of a word are not always shown and there are other differences that would appear strange to those familiar only with the orthography of the modern language. Thus Modern Irish *cogadh* 'war, battle' is written *cocad* in the orthography of Old Irish, Mod. Ir. *codladh* 'sleep' as *cotlud, póg* 'kiss' as *póc, éad* 'envy' as *ét,* etc. In the course of time the orthography developed so that these and other changes are clearly shown. Orthographical uniformity, however, is rather a modern phenomenon. Throughout the ages the Irish were willing to accept an amount of diversity in various orthographical systems used.

OGHAM

There is one other system of writing to which we should refer. This is the Ogham script found on some 400 stone inscriptions both in Ireland and in Britain. Although many theories have been offered on its origin and function, it is clear that it too is a system that is ultimately based on Latin. Ogham inscriptions bear personal names in the genitive case and were written through cutting a series of notches on the corners of standing stones. The stones evidently commemorated or marked the graves of important people. The presence of such stones in Britain is due to the fact that the Irish had a number of colonies in Britain in the early part of the Christian era. Of these the most prominent was that of Dál Riada established in Scotland in the fourth century by settlers from what is now County Antrim. These settlers were responsible for bringing the Irish or Gaelic language to Scotland where it has endured down to the present day. The Manx language of which the last native speaker died in 1974 is a form of Gaelic introduced to the Isle of Man from Scotland. On the other hand, the colonies established in Wales, where most of the British Ogham stones occur, were to die out.

Although Ogham is based on the Latin script, the form of Irish found in the inscriptions is extremely archaic. It reflects a stage of the language in which many major changes had not yet taken place. Thus names that have two syllables in early Irish may frequently have three or four syllables in Ogham, the sound represented by *f* appears as *v*, and so on. Early Irish *Conaill* (genitive) appears on Ogham inscriptions as *Cunovali*, *Fergusa* (gen. of *Fergus*) as *Verguso*, while *Eoghain* (gen. of Eoghan) appears as *Ivageni*. It is likely that Ogham was retained for a period as a archaic prestige language for use in monumental inscriptions. We might compare the use of the Latin language in inscriptions down to comparatively recent times.

HISTORICAL PERIODS

As is customary with any language that has a long written tradition, Irish is divided into different periods. Thus we distinguish the Old Irish period, extending roughly from 600-900 AD, the Middle Irish period from 900-1200, the Early Modern Irish period from 1200-1650, and the Modern Period from then down to the present day. The latter period can be divided between postclassical Irish (c.1650-1880), and the Irish of the revival period from c.1880 onwards. These are rough approximations and they do not carry with them the assumption that change was uniform or took place simultaneously throughout the country.

Not surprisingly, nearly all of the extensive material we have from the first three periods, and much from the Modern Irish period, is found in manuscript form. For the Old Irish period, however, almost all of our evidence is found not in Ireland, but resides in a number of libraries in continental Europe in the form of glosses and other material written on the margins of Latin manuscripts. These glosses consist mainly of explanatory notes or translations which Irish clergymen of the eighth and ninth centuries wrote on the various religious, grammatical and other works they were required to read. They were subsequently taken to Europe with the wave of Irish missioners who established and worked in the numerous Irish monastic foundations on the continent during this period. As time passed, the Irish influence and presence waned but the manuscripts were kept in their new homes and remained unused until the valuable linguistic evidence they provided was mined by Celtic scholars in the nineteenth century. The importance of such material is that it is contemporary with the manuscripts in which it is found. On the basis of these sources scholars have been able to write extensive grammatical descriptions of Old Irish. Manuscripts that remained in Ireland, on the other hand, were widely used throughout the ages and, when worn, were copied and discarded. Thus while our oldest surviving Irish manuscripts, compilations such as *Leabhar na hUidhre* or *The Book of Leinster*, are no earlier than the twelfth century they contain material copied from earlier manuscripts now lost. This we can tell by comparing the form of Irish in which they are written with the Irish of the eighth or ninth centuries as seen in the Old Irish glosses. Many of the tales of the Ulster Cycle, for instance, can be dated to the eighth or ninth centuries on this basis. Our extensive corpus of Early Irish law tracts can similarly be dated to this period or perhaps a little earlier, even though the earliest copies we have may be found in manuscripts as late as the sixteenth or seventeenth centuries.

Old Irish is a language of some complexity, both in its morphology and syntax. It is highly inflected, all persons of the verb have two sets of endings and compound verbs abound. Thus we have *berid* 'carries', *but ní beir* 'does not carry', *do-beir* 'gives' but *ní tabair* 'does not give', *do-gníu* 'I make' but *ní dénaim* 'I do not make', *ro memaid* 'has broken' but *ní róemid* 'has not broken' and so on. A simple verb may, in certain tenses, have in excess of twenty different forms. Many nouns show inflection in the nominative, vocative, accusative, genitive and dative, both singular and plural. In addition to the masculine and feminine genders, Old Irish also has a neuter gender. Three types of pronoun,

infixed, suffixed and independent are found, the first type having
several different forms. Three degrees of comparison are found in the
adjective, equative, comparative and superlative, and the numerals two,
three and four are inflected for gender and case.

This system is simplified considerably in the Middle Irish period (c.900-
1200). Many verbal endings are lost, original compound verbs tend to
be treated as simple verbs, and independent pronouns take the place
of infixed or suffixed pronouns. In the noun system, the neuter gender
is lost, although its trace remains vestigially in certain set phrases and
in the eclipsis that follows some nouns in place-names, certain case
forms are lost and new plural endings are developed. Inflexion in the
adjective and article is also simplified; certain prepositions converge,
e.g. Old Irish *ar* 'before', *for* 'on' and *iar* 'after', fall together as *ar*.
Very often older and more modern forms may exist side by side in texts
of the Middle Irish period a feature some writers seem to have used to
stylistic effect.

One of the main features of the Early Modern Irish period (c.1200-
1650) is the emergence of a standardized language which was used
by professional poets in their compositions and was taught in their
bardic schools. The rules for this literary dialect, commonly referred
to as Classical Modern Irish, were formulated in the late twelfth or
early thirteenth centuries and were apparently based on spoken as well
as literary forms. Although it allowed a certain amount of variety and
choice, it was a calcified language retained for certain literary purposes
while spoken dialects evolved and diverged. The significant differences
that emerged between different dialects of the language throughout
the Gaelic world are masked by this standard. Not only did Classical
Modern Irish contain many archaic forms and usages that had long
since disappeared from common usage, but its phonological system was
based on a pronunciation of Irish current in the late Middle Irish period.
The sound represented by *dh*, for instance, would have approximated
to the sound of *th* in the English words *father, that* (as pronounced in
England) whereas at an early stage in the spoken language the sound
was either lost or its pronunciation fell together with that of *gh*. The
earlier pronunciation is preserved in place-names such as *Meath*, from
Irish *Midhe*, which was taken into English at a time the medial -*dh*- was
pronounced in the earlier manner.

Not all texts from this period adhere to this strict classical norm. Prose texts show a wide variety of styles, ranging from translations or fresh compositions written in a literary language more archaic than even the classical dialect, to written registers that would have been much closer to the spoken dialects of the authors. Some linguistic features found in these texts have much to tell us about the emergence of the modern dialects, dialect boundaries and other such information.

Up to the end of the Early Modern Irish period, Irish was the language of the vast majority of the people of the island and much of its literature was written under the patronage of an independent aristocracy. The Tudor conquest, effected in the early seventeenth century, changed the circumstances of the language and its literature. Those members of the native aristocracy who had not been killed or gone into exile lived in reduced circumstances and lost much of their land, power and prestige. Plantation introduced English-speaking settlers and English now became the language of administration. The socially ambitious followed this drift and while the number of Irish speakers grew in step with the general increase in the population between the seventeenth and nineteenth centuries, the overall percentage of the national population speaking the language declined. It was fast becoming the language of a social underclass, a position it had reached by the eve of the Great Famine. Despite its reduced circumstances, we have a voluminous body of literature in Irish from this postclassical phase. This is found in many thousand paper manuscripts written mainly, but not exclusively in Munster, and often enjoying the patronage of clerics or of more well-to-do members of the middle classes. In many of these, features that mark the main present-day dialect divisions can be found.

BORROWINGS FROM OTHER LANGUAGES

During its attested history the vocabulary of Irish has been augmented by borrowings from several languages. We have already alluded to the fact that many of our terms for writing derive from Latin as writing was introduced to Ireland from without. In like manner, Latin provided many of the terms to do with religion or the ecclesiastical life and gives us words such as *eaglais* < *ecclesia, sagart* < *sacerdos, teampall* < *templum* and numerous other words are of Latin origin. The Viking incursions and settlement of the ninth and tenth centuries brought Irish into contact with Old Norse. The latter language provided Irish with a small number of terms mainly to do with seafaring, fishing or trade. Words such as *trosc* 'cod', < ON *torskr*, *ábhar* 'oarhole' < ON *hábora*, *stiúir* 'rudder' < ON *styri*, *langa* 'ling' < ON *langa* etc.were introduced to Irish at this time as were certain other words to do with trade.

The Anglo-Norman invasion and settlement brought many words of French origin in its wake. Apart from personal names, the greater part of these borrowings have to do with architecture, administration and warfare. French has given Irish words such as *áirse* 'arch' < AN 'arche', *barántas* 'warrant' < AF *warants*, *caiptín* 'captain' < AN *cap(i)taine*, *garasún* 'garrison' < AN *garisun*, *túr* 'tower' < AN *tur*, *seomra* 'room' < AN *chaumbre* etc.

While we have evidence of English loanwords from an early period, the establishment of a large and growing body of English-speakers in the country since the seventeenth century resulted in a vast increase in such borrowings. Borrowings from Latin, Old Norse and French were centred mainly on certain material, administrative, religious or cultural concepts or objects that were introduced by settlers. The nature of contact between Irish and English was such, however, that vast numbers of words to do with all aspects of life were borrowed from English, a process that has increased with the growth of bilingualism in all Gaeltacht areas. Borrowings, however, have not been all one-way. Some English words of Irish origin are galore < Ir. *go leor*, twig (to understand) < Ir. *tuig*, jilt < Ir. *diúltaím* 'I refuse', bother < Ir *bodhraim* 'I deafen' or *buaidhrim* 'I vex' and American slew < Ir. *slua* 'crowd'.

Dialects of English spoken in Ireland, moreover, often show words, features of pronunciation or structures that have been taken over from Irish. Most of our place-names and our personal and surnames derive from Irish, reminding us that the replacement of Irish through English in many parts of the country is a relatively recent phenomenon.

On the eve of the Great Famine there were probably more native speakers of Irish than at any time in the history of the language. By that stage, however, Irish had become largely the language of a social underclass and this class itself looked to progress through the adoption of English. The process was hastened by the Famine and its catastrophic consequences, and Irish has continued to decline as a community language in Gaeltacht areas despite great achievements being made elsewhere, particularly in the spheres of education, literature and the mass-media. Such achievments have ensured that in one form or another this central part of our heritage, and indeed of that of Europe, will continue to endure into what hopefully will be for it a brighter future.

Irish in the Global Context

Suzanne Romaine

INTRODUCTION

Anyone writing about Irish inevitably treads on fairly well-trodden and much contested terrain. Navigating a judicious path through a minefield of often starkly polarized opinion without losing one's balance is not easy. Not surprisingly perhaps, much of the discussion from without and within Ireland has focused on the status of Irish in the Republic of Ireland (and more recently, Northern Ireland) rather than on the language in a global context (see, however, McCloskey 2001, 2007). While the larger scene may seem bright, particularly since January 2007 when Irish became the twenty-third official language of the European Union, the home front is cloudy at best, if not gloomy at worst. I use 'home' here deliberately in an ambiguous sense to refer not just to the position of Irish in Ireland, but to its place or lack thereof in Irish homes. In view of the fact that most Irish people no longer habitually speak Irish in their everyday lives and have not done so for centuries, Ellis and mac a' Ghobhainn (1971: 143) implore us to 'remove our gaze from the terrible failure of Ireland'.

The titles of Hindley (1990), Carnie (1996), and many other works sound a similarly sombre note, in effect pronouncing the language nearly dead, and the revival movement a failure. Hindley (1990: 149-150) concludes that it is 'now incontestably apparent that the revival of Irish based on abstract ideas such as national identity, culture, tradition, and heritage divorced as they are from the forces of everyday reality for ordinary people has finally failed'. His blunt statement minces no words: 'There is no room for honest doubt that the Irish language is now dying.' If Hindley's obituary is in any sense 'qualified', as his subtitle suggests, it is to wonder 'whether the generation of children now in a handful of schools in Conamara, Cloch Chionnaola and Gaoth Dobhair, and Corca Dhuibhne are the last generation of first-language native speakers or whether there will be one more' (Hindley 1990:

248). Likewise, Carnie's prognosis is that Irish is well on its way to death and may not survive more than a generation or two. This image of Irish in its death throes goes back at least more than two centuries to Charlotte Brooke's *Irish Reliques* (1776). The 1871 Census reiterated this imminent death sentence when it opined that 'there can be no error in the belief that within relatively a few years [sic] Irish will have taken its place among the languages that have ceased to exist' (Census of Population 1871, part 3, p. 190). At that time around 20 per cent of the population returned themselves as Irish-speakers.

At the very least, accepting these regularly repeated terminal diagnoses would leave us wondering how a dying language could be declared an official language of the European Union. With 2001 marking two millennia of an Irish-speaking presence on the island, there are many good reasons why a re-assessment of the language in both the larger all-Ireland context of the Republic and Northern Ireland as well as beyond is timely. The late twentieth and early twenty-first centuries represent a time of considerable change in the position of Irish in the North in the wake of the 1998 Good Friday Agreement. Indeed, Harris (2007: 360) believes that Irish has greater vitality there, and has now captured the leadership role. The establishment of Foras na Gaeilge, the new all-Ireland statutory agency responsible for planning and development, will require policy makers to consider the language in a unitary framework. Meanwhile, beyond Ireland, the forces of globalization have made the world quite a different place at the beginning of the twenty-first century. Some of the factors responsible for the decline of Irish are now affecting other languages on a scale hitherto unanticipated. Indeed, we can see what happened to all the Celtic languages as an early example of a process now being played out on a global scale, with English, French, Spanish, and Chinese spreading through swathes of the developing world at the expense of the world's many hundreds of small, largely rural, vernaculars.

Some linguists predict that between 50 per cent and 90 per cent of the world's some 6,900 languages will disappear over the next century (Nettle and Romaine 2000, 2006). With English rapidly becoming the first preferred foreign language study at school in the European Union, and in most other parts of the world, many people are becoming bilingual in English at an increasingly earlier age through schooling.

Even speakers of large languages such as French and German, not to mention those of many small languages such as Dutch, feel that the continued use of their languages in technical domains and in many areas of higher education is threatened by English. In today's global village increasing bilingualism in a metropolitan language, particularly English, is making the majority of the world's languages in effect minority languages.

Unlike Ellis and mac a'Ghobhainn, I think Irish warrants our gaze for what it may tell us of the fate that globalization portends for the survival of the world's linguistic diversity. Much is to be gained for Ireland and the world by examining the Irish experience in a larger perspective. Few, if any, countries have the time depth of sustained experience that Ireland has with respect to what has come to be called reversing language shift. As many communities now look for expertise and guidance on what works and what does not in efforts to preserve languages, eighty some years of Irish language policy and planning, particularly in the domain of education, present unique opportunities for insight into the forces of language maintenance and shift. There have been dramatic losses, but not without some substantial gains. The prognosis on Irish ultimately hinges on what we mean by life, death, revival, restoration, maintenance and survival, and other terms still lacking clear consensus. Much also depends on where we direct our gaze. It is a truism that people looking at the same landscape will see different things. The first page of the Government of Ireland's (2006) *Statement on the Irish language* shows a photo of a young man with his back to us, standing at water's edge looking towards the mountains. An Irish manuscript is emblazoned across the reddish-orange light shining from behind the clouds. Is he looking at the rosy glow of sunrise or the waning twilight rays of sunset?

IRISH BY THE NUMBERS
It has become a cliché that there are many ways one can lie with statistics. Official statistics on Irish provide plenty of fodder for those who wish to have their cake and eat it too. Hope for the hopeful lies in the continuing rise in the proportion of people returning themselves as Irish-speakers in recent censuses after a period of almost continuous decline from 1861 to 1911. The 2006 census reports that 1.6 million of the four million population can speak Irish. This would place current

numbers well above those of the 1861 census, which recorded just over a million speakers. Proportionally speaking, the numbers represent a remarkable upsurge in the percentage of the Irish-speaking population from 24.5 per cent in 1861 to 41.9 per cent in 2006. Within the officially defined Gaeltacht comprising 91,862 persons aged 3 and over, the rate is 70.8 per cent. These proportions suggest an apparent level of recovery approaching a point similar to the last quarter of the eighteenth century when 45 per cent of the population were Irish-speakers.

Likewise, there is despair for the desperate. The 2006 numbers actually represent slight declines over the 2002 figures of 42.8 per cent for the country as a whole, and 72.6 per cent for the Gaeltacht. More telling, however, is the 2002 census finding that nearly half a million of those who said they *could* speak Irish reported that they never *used* it. Another half-million said they used it less than weekly. In 2002 only 339,541 (21.6 per cent) said they used Irish daily (Census 2002: 55, Table 30); of the 62,157 Irish-speakers in the Gaeltacht, 54.3 per cent report using Irish daily (Census 2002: 69, Table 34A). The 2002 figures do not distinguish frequency of use inside and outside education and are therefore not directly comparable to the 2006 figures. A refinement of the question in 2006 reveals that only 3.2 per cent reported using Irish daily outside the education context; in the Gaeltacht, the figure is 27.5 per cent of the 64,265 speakers.

These percentages disguise the fact that more Irish-speakers were alive during the last quarter of the eighteenth century than at any other point in history. In 1841 the population was close to 8 million, of whom some 2.5 million were Irish-speakers. This was a very sizeable minority. Seán de Fréine, one of the few early scholars attempting to situate the collapse of Irish in the context of Europe and the world at large, observed that before the famine, Irish ranked comfortably within the first 100 of the world's 5,000 or so languages in terms of number of speakers. The famine itself, lasting from 1845 to 1849 and impacting Irish-speaking communities more severely than others, killed around one million and led to mass emigration of another 1.5 million. These losses reduced the population by more than half by 1900. The collapse in the monolingual Irish population from 319,602 (4.9 per cent) to 20,953 (0.5 per cent) in 1901 was dramatic. For de Fréine (1978: 47), it constituted 'an event the like of which has not befallen any other

European nation in 1,000 years'. Yet, historians passed over it with the utmost casualness as though language shifts of such magnitude were commonplace occurrences. He ventures that if a shift on the scale of Irish had affected the national languages of Europe, half of them would now be extinct. By his estimate, there were fewer than one million speakers of Norwegian, Finnish, Lithuanian, Latvian, Estonian, and Danish in 1800.

If the pulse of a language lies in the youngest generation, then much worse is the fact that the proportion of Irish-speakers under ten years old had already dwindled to 3.5 per cent in 1891. Indeed, Hindley (1990: 35) contended that the 'true' national figures for use of Irish as the first language of pre-school children could hardly be above 1 per cent. Hindley's (1990: 173, 187) conclusions were based on his attempt to probe beyond what he called 'the snares of statistics' by assessing the number of children between six and twelve years old qualifying for the *deontas* or grant payments made to those judged by inspectors as native, or native speakers of Irish. He estimated that there were 1,473 Gaeltacht children who could generously be counted as Irish-speakers, and beyond that, even in a generously reckoned Gaeltacht population of 36,309 persons 3 years or older, 9,324 at most were effectively Irish-speaking. Thus, of the one million speakers over age 3 in the 1981 census, fewer than 10,000 habitual speakers were living in circumstances likely to enable or facilitate transmission.

Comparison of more recent figures from 2002 and 2006 reveals a continuing fundamental weakness in intergenerational transmission, within and without the Gaeltacht. Irish declines over the life cycle, beginning with 15-19 year olds and continuing through the child-bearing years of adulthood. Moreover, the loss of speakers is twice as great in the Gaeltacht (1.8 per cent) as in the country as a whole (0.9), indicating that the gains made in terms of number of people reporting themselves as Irish-speakers in the census are largely the result of school-based reproduction. The 'school age bulge' starts to be apparent in the 1926 census, the first after the declaration of the free state and introduction of compulsory teaching in Irish, but the proportion of pre-school age children who are returned as Irish-speakers has hardly budged since state intervention. It remains under 5 per cent, and was at the same level in 1991 as it was in 1926 (apart from very slight increases in 1936, 1961 and 1971). In 2002, however, it more than doubled, and continued to increase in 2006. This probably reflects the effects of pre-school immersion in *naíonraí*.

Because questions on Irish were not asked in Northern Ireland following partition in 1921, detailed statistics are lacking until 1991. The last census revealed 75,000 people who can speak, read and write in Irish, with a further 167,000 (10.4 per cent) having some knowledge of Irish. Some effects of the increasing demand for Irish-medium education are also detectable. Since its beginnings in 1971 the movement for Irish-medium schools in Northern Ireland has grown to encompass some 3,700 children in some twenty-five schools, most of them in Belfast. Irish immersion makes a difference at the secondary stage in the 12-15 age-group, and carries over into the next age-group of 16-24.

These statistics reveal a complex picture of competing forces leading to continuing loss of the remaining heartland and to a degree of renewal through school. As Hindley (1990: xvi) noted, Irish is dying at specific places among specific communities, which are hidden in the generalized data reported for the official Gaeltacht. State policies have not reversed the course of the moving frontier that creeps ever westward, and it is arguable whether they have even slowed it. More research is needed in order to assess the relative importance of various factors in supporting or hindering transmission. At this juncture, however, it is relevant to ask on whom the future of the language rests and whether survival without native intergenerational transmission is anything more than a half-life and therefore a failure. Hindley's (1990: xv, 251) view is that Irish as a living language will have expired once there are no longer mothers who speak it naturally at home to their newborn infants. Moreover, he predicts that 'a country which cannot adequately support at home the people who speak its dying language will have grave difficulties in sustaining it into the future (Hindley 1990: 182).

Irish scholars have reached similar conclusions. Ó hEithir, for instance, asserts that 'the death or survival of Irish in the Gaeltacht is now inextricably linked to the advancement of the language in the state as a whole' (cited and translated in Hughes 2001: 111-112). Likewise, Ó Riagáin (1997: 282) contends that survival requires revival because neither the school nor the community can satisfactorily replace the home as an agency of language reproduction at least when the Irish-speaking community is so small. Evaluation of these remarks also invites consideration of Irish in relation to other language communities of similar size and circumstances, but what numbers do we use in assessing the place of Irish in relation to the world's languages?

Irish in the World

Comparing Irish to other languages may also offer hope and despair in equal measure, depending on the yardstick. Scholars such as Hindley (1990) and Ó Riagáin (1997) have compared Irish with other European minority languages such as Basque, Frisian, Catalan, etc. Hindley (1990: 242-243) again contends pessimistically that 'there is not a single example of a restoration to a majority position of a language which lost it in its own well-defined territory'. Nevertheless, Irish is not a typical minority language by any means; nor, despite its status, is it a typical European national language. Ireland is the only European Union member state (apart from Belgium, which is officially trilingual in French, Dutch and German), where the percentage of the population claiming the national and/or official state language as their mother tongue is below 70 per cent (European Commission 2006).

From the outset the Irish state tried to deal with language loss by declaring Irish its national language in the hope of re-establishing it as the language of everyday life. No other European state has attempted to address minority language issues in this way. Instead, Ireland set a course that was to be followed by a number of newly independent nations of the twentieth century such as India, Tanzania and Malaysia, where shifting from the colonizers' language to the local vernacular(s) was seen as fundamental for building a new nation out of a former colony. When assessing Irish in the context of this league of languages of decolonizing nations, it is worth noting that Hindi with its some 200 million speakers, one of the eight largest languages in the world, still has not replaced English as sole official language as the framers of the Indian constitution intended. The plan for Hindi to replace English after fifteen years was unrealistic because it assumed that Hindi could achieve in a few years what English had achieved over the course of a century.

Similarly, in post-independence Tanzania, despite the strides made by Kiswahili in displacing English from most of the high domains it monopolized, the government repeatedly failed in its attempt to replace English in secondary and tertiary education. In 2003 the Malaysian government implemented a policy to switch from Malay to English as the medium of instruction in science and mathematics after having spent four decades putting considerable financial resources into modernizing Malay. While decolonization entailed rejecting colonial languages, globalization intensified and renewed the need for them. As the world's only truly global language, English is paradoxically positioned as both the key to and an obstacle to development.

Ireland's policy has proved similarly unrealistic, all the more so because the government's declaration of Irish as the official language in article 4 of the constitution framed in 1922 was clearly at odds with the actual state of the language as recorded in the 1911 census: only 17.6 per cent of the population in the 26 counties that were to form the Republic were Irish-speakers. Thus, most people had already abandoned Irish long before independence, even in the Gaeltacht area which the government was concerned to develop and maintain. Even the new official Gaeltacht boundaries redrawn in 1957 were overgenerous in their inclusion of many areas in which Irish was little used. When the new government announced its policy on Irish in schools in early 1922, the ultimate objective was to gradually replace English as the medium of instruction. This could not properly be called a restoration because Irish had not previously been the language of schooling. In hindsight it has thus become clear that the extent of the erosion of Irish severely constrained the possibilities of state intervention.

As noted at the outset, the revival of Irish has been widely judged a failure because language planning has not restored intergenerational transmission at home. This assessment is misleading and greatly oversimplified in a number of respects. Over the course of the twentieth century the position of Irish not only in Ireland, but also in Europe and the world at large has continued to undergo dramatic transformations of another kind that have led to the creation of new non-traditional users and new domains of use, largely through state education policies. Such measures have completely transformed the demography and linguistic landscape. Before the seventeenth century, the majority of the population overwhelmingly spoke Irish, and English was dominant only in a small eastern region around Dublin. By 1851, however, Irish was almost absent from the eastern half of the country, and was losing ground among young people everywhere except the far western margins. As Hindley (1990: 139) pointed out, what happens in Dublin and the surrounding area is now critical when it comes to the establishment of a sufficient and sound numerical base for creation and maintenance of Irish-speaking communities outside the Gaeltacht. Dublin is the area showing the greatest increase in Irish-speakers, almost uninterrupted since 1891. Even otherwise pessimistic Hindley (1990: 42) cannot refrain from acknowledging as a great achievement without international parallel the metamorphosis of Irish from the first language of an impoverished and geographically remote population into the modern second language of a privileged urban elite.

Even so, Hindley's and McCloskey's assessment of the uniqueness of Irish must be reconsidered in light of the fact that many languages are already surviving without their customary heartlands that once served as a resource base for transmission. More children are learning Basque, Welsh and other languages through the education system than are learning it at home as a native language. In so far as these new users may fall short of what is required in practical terms to guarantee intergenerational transmission, the main value for many small languages in the future may well be symbolic and cultural rather than practical. That is to say, many will not be widely used, if indeed at all, in everyday communication; they will cease being grounded in continuity of practice, and instead become primary vehicles for the articulation of identity (Romaine 2006).

A more nuanced measure of vitality would rely on indicators other than absolute size, which does not tell the whole story. Nevertheless, Wurm (2001) suggests that languages being learned by fewer than 30 per cent of the younger generation may be at risk. Comparing estimates of number of speakers of a language is problematic, particularly when the available numbers come from different years and contexts, but it is worth trying to place some of the Irish numbers in a larger context. There are huge disparities between the sizes of the populations speaking the world's some 6,900 languages. If all languages were of equal size, each would have about 917,000 speakers. Yet the median number of speakers for the languages of the world is only 5,000 to 6,000, and nearly 85 per cent of languages have fewer than 100,000. Fifty per cent of the population speaks one of the ten largest languages with hundreds of millions of speakers (i.e. Mandarin Chinese, Spanish, English, Hindi, Portuguese, Bengali, Russian, Arabic, Japanese, and German). More than 3,500 of the world's languages are spoken by only 0.2 per cent of the population. The majority of these smaller languages may be at risk (Nettle and Romaine 2000).

Irish is not doing badly in the world at large if we take the 2006 census figure of 1.6 million. By this yardstick, Irish would count as one of 347 languages accounting for 94 per cent of the world's population. In the European context only Maltese (371,900) and Estonian (1.08 million) are smaller than Irish, but Europe is perhaps unique in having within its borders such a large concentration of world languages (5 in the top ten) but only about 3 per cent of the world's languages. Only about 5 per cent of the world's languages have at least one million native speakers.

Nevertheless, to think of Irish as belonging to the big league of world languages with at least a million speakers makes it sound rather safer than would a comparison based on figures assessing the size of actual Irish-speaking communities. If we take the 2006 Census figure of 53,471 (3.2 per cent of the population) as the number of persons over 3 who use Irish daily outside education (Table 32A, p. 80), or the figure of 17,687 (27.5 per cent) of the Gaeltacht population over 3 years of age who use Irish daily outside education (Table 34, p. 83-84), then we should direct our gaze towards languages of a similar size (c.8,000 to 54,000) and status. By this reckoning Irish belongs in a mid-sized group comprising about 25 per cent of the world's languages with 10,000 to 99,000 speakers. This would put Irish on a par with many indigenous languages of the Americas, averaging around 47,000 speakers, including, for instance, Ojibwe (c.55,000) in Canada at the upper end and Lakota (c.8,000-9,000) in the US at the lower end. In Australia, by comparison, the very few 'strongest' Aboriginal languages are much smaller in size.

The proportion of children in Canada with an Aboriginal mother tongue is well below the suggested minimum of 30 per cent mentioned by Wurm (2001). Only about 20 languages are at or above this threshold. A few small languages with fewer than 10,000 speakers (Attikamek, Montagnais, Dene) and the three largest languages (Inuktitut, Ojibway, Cree) emerge as the strongest languages by this measure, with over 70 per cent of children having them as home languages. A few of the much smaller languages such as Chilcotin with fewer than 1,000 speakers also have good intergenerational continuity (Norris and Jantzen 2002).

If we rely on the figure of 27.5 per cent of daily users outside school in the Gaeltacht, then Irish is less like some of the larger languages such as Ojibway and Cree, whose continuity indices are between 70 per cent and 80 per cent, and more like some of the smaller languages such as Nisgha and Tsimshian. If we take the overall 2006 census figure of 3.2 per cent of Irish-speakers who report using the language daily outside school as the basis for comparison, then Irish is similar to some of the smaller languages of the Iroquoian family like Mohawk whose fate is uncertain. It is not entirely clear whether such comparisons are valid or even helpful. Speakers of Aboriginal languages represent a mere drop in the bucket of Canada's population of c.30 million in the 2001 Census, 17.5 million (59.1 per cent) of whom are mother tongue Anglophones, and 6.8 million (22.9 per cent) of whom are mother tongue Francophones. Those with other mother tongues comprise 5.3 million (18 per cent), out of which about 3.9 per cent are speakers of Aboriginal languages (Marmen and Corbeil 2004).

If Irish is demographically on a par with some of both the larger and smaller Aboriginal languages with a weak basis for transmission, the picture is dramatically different when we consider the status dimension. Fewer than 4 per cent of the world's languages have any kind of official status in the countries where they are spoken. A small minority of dominant languages prevail as languages of government and education. English is the dominant de facto or official language in over seventy countries; French has official or co-official status in twenty-nine. Most Aboriginal languages in Canada, the United States and Australia, cannot draw on official support or rely on institutions such as the school to produce new users. Although a few languages have status at the provincial level, the primary objective of Canadian federal language policy since the adoption of the Official Languages Act in 1969 has aimed at linguistic duality between English and French. Originally introduced to moderate Quebec nationalism and avoid the threat of secession, the changes brought about by measures aimed at supporting the Francophone minority have been nothing short of revolutionary. From 2005 the federal government has committed itself to positive measures to fulfill its obligation to promote linguistic duality.

In terms of status and the legal framework guaranteeing it within and
beyond Ireland, few languages rival Irish. Irish is clearly in a league
with a highly select group of world languages, and is more similar
to French in Quebec than to the Aboriginal languages of Canada. No
other Celtic language has official status in the EU because the relevant
populations are constituents of member states, whose national languages
are official languages. The language politics of the European Union
oriented as they are towards national languages which are automatically
accorded special protected status, has propelled some relatively small
languages onto a stage where at least in theory they have equal footing
with truly global languages like French and English, a status they have
nowhere else in the world. This means that relatively small national
languages like Danish with roughly 5 million speakers and Greek are,
in principle, as official community languages on an equal footing.
Outside the European Union and its own borders, Danish has a similar
status only in the Nordic Parliament, and, like Greek, it is not spoken
at international gatherings. By contrast, Catalan with roughly a million
more speakers than Danish, was not admitted as an official language
because the country in which it was officially recognized, Andorra, is
not a member of the European Union. In the member states where it is
spoken, France, Spain and Italy, it does not have official status. Were it
not for Ireland's declaration of Irish as a national and official language, it
would be fully minoritized.

The government of Ireland's most recent policy initiatives seem
to be following the Canadian example in its passing of legislation
such as the Official Languages Act of 2003, and its appointment of
a Language Commissioner (*An Coimisinéir Teanga*), an independent
official appointed by the President of Ireland and head of the *Oifig
Choimisinéir na dTeangacha Oifigiúla* ('Office of the Commissioner
of Official Languages'). The former, being implemented on a phased
basis, gives people the right to interact with state bodies in Irish and
provides a mechanism for monitoring and advising public bodies on
their responsibilities. It is too early to assess how well this is working
in practice, or what will result from the government's 20-year strategy
designed to promote a bilingual society 'where as many people as
possible use both Irish and English with equal ease' (Government of
Ireland 2006). The repercussions of the decision by the Minister for

Culture, Arts and Leisure in Northern Ireland not to introduce an Irish Language Act in 2007 also remain to be seen.

Likewise, it is also too soon to evaluate the ramifications of elevating Irish in the European Union from its former status as a treaty but not working language to that of full official and working language. This will be governed under a special regime for five years during which only regulations adopted jointly by the European Parliament and the Council of the European Union will be translated into Irish. Meanwhile, however, the renegotiation of the previous somewhat anomalous status of Ireland as the only member state not requiring translation of all community documents into the language its constitution declares as the country's national and co-official language will also eliminate a disadvantage faced by Irish nationals under EU staff recruitment policies requiring knowledge of at least two of the official working languages plus native or first language. Irish nationals were at a disadvantage by comparison with nationals of other member states because they had to have three. The EU's inclusion of Irish also opens up a new avenue for social mobility via Irish within and beyond Ireland due to the need for Irish translators and interpreters. When the new status was implemented, there were virtually no interpreters who could translate from Irish into the other official languages. This will create a market for bilingualism in Irish and languages other than English. Now that the expansion in post-primary education has run its course, continued reliance on schooling as a means of generating competence in Irish has put the language in a very vulnerable position. Creating a market value for young bilingual adults may give it a boost.

THE WORLD IN IRISH

In apparent ignorance of the richness of the world expressed through Irish, historian Arnold Toynbee (1934-1961: 511, 509) implied that Irish was never anything more than a 'peasant patois'. Referring to an 'embarrassing scantiness of material' in ancient Gaelic, he dismissed the revival of Irish as a 'perverse undertaking which has come from the nationalistic craze for distinctiveness and cultural self-sufficiency'. Toynbee's dismissal glosses over the fact that the years which historians have called the 'Dark Ages' were only so in parts of Europe outside Ireland. For Irish, this was a Golden Age in which Ireland was the centre of learning in western Europe and the language expanded and spread to Scotland and the Isle of Man. There were probably more medical works in Irish than in any other European language. The Irish Government's *Statement on the Irish language* (2006: 10) refers to it as the 'oldest spoken literary language in Europe'. After years of disuse, Irish is once again a literary language as well as a language of modern media such as radio, television and the internet. By contrast, the rich conceptual worlds residing in the oral traditions of most of the world's languages are only a generation away from extinction. When their last speakers die, such languages vanish without a trace.

While it is critically important to confront openly and realistically the actual extent of the Irish-speaking communities at the beginning of the twenty-first century, Irish would certainly be a lot worse off without all the work on its behalf. Most threatened languages will not achieve anything like the relative successes of Irish. A sign that once hung in Albert Einstein's office declared that 'not everything that can be counted counts, and not everything that counts can be counted' (Henshaw 2006: 55). The active Irish-language scene probably comprises only 5 to 10 per cent of the island's population, and around one in three people (c.1.8 million) on the island can understand Irish to some extent. This means that the world in Irish will not be lost and the world can indeed still be lived in Irish by those who choose to learn and use it. That is hardly failure.

References

Annual Report 2005-2006. *Official languages in Canada: Taking on the new challenge.* Ottawa. Office of the Commissioner of Official Languages.

Carnie, A. 1996. 'Modern Irish: A case study in language revival failure', in Bobaljik, J.D., R. Pensalfini & L. Storto (eds), *Papers on endangered languages and the maintenance of linguistic diversity. Vol. 28. MIT Working Papers in Linguistics.* Cambridge. Massachusetts Institute of Technology.

Census of Population. 1871. *Ireland.* London. Registrar General/HMSO.

Central Statistics Office. 2007 *Census 2006, Volume 11, Results.* Dublin. Stationery Office.

Central Statistics Office. 2007. *2006 Census.* Dublin. Stationery Office.

Government of Ireland. 2006. *Statement on the Irish language.* Dublin. Government of Ireland.

Ellis, P.B. & Seumas mac a'Ghobhainn. 1971. *The problem of language revival.* Inverness. Club Leabhar.

European Commission. 2006. *Europeans and their languages.* Special Eurobarometer 243.

de Fréine, S. 1978. *The great silence*. 2nd ed. Dublin/Cork. Mercier.

Harris, J. 2007. 'Bilingual education and bilingualism in Ireland North and South' in *The international journal of bilingual education and bilingualism* 10(4): 359-368.

Henshaw, J.M. 2006. *Does measurement measure up? How numbers reveal and conceal the truth*. Baltimore. Johns Hopkins UP.

Hindley, R. 1990. *The death of the Irish language: A qualified obituary*. London. Routledge.

Hughes, A.J. 2001. 'Advancing the language: Irish in the twenty-first century' in *New Hibernia Review* 5(1): 101-126.

McCloskey, J. 2001. *Guthanna in éag: An mairfidh an Ghaeilge beo? / Voices silenced: Has Irish a future?* Baile Átha Cliath. Cois Life.

McCloskey, J. 2007. 'Irish as a world language' in *Why Irish?* Galway/Syracuse. Arlen House/Syracuse UP.

Marmen, L. & J.P. Corbeil. 2004. *New Canadian perspectives. Languages in Canada 2001 Census*. Ottawa. Statistics Canada.

Nettle, D. & S. Romaine. 2000. *Vanishing voices: The extinction of the world's languages*. Oxford. OUP.

Nettle, D. & S. Romaine. 2006. 'Vanishing voices. The plight of the Celtic languages in global context' in Lloyd Jones, M. *First Language*. Llandysul. Gomer Press with the National Library of Wales.

Norris, M.J. & L. Jantzen. 2002. *From generation to generation: Survival and maintenance of Canada's aboriginal languages within families, communities and cities*. Government of Canada. Indian and Northern Affairs. Ottawa. Canadian Heritage.

Ó Riagáin, P. 1997. *Language policy and social reproduction: Ireland 1893-1993. Oxford*. Clarendon Press.

Romaine, S. 2006. 'Planning for the survival of linguistic diversity' in *Language policy* 5(2): 443-475.

Toynbee, A.J. 1934-1961. *Study of history*. Oxford. OUP.

Wurm, S.A. 2001. *Atlas of the world's languages in danger of disappearing*. Paris. UNESCO.

The State and the Irish Language: an Historical Perspective

Gearóid Ó Tuathaigh

The direction and dynamic of Ireland's 'language shift' were already well established by the time of Ireland's incorporation into the British state by the act of union of 1801. While complex factors – attitudinal and institutional – in the many domains of civil society (religious, commercial, political) contributed to the language shift, the post-union state was itself an important agent of change. Its range and penetration extended relentlessly throughout the union era into the various domains of the life of the general population: policing, poor relief (and, later, pensions), public works, agricultural improvement, regional socio-economic development, and, most crucially in terms of the language shift, the state system of elementary education. The combined impact of these seemingly irresistible forces driving the language shift, together with the decimation of the largely Irish-speaking rural underclass by the Famine ravages and by continuous heavy emigration in the following decades, determined that, as census data revealed, approaching the end of the nineteenth century, Irish as a living language seemed doomed to extinction within a relatively short interval. The language revival movement established in the final quarter of the century ensured that this did not happen.

Initially the Society for the Preservation of the Irish Language, and later the more sustained pressure of the expanding Gaelic League, succeeded in eliciting from the state a more permissive response to demands that Irish be given a presence in the state-supported education system. By the late 1870s Irish (called 'Celtic') was accepted as a subject for examinations in secondary school state exams. It was then admitted as an 'extra subject' in primary schools, but with limited impact initially. The Gaelic League maintained pressure. In 1900 Irish was accepted as an 'ordinary' subject, and in 1904 the government's Commissioners of National Education introduced a Bilingual Programme, with a detailed syllabus in Irish and English for each grade of the primary schools, taking account of differences between Irish-speaking districts and others. A further significant decision was that of the new National University of Ireland to make Irish a compulsory subject for matriculation: support from nationalist politicians at county council level for the Gaelic League's demands being crucial in this instance. For a summary of these early developments see Kelly (2002), and Ó Murchú (2001).

Training of teachers involved a series of intensive courses run in special colleges of its own by the League, and, eventually, courses were provided in the six, state-run, Teacher Training Colleges. Progress was made; the state had responded to the Gaelic League's campaigns. By 1922 some Irish was being taught in almost a quarter of all schools in the country. The Gaelic League had restated its objectives in 1900 as: the preservation of Irish as the national language of Ireland, the extension of its use as a spoken tongue, and the publication of the existing Irish literature and the creation of a modern literature in Irish. As Ó Riagáin (1997: 9) has noted, it is clear from its policy statements that the League envisaged a 'satisfactory' bilingual objective, rather than a total reverse language-shift. Furthermore:

> As the campaign (GL) developed, so emerged the basic shape of what was later to become the State language policy – a strong emphasis on education policy, teaching methods, teacher training, developing a standard language and promoting a creative literature, securing the employment of competent Irish-speakers in the public service, and maintaining the Irish-speaking heartland.

Yet, despite the League's successes, notably in the sphere of education, by the early twentieth century Irish was spoken by less than one in five of the population; its heartland was overwhelmingly in the western periphery, its core-base, of agricultural smallholders and fishing families, an economically depressed and vulnerable community, experiencing heavy emigration. The efforts of the revivalists had not arrested the emigration outflow from the enclaves of native speakers or the continuing shift to English within these communities. In fact, the total number of Irish-speakers had fallen by 18 per cent in the period 1890-1926.

With the Partition settlement of 1920-22, two states were established in Ireland. In Northern Ireland the insistence of its unionist majority on asserting the essential Britishness of their heritage resulted in the exclusion of any acknowledgment of the Irish language from the official culture or policies of the Northern state. For a portion of the nationalist minority lodged within Northern Ireland, support for the Irish language (and its use, where possible, in areas of their social life) was important for their sense of ethnic (as distinct from religious) identity, though it was generally viewed by the state as a predictable aspect of a general Catholic stance of cultural dissent. Irish cultural nationalists would find the Northern state a generally inhospitable place for the Irish language for many decades.

On the other hand, the new independent Irish state was determined from the outset to assert the distinctiveness of Irish cultural identity. For a key cohort of the political leadership of the new Free State (in government and among republicans in opposition), the Irish language was the corner-stone of that cultural identity: they had 'been to school' at the Gaelic League. Garvin's claim (1987: 78-106) that the Gaelic League, in effect, created the political elite of independent Ireland, probably exaggerates the extent and intensity of commitment to the language 'revival' across the broad spectrum of 'leadership' within the state apparatus. But, at least the leaders of the main political groupings in the new state accepted that the government of an independent Irish state had an obligation to give official support and recognition to the most irrefutable mark of a distinctive Irish 'nation', on whose behalf an independent state had been claimed and established.

Thus, Irish was given constitutional status (as 'the national language', with official recognition also for English) in the first Irish Free State constitution, and this was repeated and strengthened in the 1937 Constitution, which declared Irish the first official language. The general shape and emphasis of the language policy adopted by the new state is by now a well-rehearsed story: the main elements were, the maintenance of the Irish-speaking community of the Gaeltacht; the promotion/ revival of Irish in the overwhelmingly English-speaking country at large, through the education system; ensuring basic competence in Irish from those working in the public service, and standardizing and modernizing the language itself. In effect, 'despite the well-established dynamic of language assimilation, the small demographic base, and the rural character of Irish language communities ... [the new] 'Irish state did not legislate for a bilingual policy organized on territorial lines...

Irish language policy applied to the state as a whole and not just to a region of it' (Ó Riagáin 1997: 269).

In terms of specific government policies, the state's revivalist commitment was most aggressive in the education system. Irish was made an obligatory subject in the school curriculum (at elementary and second level), with a requirement for teaching subjects through Irish at the lower infant classes that went beyond what the Gaelic League had demanded before 1922, and well beyond what the majority of teachers were then competent to deliver. In-service courses and the establishment of special 'preparatory colleges' at second level in hitherto poorly-served Gaeltacht areas sought to ensure for the teaching profession a supply of fluent Irish-speakers to meet the declared objectives.

In the 1920s and 1930s Irish was made compulsory for passing public examinations (1927/8 for Intermediate Certificate, 1933/4 for Leaving Certificate), and from 1925 for recruitment to general grades of the civil service; a range of incentives were introduced to encourage increased competence in Irish within the apparatus of the state.

From an early date doubts and misgivings were expressed at the 'realism' of the declared objectives, the resource deficits that needed to be overcome, and the danger that an excessive emphasis on Irish (as a subject and as a medium of instruction) might compromise the achievement of other educational objectives, especially at primary level. Such criticisms would become more widespread and insistent over time. But the growth in Irish-medium schools was strong in the first two decades of the new Irish state. By the early 1940s, over 55 per cent of the combined number of primary and secondary schools were using Irish as a medium of teaching, fully or partially, within their curriculum. This was the peak of state-led Irish-medium schooling. By the 1950s it was in decline, and from about 1960 the decline accelerated, as documented by Ó Buachalla (1988: 341-367) and Kelly (2002).

Survey evidence of public attitudes and criticism from teachers and other educationalists (notably from the later 1930s) were to lead to government acknowledgement of disappointing outcomes; which eventually prompted alterations in teaching emphasis – to spoken proficiency – and to some focused research on language teaching in general and Irish in particular. In other areas of state support for the promotion of Irish within the English-speaking wider community (the revivalist objective), one can identify initial signs of progress. Irish forms were favoured in the nomenclature of many state offices, services and public companies, its use became part of the ritual of solemn state occasions, and it was used, even if generally in very limited measure, by many prominent figures in the state (the symbolism of Douglas Hyde as first President under the 1937 constitution should not be ignored). From 1929 the state gave modest support for the promotion of Irish as a medium for university education at University College Galway, subsidised an Irish-language theatre, an Irish presence in the army (again in Galway), established a state-publishing arm, and sought to promote Irish through the state-funded national broadcasting service. The standardization and modernization of the language was supported, even if progress seemed slower than many would have wished: specialist dictionaries of terms from the 1920s were followed by an official standard spelling guide in 1945, a standardized grammar guide in 1953, an official English-Irish dictionary in 1959 and in 1977 an official Irish-English dictionary. The broadcasters and, especially, the translation staff of the Dáil, also contributed to this vital aspect of language modernization. By the 1950s, despite all the shortcomings of the revivalist aspect of state policy since 1922, it may be conceded that 'a substantial cohort of secondary bilinguals, of varying levels of competence, had emerged from the schools, and Irish had achieved a degree of penetration and a presence in public domains in Ireland from which it had been excluded from centuries' (Ó Tuathaigh 2005: 50).

While the fate of the Gaeltacht under native government constitutes the most calamitous failure of state policy, and will be discussed below, progress on the wider revivalist project was already a source of disappointment to language supporters, prompting criticism of state commitment to the cause, even before the state-led revival policy based on 'permeation' of the schools and public service, was abandoned in the 1960s. The substance of this criticism by Irish-speakers of state policy is easy to identify. The constitutional status of Irish had not been elaborated, or clarified, in any legal statement of rights and entitlements, either through judicial activism generating an enabling body of case-law, or, more crucially, through the state itself making legislative provision for these language 'rights' (Ó Máille 1990; Ó Tuathail 2002). The ritual symbolic use of Irish by politicians was frequently so limited that it seemed no more than tokenism, and the degree of real penetration of Irish in the apparatus of the state continued to disappoint. Crucially, the evidence was unmistakable that insisting on 'competence' in Irish for entry to the public service did not guarantee increased use of Irish in the actual services being supplied to the public. The encouraging numbers of secondary bilinguals dispersed throughout the country were not congealing into sustainable Irish-speaking communities. In short, the 'maintenance' objective of state policy on Irish was failing spectacularly in the language's primary habitats, without Irish becoming embedded elsewhere in newly-formed communities of Irish-speakers.

In seeking to understand the relative failure of state policy to achieve its own declared objectives, one must look beyond the blunt charge of hypocrisy and bad faith (though these were not entirely absent). The confessional character of the independent Irish state was a factor: over 90 per cent of the citizens were observing Catholics, with, for historical reasons, a particularly strong sense of religious communal identity. This religious communal identity transcended class; for many Irish Catholics it also eclipsed language as the defining mark of their 'national' identity. This confessional identity (described often as Catholic nationalism) was deeply-rooted: it blunted or resisted the claims for support for the revival of Irish on 'essentialist' identity grounds. Again, given the liberal democratic nature of the Irish state, the force of public opinion was a vital determinant of what any government (or dedicated cohort of ministers) could or could not do, in terms of social and cultural engineering under state direction.

The new state from its inception was generally respectful of existing vested interests in social and economic affairs. It was also (after the end of the civil war) a stable state, with an increasingly assured voice in world affairs. The state, with its symbols and stability, itself conferred a secure sense of 'Irishness' on the bulk of its citizens. Again, the status of 'the English of Ireland' was greatly enhanced by the award of the Nobel prize for literature to Yeats and later Shaw, by Joyce's world impact, and, in popular culture, by John McCormack's stellar status, not least through his repertoire of 'Irish' songs, throughout the Anglophone world. English had become the language of the majority of the Irish diaspora, and of Catholic Ireland's missionary project. Indeed, the very geocultural location of Ireland in the century when English was becoming the dominant world language (a function of the 'reach' of American power in all aspects of global communications), must be recognized as central to any serious contextual appraisal of the Irish state's language policy in the twentieth century.

Yet, allowing for this wider context, there are questions that may be fairly asked regarding the effectiveness of state policy on Irish. A central issue in the extension of competence in any language, through the education system, is the issue of motivation. But motivation for language acquisition is, inter alia, inextricably linked with real prospects for the purposeful use of the language being acquired. The credibility of the state language policy on this precise issue of ensuring opportunities for purposeful use of Irish deserves notice. For many pupils (as for their Irish teachers, or their parents) it must have seemed at times that, in learning Irish, they were being brought up several staircases only to discover that the final landing (i.e. leaving school) had nothing above it or attached to it. Those areas where competence was translated into the obligation or opportunity for regular use, even within the 'domain' of the state's own 'business', were too few, uncertain and sporadic to constitute a 'credible' defence of the emphasis on Irish for state examination or public service employment purposes.

This issue of the 'credibility' of the declared objectives of a policy that placed such emphasis on the acquisition of basic competence in Irish at school, went to the heart of the state apparatus. The legislature conducted only the tiniest portion of its business through Irish; the higher echelons of all branches of the state – civil service, the legal system, local government, security – conducted their business overwhelmingly, if not exclusively, in English, as did the growing number of agencies (state or semi-state companies) established under state auspices for specific, largely developmental, purposes from the 1920s onwards. Indeed, even where these agencies of the state operated in officially designated Gaeltacht areas, it was not guaranteed that they would be capable or obliged to do so through Irish. The corrosive effect of these contradictions – leading to cynicism or charges of hypocrisy, opportunism, tokenism – sapped the language policy of much goodwill, an asset which it could not afford to lose or seriously deplete. This would become increasingly apparent from the 1950s.

But whatever disappointments or frustrations marked changing public attitudes to the 'revivalist' part of the language strategy in the state at large, the failure to maintain a healthy Irish-speaking community in the Gaeltacht was the most obvious and gravest indictment of the declared state language policy. The government-appointed Coimisiún na Gaeltachta in 1926, in addition to providing an estimate of the population of Irish-speakers in the Gaeltacht, made recommendations for, inter alia, state intervention in areas of economic and social (including educational and general infrastructural) improvement, in the interests of maintaining a viable Gaeltacht. The Coimisiún's ideas and recommendations were of their time (with the work of the Congested Districts Board of 1891-1923 very much in mind). Certainly they did not amount to a coherent plan of language-sensitive socio-economic regeneration for the Gaeltacht; nor, perhaps, should we expect such at that time. In the decades following the Coimisiún's report, some of its recommendations were partially implemented by various government departments (often under the sporadic pressure of cohorts of Gaeltacht and Irish-language activists, as in the case of the 'transplanting' of Gaeltacht migrants to Co. Meath during the 1930s). But state action fell far short of what was needed to stem the flow of emigration, or to arrest the language shift to English within the Gaeltacht in the immediate post-independence decades. For further comment see Ó Conghaile (1986); Ó Tuathaigh et al (2000); and Walsh (2004).

From the late 1950s one can identify a decisive shift in the ideological basis of state policy, and rhetoric, in independent Ireland. The socio-economic crisis of the 1950s – with an emigration haemorrhage of over 400,000 souls within that decade – shattered the de Valera vision and rhetoric of national sovereignty with its attendant cultural agenda. An inter-generational shift in leadership was taking place. By the early 1960s the state's principal objectives were being articulated in new terms, strongly focused on economic performance and improved living standards, in the interests of economic growth and population retention. Protectionism of all varieties gave way to 'openness', to cultural no less than economic forces: the application was being prepared for membership of the European 'Common Market', the new setting in which Irish identity would be refurbished and reconfigured. Approaches to state policy formulation and implementation were also changing:

more reliance on expertise, planning, evaluation, with a plethora of new agencies advising and monitoring external and internal factors relevant to state policy in all areas. These changes were reflected, in varying degrees, in state language policy.

In considering the new directions – and instruments – of state policy towards the Irish language from the late 1950s, we are confronted by evidence of considerable activity and innovation, but with little sign of clarity or coherence in enunciating state language policy. A government-appointed Commission (1958), to examine progress to date on the language revival policy, reported at the end of 1963. It reaffirmed the *raison d'être* of the revival policy in traditional 'essentialist' identity terms, and reiterated the link between the 'maintenance' of the Gaeltacht and the prospects for the extension of Irish throughout the rest of the country in unequivocal terms: 'there can be no survival without revival'. The Commission made many useful recommendations for supporting the wider use of Irish, including increased use by the state and its agents. But in responding to the Report, the Government emphasized the role of public opinion, and accordingly the importance of attitudes and actions in the several domains of civil society (churches, trade unions, voluntary bodies etc.), in determining the use and the fate of Irish as a living language. As Ó Riagáin (1997: 23) has put it: 'The emphasis on public attitudes clearly reflected the government view that the major constraint on policy development was the absence of sustained public support and not state action per se'.

Thus, on the one hand, committees and new bodies were established (even if they were not always adequately resourced) to advise, coordinate, evaluate and conduct research on different aspects of the state's language policy. Following the 1963 Commission Report, Comhairle na Gaeilge (1969) was established, followed by The Committee on Irish Language Attitudes Research (CILAR) in 1970, and Institiúid Teangeolaíochta Éireann (ITÉ) in 1967, all, it seemed, intended to provide better quality (more scientific) data and advice for language policy, drawing on international expertise and research in sociolinguistics and applied linguistics, better measurement of progress (in the education sphere, and in other areas), better teaching methods and materials. In 1975 the state established Bord na Gaeilge, to promote Irish, particularly through 'extending its use by the public as a living language' (Tovey 1988: 53-68). All of these initiatives were undertaken with a view to achieving a still tantalisingly vague version of 'bilingualism'. A coherent, authoritative statement on the strategic aim of bilingualism did not come from the political leadership, but from expert advisors: see, for example, Ó Murchú (1970).

In the case of the Gaeltacht , the ravages of the emigration haemorrhage of the 1950s, together with the more deep-seated failure over many decades to address economic and social regeneration, had utterly devastated these communities. But by the late 1950s a revised definition of the territorial extent of the Gaeltacht had been accompanied by a special Department of State for Gaeltacht affairs and by a dedicated development agency (Gaeltarra Éireann) for the economic and social regeneration of the Gaeltacht. Such steps came very late – perhaps too late – but they at least ensured that targeted initiatives at employment creation (if not always language-sensitive) were now being directed at the fast-dissolving core communities of Irish native-speakers. By the later 1960s a cadre of young educated Gaeltacht men and women (stimulated by 'civil rights' movements and rhetoric from the USA and Paris and Northern Ireland) raised their voices and their demands for a more robust and multi-faceted response to the predicament of their communities, as Irish-language communities under threat. They achieved results: a dedicated Gaeltacht–based radio station (1972); a development authority (Údarás na Gaeltachta) with a wider remit and a more democratic base than Gaeltarra Éireann; a state-supported, substantially Irish-language television service (1995) – all of these, incidentally, with their headquarters in the Conamara Gaeltacht.

The past thirty years have seen remarkable progress in economic and social development – per capita incomes, educational and social infrastructure (including university centres in recent years), improved housing stock and employment opportunities – in most Gaeltacht areas. But the evidence is irrefutable that the language shift to English has continued unabated – may, in fact, be accelerating – even as the population grows and prosperity and improved living standards become strikingly obvious. Among the factors that account for this situation one may note immigration (including returned Gaeltacht emigrants whose family language had shifted to English), urban spill-over, unchecked holiday and retirement home development; increased daily mobility in and out of the Gaeltacht for work and leisure purposes; excessive concentration until recently by Údarás na Gaeltachta on job-creation, without adequate attention to language-maintenance; and, of course, the sheer sunami-like wave of English-language media of popular entertainment and information. There is also the argument that the very belatedness of these recent socio-economic and language-maintenance supports meant that they were simply unable to arrest, still less to reverse, historic patterns of language shift.

These discrete policy initiatives directed at Gaeltacht regeneration cannot be taken in isolation from overall state policies, either in relation to regional socio-economic development, or specifically in relation to language. Here we may say that from the 1960s there was a discernible shift in state policy (and attitudes) in relation to Irish. Increasingly the language issue has become less a matter of identity-formation for a 'national community' (an indispensable mark of ethnicity, in which the policy objective was to secure universal competence in the hope of achieving widespread use), and more a matter of the state's dealing with the Irish-language community as a sectional interest, with distinct needs and demands. In the early 1970s the requirement that competence in Irish be obligatory for passing state examinations and for entry to the public service was abolished, and requirements were relaxed in other branches of the public service. This retreat by the state came at time of widening access and new institutional structures in education at second and third level.

The state did not seek for Irish the status of an official language at the time of Ireland's accession to the then 'Common Market' in 1973. Different commentators have written of the state's stance on Irish in these decades in terms of 'benign neglect' (Ó Riagáin 1997: 23) and 'the de-institutionalization of the Irish language from the nation-state' (Mac Giolla Chríost 2005: 111-133; 175-198), a position reflecting a more general shift from essentialist ethnic nationalism to contractual civic nationalism in state ideology, discourse and policy. So far as language policy is concerned, the evangelical impulse of the 'revival' decades was being replaced by the state's understanding of itself and its services as functioning in a predominantly market-place environment: a provider of services on a cost-efficient basis, and a facilitator and supporter, as resources permitted, of initiatives for promoting the use of

Irish in the wider civil society.

As it happened, as the state retreated from a proactive 'lead' role in language promotion, the Irish language community began to undertake new initiatives and to exert political pressure on successive governments to provide better support and services and to vindicate the language rights of Irish-speakers. We have noted the effects of this in the Gaeltacht. But throughout the state as a whole, the voluntary efforts of parents and language-activists, rather than state planning or policy, has been the driver of an expanding Irish-medium school movement ('Gaelscoileanna' at elementary, and 'Gaelcholáistí' at second level). The state has been generally – though hardly systematically or urgently – supportive of this movement, at primary and, more circumspectly, at post-primary level. In most areas, however, throughout the 1970s, 1980s and 1990s, the Irish-speaking community had to mobilize itself, and exert pressure as a lobby group, in order to secure the attention, and in certain areas the support of the state. In sum, the state's position on Irish in these decades was essentially responsive rather than directive.

Turning briefly to Northern Ireland, language rights were always likely to emerge as a sensitive element in the larger conflict on ethnicity, power, state legitimacy and rights (communal and individual), which convulsed Northern Ireland from the late 1960s. The fraught circumstances of conflict and community polarization encouraged cultural assertiveness. A re-energized Irish-language community, with strong growth in the most republican urban areas of Belfast and Derry, and generally within the wider nationalist community, ensured that language would be a feature of any political accommodation based on parity of cultural esteem. Accordingly, the parties to the 1998 Belfast Agreement committed themselves to 'understanding and toleration' in respect of cultural diversity, including language. The North-South bodies, established following the 1998 Agreement, together with the scope for progress on 'minority' language rights inherent in the European Charter for Regional or Minority Languages, provide the overarching framework within which new relationships between Irish-speakers and the state in Northern Ireland are evolving. Given the historical circumstances, this evolving accommodation of the language rights of Irish-speakers in Northern Ireland is likely to involve patience and fortitude all round, in working through difficulties as they arise.

See, in particular, Mac Giolla Chríost (2005: 134-171) and Kirk et al
(2001).

Finally, in considering state policy (and the effectiveness of its
implementation) in the Republic, it is necessary to refer to a number of
significant recent developments. Firstly, the Planning and Development
Act of 2000 imposed, for the first time, a duty on planning authorities
to 'protect the linguistic and cultural heritage of the Gaeltacht' in
future development plans. The experience to date would suggest
variability between planning authorities in the rigour and consistency
of its implementation. It may have a positive impact on language
maintenance in the Gaeltacht in the future: but the troubling sounds of
galloping horses and the bolting of stable doors are hard to ignore. For
a sharply critical perspective on state priorities, see Ó hÉallaithe (2004:
159-192).

In 2003 a long-sought Official Languages Act (Acht na dTeangacha
Oifigiúla) was passed, providing a statutory framework for the
provision of public services through the Irish language. While the Act
includes a number of provisions of 'universal applicability' (relating to
correspondence, state obligations in bilingual publications, etc.), the
key aspect of the Act is the obligation it places on Departments of State
and designated public bodies to provide a range of services through
Irish to the public, these to be specified in a 'scheme' to be agreed by the
Minister in respect of each Department or public body; such schemes
are to be reviewed and renewed at three-yearly intervals. Compliance
by the relevant bodies is monitored by a Language Commissioner.

The immediate impact of the Act (despite certain shortcomings) ought
to strengthen the entitlement of Irish-speakers to conduct their business
through Irish, if they so choose, with various parts of the state apparatus
of government and designated public bodies. As always, the devil is in
the detail. The obligations specified in these 'schemes' will be much
more demanding when being applied within the Gaeltacht than in
other parts of the state. How significant the enhanced provision may
be outside the Gaeltacht remains to be seen. Clearly, much will depend
on the strength of demand. But as these schemes come up for regular
renewal in different sectors of the public service, it would be naive to
imagine that considerations of 'cost-benefit' will not arise. A second
development of more recent years was the Irish state belatedly seeking

and securing recognition for Irish as an official language of the EU, prompted by a focused lobby campaign at home and by the insistence by a host of new entrants to the EU on recognition for their languages as 'official' languages of the Union.

We may note briefly the possible (indeed likely) positive effects of these latest initiatives in state policy. They will enhance the status of the language at EU level; and, domestically, give greater immediate precision to the actual entitlements of Irish-speakers. On the other hand, the Language Act may be seen as 'limiting', even if not in a strictly constitutional sense, the rights which can be easily claimed by Irish-speakers in dealing with the state services, in the widest sense.

Certainly, the new initiatives (at European and national level) should, if nothing else, create or enhance employment opportunities for qualified Irish-speakers across a broad range of translation needs (print and electronic). To the extent that this will increase the 'transactional value' of Irish, it may well be an incentive to its maintenance or thorough acquisition by a cohort of the educated young, seeking good employment in the language service sector of the EU and of the state.

The designated state agency for the general promotion of Irish has, understandably, been left a little in the shade in recent years by the legislative initiatives of the Dublin government and the energetic public advocacy of Irish by Minister Ó Cuív. Moreover, the fact that this agency, entitled Foras na Gaeilge, has been positioned within the cross-border, inter-governmental institutions, established as part of the new structures of political accommodation in Northern Ireland, must inevitably have an impact on the way in which the agency operates (the resources it can deploy, and the aggressiveness, so to speak, of its activities, across two jurisdictions with such radically different histories of language policy – and of language 'platforms' – for more than eighty years). The restoration of a reconfigured cross-community Executive in Northern Ireland will require Foras na Gaeilge to operate in a highly politically-sensitive environment for the foreseeable future.

Whether the recent positive initiatives in the Republic are part of an emerging new state strategy, or will make a decisive difference in the established patterns/directions of language-behaviour in Ireland, is difficult to predict. Here, as we have stated at various points throughout this essay, the issue is one of coherence; that is to say, the issue is whether language (i.e. sensitivity to or concern for the language consequences of decisions made) will be an integrating imperative across a broad range of state policies impacting on social cohesion and social reproduction.

But if we are to ask ourselves honestly what are the prospects of seeing such sustained coherent state policy being adopted and implemented, with a view to ensuring that Irish as a living community language should survive into an indefinite future, it would be difficult to take an optimistic view in the light of experience to date. The evidence is incontrovertible that the 'base communities' of native Irish-speakers in the Gaeltacht are experiencing relentless language shift to English as the dominant vernacular among school-going children. With a very few exceptional pockets, the officially-designated areas called Gaeltacht are witnessing the replacement of Irish by English as the dominant everyday language of school-children socializing among themselves, and among teenage cohorts, and within an increasing number of Gaeltacht households, even those in which both parents are native speakers of Irish.

The trend is not universal. Counter-forces can be identified: a strong indigenous educational and communications infrastructure has acted as an increasingly active site of affirmation of Irish and as arteries for its transmission as a community language within a number of the core Gaeltacht communities. But, in general, the omens are not reassuring: the 'maintenance' mission (of the traditional Irish-speaking communities), of the language revival movement of the 1880-1920 period, and of the Irish state since its inception, is perilously close to having to be declared a failure. The findings of the most recent research (Ó Giollagáin et al 2007), confirm earlier evidence that the Gaeltacht is melting away as inexorably as the polar ice-cap.

The more encouraging evidence of 'revival' among the greater, dispersed population throughout predominantly English-speaking Ireland, needs to be acknowledged. Gaelscoileanna have generated strong networks (as have the summer colleges). Irish has achieved penetration (albeit uneven) in many domains of 'ordinary living' – the media, business and professional life, publishing, leisure activities, voluntary bodies, and the 'culture industries'. There is scarcely an aspect of the world-experience of contemporary Irish people that one cannot find discussed in the Irish-language media. But nowhere among the widely dispersed community of real (and aspiring) Irish-speakers throughout Ireland has a self-sustaining urban community been established in which Irish runs uninterrupted through the main communication arteries of that community.

In short, the large number of Irish-speakers dispersed throughout Ireland still have not succeeded (nor has state policy seriously attempted to plan for or to assist them) in establishing settlements of Irish-speakers of sufficient critical mass to generate the kind of 'credible acoustic reality' of Irish, that would affirm the young in a language reflex favourable to using Irish, or that would ensure that the stranger, newcomer or language-learner would accept the normalcy of linguistic conformity in the interests of living 'the full life' in such a community. The fragile nature of these relatively thin urban networks of Irish-speakers (dispersed native-speakers and secondary bilinguals) presents serious questions for those concerned with inter-generation transmission of Irish or the 'reproduction' of these networks. The social 'porosity' of these networks, their vulnerability to disruption in a highly mobile society, are only the more obvious signs of this fragility. Again, these networks are frequently generated and sustained (in so far as they are sustained) through association with a particular Gaeltacht community/experience. What would be the consequence for these dispersed (largely urban) networks if the remaining Gaeltacht enclaves were, in effect, to wither away as viable Irish-speaking communities?

Whether in the liberal-democratic Irish state of the early twenty-first century there exists the political will (at local no less than at state level) required for adopting the kind of radical measures which any credible 'rescue' plan for arresting the seemingly definitive language shift in the surviving Gaeltacht must entail, or for creating a sustainable Irish-speaking community in the country at large, only time will tell.

REFERENCES

An Coimisiún um Athbheochan na Gaeilge. 1963. *An Coimisiún um Athbheochan na Gaeilge: An tuarascáil dheiridh*. Baile Átha Cliath. Oifig an tSoláthair.

Garvin, T. 1987. *Nationalist revolutionaries in Ireland, 1858-1928*. Oxford. Clarendon Press.

Kelly, A. 2002. *Compulsory Irish: Language and education in Ireland, 1870s-1970s*. Dublin. Irish Academic Press.

Kirk, J.M. & D.P. Ó Baoill (eds). 2001. *Linguistic politics: Language policies for Northern Ireland, the Republic of Ireland, and Scotland*. Belfast. Cló Ollscoil na Banríona.

Mac Giolla Chríost, D. 2005. *The Irish language in Ireland: From Goídil to globalisation*. Oxford. Routledge.

Ó Buachalla, S. 1988. *Education Policy in twentieth century Ireland*. Dublin. Wolfhound Press.

Ó Conghaile, M. (ed). 1986. *Gaeltacht Ráth Cairn: Léachtaí comórtha*. Indreabhán. Cló Iar-Chonnachta.

Ó hÉallaithe, D. 2004. 'From language revival to language survival' in Mac Murchaidh, C. (ed). *Who needs Irish?* Dublin. Veritas.

Ó Giollagáin, C., S. Mac Donnacha et al. 2007. *Staidéar cuimsitheach teangeolaíoch ar úsáid na Gaeilge sa Ghaeltacht*. Baile Átha Cliath. Oifig an tSoláthair.

Ó Máille, T. 1990. *The status of the Irish language: A legal perspective*. Dublin. Bord na Gaeilge.

Ó Murchú, M. 1970. *Language and community / Urlabhra agus pobal*. Dublin. Comhairle na Gaeilge.

Ó Murchú, M. 2001. *Cumann Buan-Choimeádta na Gaeilge: Tús an athréimnithe*. Baile Átha Cliath. Cois Life.

Ó Riagáin, P. 1997. *Language policy and social reproduction: Ireland 1893-1993*. Oxford. Clarendon Press.

Ó Tuathaigh, G. et al (eds). 2000. *Pobal na Gaeltachta: A scéal agus a dhán*. Indreabhán. Cló Iar-Chonnachta.

Ó Tuathaigh, G. 2005. 'Language, ideology and national identity' in Cleary, J. & C. Connolly (eds), *The Cambridge companion to modern Irish culture*. Cambridge. Cambridge University Press.

Ó Tuathail, S. 2002. *Gaeilge agus bunreacht*. Baile Átha Cliath. Coiscéim.

Tovey, H. 1988. 'The state and the Irish language: The role of Bord na Gaeilge' in *The international journal of the sociology of language* 70: 53-68.

Walsh, J. 2004. *Cás na Gaeilge agus cás na hÉireann: An teanga, an cultúr agus an fhorbairt*. Baile Átha Cliath. Coiscéim.

Census Data on the Irish Language

Aidan Punch

INTRODUCTION

The Census of Population is the most comprehensive source of data on Irish language ability and usage. The census figures provide a data series which extends from the middle of the nineteenth century right up to the present day thereby enabling the changes which have occurred during this period to be monitored.

The first section of the present chapter provides a brief historical background to the census and explains the formulations of the Irish language questions used in the various censuses since the question was first asked in 1851. In the next section attention is drawn to how changes in question wordings and layout may have affected comparisons over time. The criticisms, which have been levelled against the veracity of the census data on the Irish language, are considered in the next section while the final part of the chapter examines some of the data with particular focus on the period since 1996. Gaeltacht areas are separately distinguished where appropriate. All the data used in the present chapter are taken from the CSO website www.cso.ie.

HISTORY OF THE CENSUSES OF IRELAND

The first major census, using a household form, was the so-called Great Census of 1841 (for a comprehensive history of the census in Ireland see Linehan, T.P. (1991)). Censuses were subsequently taken at ten-year intervals up to 1911. Plans for the 1921 census were disrupted by the civil war conditions prevailing in Ireland at that time. The first census following the formation of Saorstát Éireann was undertaken in 1926 after which the ten-year frequency was resumed with censuses in 1936 and 1946.

The 1951 census was the first in a series of censuses carried out at five-year intervals. This five-yearly frequency has been observed since 1951 other than on two occasions. The census planned for 1976 was cancelled at a late stage as a Government economy measure. However, the need for up-to-date population figures was soon recognized thereafter and resulted in a census being undertaken in 1979 with a restricted number of questions. This was followed by a full census in 1981. The census originally due to take place in April 2001 was postponed until 2002 due to the foot and mouth disease situation at that time. The most recent census was carried out in 2006.

To summarize, twenty-three censuses have been held between 1841 and 2006 inclusive. The first eight of these: 1841, 1851, 1861, 1871, 1881, 1891, 1901, 1911 were held in respect of the island of Ireland at a time when Ireland was part of the United Kingdom of Great Britain and Ireland. The last fifteen censuses refer to what is today the Republic of Ireland. They were held in 1926, 1936, 1946, 1951, 1956, 1961, 1966, 1971, 1979, 1981, 1986, 1991, 1996, 2002 and 2006.

THE IRISH LANGUAGE QUESTION

1851 was the first year in which the Irish language question was asked in the census. In that year the topic was introduced as part of the education question with an instruction which read:

> The word 'Irish' is to be added in this column to the name of each person who speaks Irish but who cannot speak English; and the words 'Irish and English' to the names of those who can speak both the Irish and English Languages.

This version was retained unchanged in 1861 and 1871. In 1881 a separate question headed 'Irish language' was introduced with the same categorization as the one used in the previous three censuses and the additional instruction that 'In other cases no entry should be made in this column.' This layout was followed in 1891, 1901 and 1911.

The 1926 census expanded the categories as follows: 'Irish only', 'Irish and English' for native speakers who could speak English also, 'English and Irish' for others who could speak both languages, and 'read but cannot speak Irish'. The following instruction was also given: 'Do not write anything opposite persons who can neither speak nor read Irish'. However, this elaboration was short-lived. From 1936 the second and third categories were combined into one, 'Irish and English'. This version of the question was retained unchanged up to and including the 1991 census with the coverage being restricted to those aged 3 years and over from 1961 onwards.

THE IRISH LANGUAGE QUESTION

Following contact between Roinn na Gaeltachta (as it then was) and the Central Statistics Office a number of different question layouts were tested on a sub-sample of respondents to the 1993 annual labour force survey. After analysing the results and following further consultation between both organizations the following question was included in the 1996 census form:

> **Ability to speak the Irish language**
> Indicate whether the person can speak Irish by inserting ✓ in the appropriate box.
> If the person can speak Irish please indicate frequency.
> (See notes)
> Can the person speak Irish
>
> | | |
> |---|---|
> | Yes | ☐1 |
> | No | ☐2 |
>
> If Yes, does the person speak Irish?
>
> | | |
> |---|---|
> | Daily | ☐1 |
> | Weekly | ☐2 |
> | Less often | ☐3 |
> | Never | ☐4 |

The following note was included in the notes section at the back of the 1996 census form:

> This question should be answered for persons aged 3 years and over. Leave blank for children under 3 years of age. Persons who can speak Irish only or Irish and English should tick the '**Yes**' box.

The Irish language question therefore changed in a substantial way compared with previous censuses. Some of this change was part of a general policy to ease respondent burden and at the same time speed up the processing of the census results by placing a greater emphasis on the use of tick boxes throughout the census questionnaire. The specific implication of this policy for the Irish language question was that the respondent no longer had to write in one of the following responses: 'Irish only', 'Irish and English' or 'Read but cannot speak Irish'. Instead all that was required was that a box be ticked. In addition the opportunity was taken to inquire about the frequency of speaking Irish – the first time that this facet was covered in the census. So while most of the wording changes introduced in the Irish language question, since its introduction in 1851, were gradual, the new wording used for the first time in 1996 represented a major break with the versions which preceded it.

The formulation of the 2002 census Irish language question was the same as that used in 1996 although the overall questionnaire design differed markedly. Up to and including 1991 the census questionnaire was a large booklet organized in a matrix layout with the questions in the columns and persons in the rows. The 1991 form catered for seven persons in the household (i.e. it had seven rows in which to record responses). The 2002 and 2006 forms contained 24 pages organized in an A4 booklet with three pages of questions for each person for up to six persons in the household.

The most recent census in 2006 also marked a further change in the Irish language question with a distinction being drawn between those who spoke Irish on a daily basis within and outside the education system. Specifically, it allowed for more than one box to be ticked in the frequency part of the question.

2002	2006

11 Can you speak Irish?
Answer if aged 3 years or over.

1   Yes

2   No

IF 'Yes', do you speak Irish?

1   Daily

2   Weekly

3   Less often

4   Never

12 Can you speak Irish?
Answer if aged 3 years or over.

1   Yes

2   No

IF 'Yes', do you speak Irish?
✔ *the boxes that apply.*

1   Daily, within the education system

2   Daily, outside the education system

3   Weekly

4   Less often

To summarize this section, an Irish language question was asked in 1851, 1861, 1871 as part of an education question and in 1881, 1891, 1901 and 1911 as a question in its own right. The first three censuses held after the foundation of the State – 1926, 1936 and 1946 – contained an Irish-language question. So too did 1961, 1971, 1981, 1986, 1991, 1996, 2002 and 2006. Therefore eighteen of the twenty-three censuses conducted since 1841 have contained an Irish language question. In the next section the strengths and weaknesses of the census as a medium for asking an Irish-language question are examined.

STRENGTHS AND WEAKNESSES OF CENSUS

The main advantage of the census compared with other methods of inquiry such as sample surveys is its comprehensive coverage. The fact that a complete enumeration takes place means that a high degree of confidence can be placed in the derived data. Comprehensive coverage also implies that the results can be produced at small area level. This is particularly important in the case of the Irish language where the Gaeltacht areas as currently defined consist of Electoral Divisions (EDs) and parts of EDs located in eight different administrative counties.

Asking questions on the Irish language in a census environment also allows the results to be analysed by a range of geographic, demographic and socio-economic characteristics. This is important in attempting to explain the factors which influence changes in Irish language ability or usage.

Looking at the other side of the equation, one of the major drawbacks of the census is the fact that the scope for asking refined or nuanced questions is somewhat limited. The census questionnaire is completed by adult persons of varying educational attainment some of whom may not be familiar with form filling. Using this self-completion approach precludes trained interviewers from probing responses in depth which they might do as part of their duties in a sample survey.

The trade-off between the relevance of the questions being asked and the need to maintain as much continuity as possible in what is an infrequent inquiry is a real problem for census takers. We have seen in the previous section that the same version of the Irish language question was used in censuses between 1936 and 1991 inclusive. However, to have retained this version in 1996 would have called into question the on-going relevance of the question (e.g. the use of 'Irish only' as a category). The price which was paid for the change in question layout introduced in 1996 was a complete break in continuity between 1991 and 1996 in a series of data extending back to 1851. A similar break was introduced between 2002 and 2006 in the frequency of speaking Irish part of the question. We will return to both these issues in the data analysis section.

The subjective nature of some census questions has been commented on in successive census reports. The Irish-language question has attracted most of this comment. For instance, the 1926 volume contained the following passage:

> Personal judgement must necessarily enter so largely into the replies to this question that the number of 'Irish speakers' would appear to be far less susceptible of exact measurement than any of the other matters into which it is the purpose of the Census to inquire. To every other query (place of residence, age, birthplace, religion, occupation etc.) on the Census Schedule it is possible to give an exact reply. With regard to language it is extremely difficult to devise a method simple enough for census purposes which would permit a rigid distinction being made between those who 'know Irish' and those who do not. At the same time the statistics have a considerable value for purposes of comparison as between one part of the country and another, between this and previous censuses, between one age group or occupation and another, etc.

This caveat remained in the 1936 and 1946 census reports on the Irish language. In the 1961 report the language was modified somewhat but still drew the readers' attention to the shortcomings of the question:

> Whereas the questions on the Census schedule relating to Sex, Date of birth, Marital condition, Occupation etc. can be answered precisely, the replies given to the question on 'Ability to speak the Irish language' depend to a large extent on the judgement of the person completing the form. It has not been found possible to devise a method, simple enough for Census purposes, to provide an invariable standard for classifying persons into those who 'can speak Irish' and those who cannot. Consequently the statistics contained in the present volume cannot be regarded as being precise in the same degree as those in other volumes of the Census. The statistics of Irish language may, nevertheless, be of interest for purposes of comparison between different areas of the country and between this an previous Censuses but in any use of these data the lack of objective precision referred to above must be borne in mind.

The 1961 drafting was reproduced in the 1971, 1981, 1986 and 1991 reports but was dropped in 1996 when the question layout changed. The sole comment in the 1996 report was a footnote in Tables 1 and 2 as follows:

> A new question on ability to speak the Irish language and frequency of speaking Irish was introduced in the 1996 Census of Population (see Q.14 in Appendix 1). The new version of the question marked a major departure from the version used in previous censuses.

However, as a counterpoint to the self-criticism contained in the various census reports Ó Gliasáin (1996) in his study of the Irish language question in the Census of Population compared the results of seven national surveys covering the period 1968-1993 and concluded:

> There cannot be any doubt that CLQ (census language question) data constitute real information about ability to speak Irish in the Population. How much information, and how heavily we can depend on its secondary analyses, is not clear.....

Furthermore, many of the analyses, especially those based on age and sex, are consistent with other studies on language ability. The next section explores some of the trends shown by the data.

CENSUS DATA FROM 1851 TO THE PRESENT

One of the most basic statistics from the census in relation to the Irish language is the percentage of the population for whom an ability to speak the language is indicated. Figure 1 is based on the numbers returned as Irish speakers in the various censuses since 1851 expressed as a percentage of the relevant populations.

Figure 1: Percentage of Irish speakers in each Province at each census since 1851

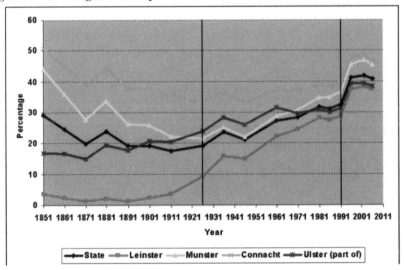

Population 3 years and over since 1926. The vertical lines represent breaks in the series.

Of the two discontinuities introduced in the series in 1926 and 1996 the impact of the latter is more serious. The new question introduced in 1926 did not appear to have had a marked impact on the continuity of

the series. By way of contrast, the results of the new question introduced
in 1996 are not comparable with those for previous censuses. The
1991-1996 increase from 32.5 per cent to 41.1 per cent in the overall
percentage of persons able to speak Irish is undoubtedly due more to a
questionnaire effect than an Irish language ability effect – although it is
not possible to precisely allocate the change between the two factors.

Despite these discontinuities the graph does show that the inter-censal
trends at provincial level are broadly similar. The traditional dominance
of Connacht and Munster is also apparent with the differential between
all provinces narrowing over time reflecting the impact of the education
system as a source of language learning in more recent times compared
with language spoken in the home in the earlier period.

Analysing the data on ability to speak Irish by age group (Figure 2)
illustrates the robustness of the census-based data. Focusing on the
results from the last three censuses shows clearly that ability is at a peak
during the school-going years, especially the early teens. Ability then
declines but experiences a slight recovery around the ages at which the
parents of young school-going children may be helping their children
with their Irish lessons. This pattern is replicated from census to census
implying a consistency among the public in their responses to what
might be interpreted as a subjective question.

Figure 2: Percentage of Irish speakers by age group, 1996, 2002 and 2006

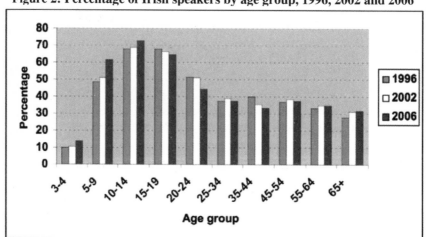

Another illustration of the consistency of the census data on ability to speak Irish is the gender difference. The data in Table 1, which represents the difference between female and male percentage ability analysed by age group, is in conformity with international experience in language ability and confirms the validity of the census language question. The female differential is highest for those in their late teens and early twenties, which is consistent with the higher female education participation rates observed for these age groups.

Table 1: Female less male percentage ability to speak Irish, 1996, 2002, 2006

Age group	1996	2002	2006
	Percentage		
3-4	1.5	1.9	2.7
5-9	3.3	4.1	4.3
10-14	4.8	6.7	6.5
15-19	9.5	11.4	10.9
20-24	9.1	10.8	10.3
25-34	6.5	9.5	10.6
35-44	5.4	7.8	9.5
45-54	4.1	4.7	6.4
55-64	2.5	3.3	4.1
65+	2.0	2.5	2.8

As alluded to earlier in the chapter a distinction was made in the 2006 census between those Irish speakers who spoke Irish within the education system and those who spoke it outside the education system by offering a choice to tick more than one box in response to the question. Table 2 summarizes the data for daily Irish speakers for 2002 and 2006 distinguishing Gaeltacht areas and the rest of the country. The table also separately distinguishes the school-going population, approximated by the age group 5-19, and the rest of the population.

The data on the number of Irish speakers is well behaved with the decline in the number of 5-19 year olds in Gaeltacht areas who were able to speak the language being caused by a drop in the underlying population. In fact the percentage able to speak the language actually increased from 84.1 per cent in 2002 to 85.8 per cent in 2006.

Table 2: Daily Irish speakers, 2002 and 2006

	2006			2002			2006 less 2002		
	Gaeltacht	Elsewhere	Total	Gaeltacht	Elsewhere	Total	Gaeltacht	Elsewhere	Total
Irish speakers									
5-19	17,373	533,101	550,474	17,580	510,171	527,751	-207	22,930	22,723
3-4 and 20+	46,892	1,059,424	1,106,316	44,577	998,566	1,043,143	2,315	60,858	63,173
Total	64,265	1,592,525	1,656,790	62,157	1,508,737	1,570,894	2,108	83,788	85,896
Daily within education only									
5-19	9,566	388,982	398,548	N/A	N/A	N/A	N/A	N/A	N/A
3-4 and 20+	4,416	50,243	54,659	N/A	N/A	N/A	N/A	N/A	N/A
Total	13,982	439,225	453,207	N/A	N/A	N/A	N/A	N/A	N/A
Daily outside education									
5-19	4,460	13,082	17,542	N/A	N/A	N/A	N/A	N/A	N/A
3-4 and 20+	18,055	36,551	54,606	N/A	N/A	N/A	N/A	N/A	N/A
Total	22,515	49,633	72,148	N/A	N/A	N/A	N/A	N/A	N/A
Daily speakers									
5-19	14,026	402,004	416,090	12,163	248,553	260,716	1,863	153,511	155,374
3-4 and 20+	22,471	86,794	109,265	21,626	57,199	78,825	845	29,595	30,440
Total	36,497	488,858	525,355	33,789	305,752	339,541	2,708	183,106	185,814
Daily as a percentage of Irish speakers									
5-19	80.7%	75.4%	75.6%	69.2%	48.7%	49.4%	11.5%	26.7%	26.2%
3-4 and 20+	47.9%	8.2%	9.9%	48.5%	5.7%	7.6%	-0.6%	2.5%	2.3%
Total	56.8%	30.7%	31.7%	54.4%	20.3%	21.6%	2.4%	10.4%	10.1%

N/A indicates not applicable.

Adding the figures for daily use within the education system only and daily use outside the education system gives a total of over 525,000 daily speakers in 2006 compared with 339,500 in 2002. This represents an increase of over a half in the number of daily Irish speakers over the four year period in question. However this increase is more illusory than real! Including a new tick box 'Daily within the education system' elicited the correct and appropriate response from respondents. However, the absence of this category in 2002 (and 1996) would appear to have implied that a sizeable number of students (and teachers?) might not have considered their usage of the language in the class situation as being daily usage of the language. This is borne out by the fact that there were 155,000 fewer 5-19 year olds speaking the language on a daily basis in 2002 compared with 2006.

Despite the discontinuity it can be strongly argued that the 2006 version of the question is more meaningful than the previous one. In particular the level of concordance for Gaeltacht dwellers other than school-going children is quite good – 22,471 daily speakers in 2006 compared with 21,626 in 2002. Of particular note is that among the 72,000 daily Irish speakers outside the education system, 22,500 are Gaeltacht dwellers and 49,500 live elsewhere in the State. A possible worrying feature is that over two thirds of the 14,000 daily speakers of school-going age in the Gaeltacht do not speak the language on a daily basis outside of school.

CONCLUSION

The principal focus of the chapter was the census as a source of information on the Irish language. The census was found to have many advantages not least the long time series of data and the comprehensive national coverage achieved. However, the wording changes introduced from time to time have proved problematical from the point of view of maintaining the consistency of the data series. The two most recently introduced changes – in 1996 for ability to speak Irish and in 2006 in relation to frequency of speaking the language – have resulted in a complete break in both data series.

From the point of view of optimizing the data on the Irish language coming from the census it is important that the present version of the question is retained, at least for 2011. This will enable trends in the number of Irish speakers and the frequency with which they speak the language to be monitored effectively.

REFERENCES

Census of Population, 1926. Volume VIII, Irish Language. P. No. 783. Stationery Office, Dublin.

Census of Population, 1961. Volume IX, Irish Language. Pr 8669. Stationery Office, Dublin.

Census of Population, 1996. Volume 9, Irish Language. Pn 6456. Stationery Office, Dublin.

Linehan, T.P. 1991. 'History and development of Irish population censuses' in The journal of the statistical and social inquiry society of Ireland 26 (4).

Ó Gliasáin, M. 1996. The language question in the Census of Population. Dublin. Institiúid Teangeolaíochta Éireann.

Irish-language Policy 1922 – 2007: Balancing Maintenance and Revival

Pádraig Ó Riagáin

INTRODUCTION

There has always been a good deal of confusion about the ultimate objective of Ireland's Irish-language policy. It has been taken by many in the past, and maybe still is by some, to mean the displacement of English by Irish among the national population (Ó Cuív 1969: 130). However, whatever may have been the views of individual politicians or language organizations, the constitutional and legislative provisions made for Irish since the 1920s and 1930s do not suggest that anything other than the establishment of a bilingual state was ever envisaged. For example, the letter from the Irish President to the Chairman of the Gaeltacht Commission speaks simply of a national policy 'to safeguard and cultivate' or, a few lines later 'to uphold and foster' the Irish language (Gaeltacht Commission 1926: 3). The first Constitution of Ireland in 1922, and all subsequent revisions, designated two official state languages – English and Irish. A half-century later, the policy objective was expressed in the *White Paper on the Restoration of the Irish Language* (1965) as the restoration of the Irish language 'as a general medium of communication' and, most recently (2006) as an objective 'to increase on an incremental basis the use and knowledge of Irish as a community language.'

Although the constitutions of many states recognize more than one official language, territorial considerations usually frame the application of these basic provisions. It is in this respect, and not in the constitutional status accorded to a minority language, that the Irish case is unusual in the international context. Despite the marked regional bias in the distribution of Irish-speakers at the time towards western areas, the Irish state did not, as happened in several other countries (e.g. Belgium, Switzerland, Spain) legislate for a language policy organized on territorial lines. That is to say, it did not designate two language regions, one Irish-speaking and the other English-speaking, within which each language would be defined as the official standard and norm. While an Irish-speaking region was defined (*Gaeltacht*) and special measures were formulated to deal with it, Irish-language policy applied to the state as a whole and not just a region of it. Of course, outside the Irish-speaking areas, Irish-speakers formed negligible proportions of an almost entirely English-speaking population. In this region, the bilingual policy was not, therefore, one designed to meet the needs of an already existing bilingual community, but rather *it sought to create one*. This feature gave an unique character to Irish-language policy. It is, however, easy to push this distinction too far. National or regional policies for minority languages in other states usually have a restorative or revitalizing element, in addition to a maintenance dimension, and differences between them and the Irish case are often more of degree than of kind.

Nonetheless, from an international perspective, the bilingual policy pursued by the Irish state can be seen to contain two key objectives. The first was the maintenance of Irish as the spoken language in those Gaeltacht areas where it was still the community language. This part of the policy quickly took on the character of a regional economic development programme. Elsewhere the objective was the revival of Irish, and the state looked to the educational system for an increase in the numbers of Irish-speakers in society. It is fair to say that the history of Irish-language policy since 1922 can be summarized as a continuing struggle to find the most efficient, fair and appropriate balance between these two objectives of maintenance and revival.

In order to develop this thesis further, the following sections will first look briefly at the changing pattern of bilingualism in Ireland and, secondly, shifts in public attitudes towards Irish.

THE CHANGING PATTERN OF IRISH-ENGLISH BILINGUALISM
The Gaeltacht

In the 1926 Census of Population, some 18 per cent of the population of the new state was returned as Irish-speakers. The Gaeltacht Commission, which also reported in 1926, although in advance of the census publication, estimated that nearly half of the number of Irish-speakers were concentrated in western areas and roughly half again lived in core Irish-speaking districts, i.e. about 5 per cent of the total population in the state. However, a reanalysis of the 1926 census data in Galway and Kerry Gaeltachtaí (Ó Riagáin 1997) would suggest that no more than 3 per cent of the national population lived in the core Irish-speaking districts (called *Fíor-Ghaeltachtaí* by the Commission) and, at most, another 3 per cent lived in bilingual districts (or *Breac-Ghaeltachtaí*). In many of the Breac-Ghaeltachtaí, Irish-speakers constituted only a small minority and were found mainly in the older age-group.

The drastic revision of Gaeltacht boundaries which was undertaken in 1956 was, therefore, in large measure simply correcting the earlier inaccuracies. However, some language shift had undeniably occurred in the period between 1925 and 1956, especially in the so-called 'Breac-Ghaeltacht' areas. There was also a significant fall in population in all Gaeltacht districts although this was a feature of Irish rural areas generally, and not just the Gaeltacht. However, these linguistic, demographic and administrative facts should not be allowed to conceal the further fact that the majority of the 1926 Fíor-Ghaeltacht areas remained stable, in linguistic terms, until the 1960s.

The small-farm economy of Gaeltacht areas, in the first half of the twentieth century, supported a pattern of social networks which was very localized. The relative stability of these networks was an important factor in sustaining Irish-speaking communities. But as economic development began to percolate into rural areas in the post-1960 period, the minimum threshold population levels were no longer available in many rural communities to support traditional activities (primary school, parish, etc.), even less so new functions such as post-primary education. The growth in non-agricultural employment resulted in increases in commuting to nearby towns. These changes in employment, education, shopping and recreation patterns all reflected a major transformation of social-network patterns in the Gaeltacht which intensified the frequency of interactions between Irish-speakers and English-speakers. The overall effect was to diminish the possibility of maintaining Irish. For example, the proportion of married couples with joint native-speaker ability in Irish declined due to English-speakers marrying into Gaeltacht families. It would appear that only about half of Gaeltacht children learned Irish in the home and a decline in the proportion of Irish-speakers in other age-groups was also occurring.

This was related to the high level of in-migration and return migration which has accompanied the economic restructuring of the Gaeltacht in recent decades (APC 1988).

As a result, it would seem that the linguistic distinctions between the Gaeltacht and the rest of the country are weakening. 'In the Gaeltacht the historical process of language shift is progressing to the point where Irish is ceasing to be a community language and becoming instead the language of particular social networks' (APC 1988: xxvi).

Outside the Gaeltacht

In 1926, about one-eighth of the total population outside of the Gaeltacht was recorded in the census as Irish-speakers. Almost all spoke Irish as a second language; they tended to be young and resided in an English-speaking environment. Successive censuses since then have shown a steady increase in the proportion of Irish-speakers to 41.9 per cent in 2006. The proportion of Irish people now claiming a competence to speak Irish is higher than the proportion of Irish-speakers recorded by the census in 1851. However, in 1851 Irish-speakers were predominantly persons who had acquired Irish as the first language in the home; their 2006 counterparts are mostly persons who have acquired Irish as a second language in school.

Furthermore, survey research conducted since 1970 would suggest that those who speak Irish as second language have mostly achieved only limited or moderate speaking skills, as measured in the CILAR/ITÉ national language surveys (i.e. they are able to speak 'a few simple sentences' and/or negotiate 'parts of (general) conversations' in Irish). At most, only about 10 per cent of national survey respondents claim levels of speaking ability in Irish that reach, or even approach, real native-like fluency in the language. Given the limited number of fluent Irish-speakers in Irish society, it is not surprising to find that the proportion of adults who use Irish as their first or main language is about 3 per cent. However, while speakers with limited proficiency do not normally use Irish in general conversation, significant numbers appear to be comfortable with Irish when the context requires a listening, or understanding, engagement. For example, about 18 per cent of the population listen to Irish-language radio programmes at least once a week, and a larger proportion (70 per cent) watch the Irish-language TV channel, TG4, at least once a week (BCI 2004).

Two other features of the present pattern of bilingualism are significant. Spatially, the small minority of Irish-speaking families are not sufficiently numerous or concentrated to form a fully-fledged community (i.e. capable of supporting a full range of social domains) at any non-Gaeltacht location. Secondly, for a combination of reasons, many of which have more to do with the structure of the Irish educational system rather than operation of language policy per se, Irish-speakers are predominantly middle-class. Although the social class base of educational participation (and of Irish-speakers) has widened in recent decades, as post-primary and third-level opportunities expanded, the middle-class bias persists.

Strengths and Weaknesses in the Structure of Bilingualism
From the viewpoint of developing, or even maintaining, bilingualism in Ireland, the present pattern has both strengths and weaknesses. Following the approach adopted by the European Commission in the 'Euromosaic' report (1996), we can assess the situation in terms of 'language reproduction' (i.e inter-generational transmission of the language in the home), and 'language production' (i.e. learning the language in the school rather than the home).

Rates of language reproduction, even when Gaeltacht and non-Gaeltacht areas are combined, are no higher than, and probably under, 5 per cent. This ratio of home use of Irish is approximately the same as that which obtained in the 1920s. While the evidence in this respect indicates stability rather than the expansion envisaged in government objectives, it is nonetheless a sociolinguistic achievement that would have been inconceivable prior to the establishment of an independent state. However, while bilingualism, so measured, appears to be relatively stable, outside the Gaeltacht only one quarter of those who grew up in Irish-language homes use Irish with the same intensity in their current homes.

The maintenance of more or less stable rates of home bilingualism over recent decades is therefore due more to the capacity of the schools to produce competent bilinguals rather than the capacity of the bilingual community to reproduce itself. Most Irish children learn Irish in both primary and post-primary school as a subject. However, research studies have consistently shown that the education system's capacity to produce competent bilinguals is closely related to the number of years an individual spends in school and, of course, the type of Irish-language programme followed. In 1993, nearly three-quarters of current users of Irish had post-primary schooling and nearly half had taken the higher level Leaving Certificate course in Irish. However, since 1980 only 10-15 per cent of a cohort opt for the higher level courses in Irish in post-primary schools and even after thirteen years' study of the subject the speaking ability of the majority of the cohort is only moderate or, in the case of a growing minority, negligible. While the Irish-medium school sector has experienced significant growth since 1970, it is still too small to greatly affect the national pattern.

Thus, Irish-speaking networks have been characterized by a marked degree of impermanence, openness and instability. While the class distribution of bilinguals has some elements of Hechter's (1978) cultural division of labour model, both hierarchically (middle-classes) and segmentally (public service), 'no social class (or class fraction) has emerged in Ireland which uses Irish primarily rather than English, or where the use of one language as against another is a central element in the processes of class formation and class closure' (APC 1988: 37).

Nonetheless, the relationship between social class and Irish has been a contributory factor in the formation of Irish-speaking networks outside the Gaeltacht. First, because the proportion of Irish-speakers is higher than average in some middle-class groups, the likelihood of Irish being spoken within these groups is also higher. Secondly, because social classes tend to concentrate in different residential areas, the spatial distribution of Irish-speakers in large urban areas is also, relatively speaking, more concentrated in middle-class areas. One of the few studies of Irish-speaking networks in urban areas found a strong relationship between the distribution of Irish-language schools and socio-spatial concentrations of Irish-speakers. Furthermore, there is some evidence that Irish-speaking networks are capable, in these circumstances, of recruiting new members, especially 'novice' or 'reluctant' bilinguals. This must be set against their acknowledged inability to secure a permanent character that could ensure the reproduction of Irish-speakers and absorb the bilingual output of homes and schools (APC 1988: 31).

For this reason, it has been argued (APC 1988: 26) that bilingualism in Ireland was 'institutionally-based'. That is to say, some specific organizations, schools, clubs and families operate as Irish-medium institutions, although these institutional areas in their totality (education, recreation, homes, work, etc.) are not Irish-speaking. However, as institutions they appear able to survive changes in personnel, unlike Irish-speaking networks per se.

ATTITUDES TOWARDS IRISH

One can view the history of the Irish language over the last century and a half as a struggle between two conflicting socio-cultural processes. Throughout the nineteenth and early twentieth century the economic and political incorporation of Ireland into the wider British system intensified. While much historical work still needs to be done before a full understanding of this process becomes available, it is clear that the language shift occurred in circumstances that created very unfavourable views of the utility of Irish among the public and that the all too clearly visible evidence of decline itself added to the strength with which these views were held. These beliefs and opinions have persisted from way back but since the early part of the twentieth century the counter-process of state intervention has been cutting across this process of decline, generating its own very different mixture of positive and negative attitudes. In the post-colonial period two ideological and status systems have been competing for dominance, one deriving from the pre-independence British connection and the second arising from an attempt to establish an alternative based upon 'Irish' ethnic identity (Tovey, Hannan & Abramson 1989). As might be expected each of these two systems accord different significance to the minority but indigenous language. The relationship between the Irish language and ethnic identity on the one hand, and perceptions of its limited value as cultural capital on the other, form two opposing attitudinal predispositions which determine attitudes towards policy. Support for the Irish language is higher in many respects than would appear to be justified by the objective position of the language in society. Yet support is not high enough in regard to those policy options which could significantly alter the linguistic picture.

Public support for Irish is shown to be very positive when attitudinal questions in surveys tap into the role the Irish language is perceived to have in defining and maintaining national cultural distinctiveness. While there is a weak relationship between this dimension of the attitudinal and actual language use, their positive relationship with public support for language policies is important. Successive surveys have shown that a majority of the public supports policies to maintain Irish in the Gaeltacht, to provide Irish-language services on the national television channels, to use Irish on public notices etc., to provide state services in Irish, to employ public officials who could speak Irish, and to support the voluntary Irish-language organizations. In all of these matters, there was an increase in public support between 1973 and 1993. Thus, the Irish public is willing to accept a considerable commitment of state resources to ensuring the maintenance of the Irish language and even to support a considerable imposition of legal requirements on certain groups within the society to know or use Irish, such as teachers and civil servants.

For most people, it is within the educational system that they have the most direct contact with Irish-language policy. Not surprisingly, given the relationship between educational achievements and the qualifications needed for entry into the largely English-speaking labour market, the public is not prepared to support policies which would discriminate strongly in favour of Irish. While the policy presently in operation is supported by a large majority, this policy does no more than ensure that Irish is kept on the curriculum of all recognized schools. It does not, by and large, produce large numbers of competent bilinguals and, on the other hand, the sanctions incorporated in the policy appear unable to prevent a steady growth in the proportion of pupils who either fail the subject in state examinations or do not present for the Irish paper at all. Although about one quarter of the public would support more intensive, including immersion, programmes only a fraction of this minority is currently being accommodated.

The attitudes to school Irish suggest that where such requirements directly affect respondents' own material opportunities, or those of their children, they are less easily supported. Therefore, although a majority of the Irish public would appear to espouse some form of bilingual objective, the evidence from surveys would suggest that many of this majority seek at best to simply maintain the status of Irish in the Gaeltacht, in artistic life and within the low levels of social bilingualism now pertaining. The survey evidence would indicate that this viewpoint may now be the dominant consideration for those favouring a general bilingual objective. When taken in conjunction with the increase over the past few decades of those favouring an 'English only' objective, it would appear that the proportion holding the revival position as traditionally understood has slipped and may no longer represent the majority viewpoint.

SHIFTS IN POLICY SUPPORT

At the policy level, a significant re-alignment has been apparent for several decades. There has been a shift towards the maintenance pole of the overall strategy and a consequent weakening emphasis on the revival dimension. The underlying principle is tending towards one of servicing the bilingual population primarily at those locations where the most obvious concentrations of Irish-speakers occurs, i.e. where a community of speakers is presumed to already exist.

This is most clearly seen in the types of policy which have received support since 1970. An Irish-language radio station has been established, followed by an Irish-language television service. But the amount of Irish-language material on mainstream radio and television services has been reduced.

One can see a similar development within the education system. The long-term drift from the objective of Irish-medium education for all seemed to have receded to the last line of defence in 1973, when Irish ceased to be a compulsory subject in state examinations, but was retained as a required subject on the curriculum of schools in receipt of state funds. But the pattern of recent examination results in Irish – which show a growing percentage of pupils failing or not taking the paper – together with a number of recent policy decisions suggest that this line is itself showing signs of erosion. While the government is careful to support the expanding Irish-medium schools sector, it has also relaxed further the requirements for pupils to study Irish and the requirements for teachers to have a professional competence in Irish. The proposals to re-structure the National University of Ireland raise questions about the continued status of Irish as a required matriculation subject. There is now a clear possiblity that Irish as a school subject will revert to its pre-independence status as a voluntary subject.

Public statements about the strategic direction of language policy are rare and extremely general in nature (see, for example, the Government

Statement on the Irish Language, 2006). While Minister Ó Cuív, speaking in October 2007, announced that a cabinet sub-committee would be established 'to agree an integrated plan ... to secure the future of Irish as the community language in the Gaeltacht' there is still no cross-departmental framework in the overall field of Irish-language policy of the range and scope, for example, of *The National Action Plan Against Racism, 2005-2008* (Department of Justice, Equality and Law Reform).

As a result, each of the main agencies responsible for implementing key policies (in e.g. education, the Gaeltacht and media) is left in a policy vacuum and increasingly tends to act autonomously. Policies are left vulnerable to assessment solely within the context of the sponsoring agency's operational environment and without reference to any wider societal goal. Thus, for example, Irish-language programmes on television are ultimately left to fight their corner in terms of the audiences they attract and the advertising revenue they bring in. The possibility that they may have a function within a national bilingual policy – irrespective of its shape – is increasingly difficult to articulate and sustain.

CONCLUSION

There are dangers in this development. Tovey (1988: 67) points out that the more policy singles out 'Irish-speakers' as the target for language policies on the grounds of their rights as a minority group, the less plausible it becomes to sustain existing policies to revive Irish. Nor is it easy, in political terms, to move from a universal policy, which has been in operation for eighty years, to one which is more selective without severely damaging public confidence in the overall policy objective.

A short reflection on the structural limits and inherent weakness of the present pattern of bilingualism in Ireland clearly indicates that there are major problems with both the processes of bilingual production and of bilingual reproduction.

The stability of current Irish usage is dependent on the stability of the social networks of users, that is, on the series of interlinked social relationships that may grow out of contacts in an institutional setting, but whose survival depends on the achievement of some degree of friendship, intimacy and interpersonal knowledge among participants.

It seems unlikely that these are strong enough at present to guarantee the reproduction of spoken Irish, or its expansion, into the next generation. A policy built around the provision of state services to Irish-speakers will, I feel, ultimately find that they do not exist in large enough numbers nor are they sufficiently concentrated to meet the operational thresholds required to make these services viable. A sustainable, bilingual language policy has to aim always to recruit from the ranks of those currently speaking English, rather than simply service those currently speaking Irish. That is why I think that the Official Languages Act 2003 signals a false dawn or, maybe, a last hurrah.

NOTE

Unless otherwise stated, all statistics and the analysis presented here can be found in fuller detail in Ó Riagáin, 1997.

REFERENCES

(APC) Advisory Planning Committee. 1988. *The Irish language in a changing society: Shaping the future*. Dublin. Bord na Gaeilge.

(BCI) Broadcasting Commission of Ireland. 2004. *Turning on and tuning in to Irish language radio in the 21st century*. Dublin. BCI.

Central Statistics Office. 2007. *Census 2006, Principal demographic results*. Dublin. Stationery Office.

European Commission. 1996. *EUROMOSAIC: The production and reproduction of the minority language groups in the European Union*. Luxembourg. OOPEC.

Gaeltacht Commission. 1926. Commission of inquiry into the preservation of the Gaeltacht, *Final Report*. Dublin. Stationery Office.

Hechter, M. 1978. 'Group formation and the cultural division of labour' in *The American journal of sociology*, 84(2): 293-318.

Ó Cuív, B. (ed). 1969. *A view of the Irish language*. Dublin. Stationery Office.

Ó Riagáin, P. 1997. *Language policy and social reproduction: Ireland 1893-1993*. Oxford. Clarendon Press.

Tovey, H., D. Hannan & H. Abramson. 1989. *Why Irish? Irish identity and the Irish language*. Dublin. Bord na Gaeilge.

The Irish Language and Identity

Iarfhlaith Watson

INTRODUCTION

In 2007 comedian Des Bishop 'took the ultimate step towards Irishness by moving to the Gaeltacht to learn his mother tongue' (www.aikenpro motions.com). This statement is interesting at a number of levels, but, in the context of this chapter, it is of interest primarily because it links the Irish language to Irish identity. Arguments in favour of learning Irish, or of reviving it, tend to be founded on the assertion that Irish is an essential element of Irish identity.

Languages are primarily means of communication. In Ireland the principal language of communication is English. In that context the Irish language is superfluous and reviving it as the primary means of communication appears futile. As the renowned sociolinguist Joshua Fishman (1991) argued, reviving a language for the sake of the language is not sufficient for the average person. Therefore, efforts to learn or to revive Irish as a means of communication have tended to be bolstered by arguments about its symbolic importance for Irish identity.

Since the beginning of the Irish language revival in the late nineteenth century the idea of 'revival' has incorporated much more than language. The revival of the Irish language went hand-in-hand with the construction of an Irish identity which contained a variety of cultural elements. In fact, to a large extent, Irishness was constructed in contrast with notions of Englishness. The image of Englishness against which Irishness was contructed was of Protestant people living in cities, playing sports like rugby, football (soccer) and cricket and speaking English. The Irish idyll was a rural, Catholic society playing sports like (Gaelic) football and hurling and speaking Irish.

Since that time, the argument has frequently been made that the revival of the Irish language should go hand-in-hand with a kind of cultural renaissance. More recently Michael Cronin argued that:

> cultivating a culture of engagement, continuity and memory could in fact
> be a bold move in elaborating a radical, dissonant modernity for Ireland, a
> move that would of course involve a central role for Irish. (Cronin 2005:
> 30)

The idea here, and in other such approaches, is to find a more 'modern' culture with which to associate the Irish language – if the Irish language cannot be revived for its own sake, perhaps it could be packaged with a whole cultural renaissance. National identity is often mentioned along with the unfashionable and old-fashioned (dancing at the crossroads) cultural elements with which the Irish language had been associated, as if to suggest that the Irish language should be divested of national identity. This appears to be a misunderstanding of how identity works, and is worth examining more closely.

NATIONAL IDENTITY

There are a number of elements fundamental to a social scientific understanding of identity. One of these has been alluded to already: identity tends to be about not only the 'us' who are included, but also there tends to be a (particular) 'them' who are not included and against whom the 'us' is compared. The 'them' in the context of Irishness was the English. The construction of Irishness in opposition to Englishness can be understood in the context of a second element of identity, which is particular to national identity: national identity tends to be constructed as part of a project. National identity functions as a component within the argument in favour of that project. Reicher and Hopkins (2001), for example, discussed how the same environment could be drawn on in two opposing ways in the construction of Scottishness. In the first instance it was claimed 'The Scots are communal, not defensive, due to their harsh environment' and on the other side of the same construction of Scottishness it was argued that 'living in a tough environment makes people independent and opinionated' (Reicher and Hopkins 2001: 114).

The Irish national identity which was constructed in the late nineteenth and early twentieth centuries was a base on which the argument or project of political independence was constructed. In that project the most logical 'them' against which Irishness could be compared were the British and, more particularly, the English. The Irish language was a component in the argument of that project. The Irish national identity (including the Irish language and particular cultural forms), which was constructed in that era, was a product of the time.

A third element of identity is that it is a process. That means that identity is in a continual state of flux, always changing and never fixed. Despite this, identity appears to be fixed and natural. This is what gives it strength. Identities are regarded, by the people who share those identities, as natural and fixed essences of themselves. Identity holds us together because we believe that within each of us is that same something that constitutes that identity.

Hugo Hamilton opened his book *The Sailor in the Wardrobe* with:

> People say you're born innocent, but it's not true. You inherit all kinds of things that you can do nothing about. You inherit your identity, your history, like a birthmark that you can't wash off. We have our Irish history and our German history, like an original sin. We are born with our heads turned back, but my mother says we have to face into the future now. (Hamilton 2006: 1)

That is how identity, and particularly national identity, is. It is Janus-faced – looking to the past and the future at the same time. Identities are social constructions and the Irish national identity, within which we see the Irish language associated with an 'old-fashioned' culture, is an identity which was forged in a revolutionary period a century and more ago. There were certain individuals proactively involved in the construction of that national identity. These individuals have sometimes been referred to as intellectuals.

THE ROLE OF INTELLECTUALS

Although national identity appears to be 'natural' and pre-existing, it is a social construction. This means that our national identity exists because we accept it as a legitimate identity in our social interaction. It doesn't exist as a thing in itself, but rather in our social relationship with one another. Our identity exists in the context of our social interaction, it can be different from one social interaction to the next and the overall pattern can change over time. Nonetheless, certain individuals can have a leading role in the construction of identity.

The role of intellectuals has been discussed in the sociological and political scientific literature (see O'Dowd 1996; Gellner 1964: 169; Smith 1981: 90) and it also has been discussed in relation to the revival of the Irish language (see Cronin 2005 and Ó hÉallaithe 2004). As

Smith (1994) argued, national identity is not created out of nothing – history is not a pick-'n-mix sweetshop. National identity depends on the resources provided by history. Hence the importance of professional intellectuals such as historians, archaeologists and folklorists during the emergence of nationalist movements. Intellectuals tend to draw on the resources of history to construct a national identity, but this identity must resonate with the masses. After all, nationalist movements are mass movements in the end. The inclusion of the Irish language in the national identity constructed in the late nineteenth and early twentieth centuries created a bond with the past, which gave the Irish nation an appearance of natural antiquity.

More recently Cronin discussed the importance of the Irish language in terms of unlocking 'the storehouse of an extremely distinguished ancient, medieval and baroque civilization' (Cronin 2005: 24), but he was careful to raise the question that associating Irish with the past could mean 'that the language is forever hostage to antiquarian defensiveness' (Cronin 2005: 26). Instead, Cronin considered the issue of the past appositely in the context of the currently dominant utilitarian worldview – he emphasized the 'cognitive and aesthetic resources' contained in that Irish language 'storehouse' on which the current 'knowledge society' could draw.

Despite efforts in recent decades to dissociate the Irish language from what was perceived to be an obsolete national identity, it will not prove fruitful to attempt to dissociate the Irish language from Irish national identity per se. Indeed, national identity will be a relevant force for the foreseeable future, notwithstanding current processes of globalization. Fundamentally, the effort to associate the Irish language with a culture with contemporary resonance is an intellectual endeavour to elaborate and construct a national identity for today. As long as the Irish nation exists there will be a place for Irish national identity.

NATIONS AND DIVERSITY

Interestingly, Cronin's argument in favour of a culture which would be a 'counter-move to globalising uniformity' is reminiscent of Johann Gottfried von Herder's argument in the eighteenth century about defending diversity from uniformity. Herder argued that language is what makes people human. He went on to argue that language is thought and, that being the case, each linguistic community has its own mode of thought. Furthermore, he argued that individual governments are the result of an organic historical development as the folk-nation comes into existence on its own (see Breuilly 1982: 336). Many nationalist movements (including the Irish nationalist movement) drew on Herder's romantic nationalism in which language was an important marker of a nation.

Nationalist movements, by their aspirations, tend to be primarily about self-determination. A consequence of dividing the globe into separate nation-states is that a limited diversity is constructed on the global level, while, at the same time, uniformity and homogeneity comes from nation-building efforts within nation-states.

It appears that the basic structure of arguments about the Irish language today is similar to the structure of such arguments in the past (e.g. defending diversity from uniformity or associating the Irish language with cultural forms). As the French say *plus ça change, plus c'est la même chose*. Nonetheless, the form of globalization in existence today must be borne in mind. This is evident in McCloskey's argument for the maintenance of the Irish language:

> the effort is worth making because it is our contribution to a much larger effort, a global struggle to preserve a kind of diversity which human society has enjoyed for millennia, but which is being lost in our time. (McCloskey 2001: 41)

This statement about linguistic diversity reflects arguments about maintaining biodiversity. As an element of global diversity, the Irish language should be protected, and, because it happens to exist in Ireland, the people of Ireland should take responsibility for protecting it. This sounds like a more sophisticated version of protecting the language for the sake of the language. At the same time it is clear that there is an element of pride suggested in McCloskey's argument, especially when he uses words like 'celebrated' (p. 47) and 'extraordinary' (p. 51), but he was attempting to get 'beyond nationalism' (p. 43). The kind of nationalism he was trying to overcome, however, is what has been called 'hot' nationalism, but a more 'banal' type of nationalism (Billig 1995) can include pride in things that are unique to the territory of that nation, such as special areas of conservation, archaeological treasures or a language.

A NATIONAL SYMBOL

Various things can be employed as symbols of identity and 'worn' with pride. The Irish language has been a symbol of Irish national identity since the nineteenth century (and before) and, to a large extent, the revival of the Irish language has been predicated on such national pride. As a symbol of Irishness, however, the Irish language would not need to be adopted as the primary means of communication in Ireland, as was intended by 'revival', but, rather, could be spoken by a linguistic minority and on 'special' occasions. There has been a contradiction, therefore, between, on the one hand, reviving the Irish language because of its symbolic importance and, on the other hand, an emphasis on its symbolic importance while disregarding its revival. That contradiction is evident in the favourable opinions about the Irish language expressed by the adults of Ireland while they (as the state and parents) attempted to use the education system to revive the Irish language in the next generation rather than making the effort to revive it in their own generation.

The Irish language continues to be regarded as an important aspect of Irish national identity. To the majority of people in Ireland the Irish language is primarily of symbolic importance. In a recent survey 89 per cent of the respondents agreed that 'promoting the Irish language is important to the country as a whole' (MORI Ireland 2004: 7), but this percentage is divided between 57 per cent who also agreed that 'promoting the Irish language is important to me personally' and 32 per cent who also agreed that 'promoting the Irish language is not important to me personally'. Although 57 per cent of that sample regarded the promotion of the Irish language as important to them personally, only 39 per cent of another sample agreed that the ability to speak Irish is important or very important to being Irish (International Social Survey Programme 2003 national identity data – down 3 per cent from 1995).

It seems that the majority of people in Ireland believe that promoting the Irish language is important to the country and to them personally, but a lower percentage believe that actually speaking Irish is important to being Irish. Overall, the majority of Irish people appear to regard the Irish language to be of symbolic importance for Irish national identity and a very large minority regard the actual speaking of Irish as important.

SYMBOLIC TRANSMISSION

Although recent censuses have recorded responses about how frequently people speak Irish, the main question about ability to speak Irish appears to be more an expression of attitude than ability. The percentage of the population returned as Irish speakers in the most recent census (2006) is 42 per cent. This percentage has remained relatively stable over the past three censuses since 1996. This is about three or four times higher than the figures returned from other surveys such as the Committee on Irish Language Attitudes Research (CILAR) in 1973 and continued by Institiúid Teangeolaíochta Éireann (ITÉ, the Linguistics Institute of Ireland) in 1983 and 1993, as well as the International Social Survey Programme (ISSP) modules on national identity in 1995 and 2003. In the most recent ISSP survey on national identity, 16 per cent of the sample claimed that Irish was one of the languages that they speak well.

Most surveys tend to include only adults in the sample, but the national census, of course, includes everyone. If we compare the percentage of people in full-time education who can speak Irish with the percentage of people finished full-time education who can speak Irish we get 53 per cent and 39 per cent respectively (Census 2006). The contrast is even more extreme if we compare people aged 5 to 19 years old with people aged over 19, we get percentages in the range 60 to 70 and 30 to 40 respectively (calculated on Census 2006 data). The contrast between the younger and older age groups is not because of an increased ability to pass on the language to the next generation, but is a reflection of the symbolic (as opposed to the actual) transmission of the Irish language to the next generation.

IDEOLOGICAL SHIFT

Efforts to revive the Irish language have rested largely on the education system. This was compatible with the ideology of the time. From a critical view, ideology:

> is primarily concerned with the ways in which symbolic forms intersect with relations of power. It is concerned with the ways in which meaning is mobilized in the social world and serves thereby to bolster up individuals and groups who occupy positions of power. (Thompson 1994: 135)

During the first few decades following independence a conservative and protectionist ideology (which served those in power) dominated.

The main unit of this ideology was the nation. In this context the efforts made to revive the Irish language were national efforts employing the national education system and the national broadcaster. Although the efforts of that era have had an effect which has lasted up to the present, some of the most compulsory elements in education (see Kelly 2002), in mass media (see Watson 1996, 2003 and 2007b) and in state employment, have been eroded during the past forty years.

During the 1950s the conservative ideology came under attack and there was gradually an ideological shift to a more liberal and social democratic ideology in which people were believed to have the right to certain choices. This ideological shift was reinforced when Ireland joined the European Economic Community in 1973. The ideological approach within Europe was to overcome national(ist) conflict by focusing on economic cooperation. Within the European community, and particularly in the context of the violent conflict in Northern Ireland, nationalism – even its more banal symbols – was de-emphasized. During this era, although the Irish language remained an important national symbol, a new approach to it emerged in which the Irish language was regarded as the language of a linguistic minority and the speaking of the Irish language a minority right rather than a national obligation. This perspective is evident in the emphasis placed on the Gaeltacht during this era (e.g. Gaeltarra Éireann (1957), the Gaeltacht civil rights movement (late 1960s), Raidió na Gaeltachta (1972), Údarás na Gaeltachta (1980)). During that time, the Irish language also came to be regarded as a European minority language.

In more recent years there has been a shift toward a more neo-liberal ideology in which Ireland flows with the currents of globalization. Within this ideology there is a fervent 'rational' individualization which is evident in some economic policies over the past decade (such as tax individualization). It is also evident in a new approach to the Irish language in which learning and speaking Irish is a 'rational' choice made by individuals. This new approach is manifest in the Official Languages Act 2003. The purpose of the Act is to promote the use of the Irish language for official purposes in the state as well as in communicating with or providing services to the public. Effectively the Act makes it possible for Irish speakers as individuals to conduct their business with the state in Irish. (See Watson 2007a for a further discussion of these ideological shifts).

In the current era of globalization more stock is taken of global diversity. This is the argument McCloskey (2001) made in relation to maintaining global linguistic diversity (discussed above). The perspective which had been staunchly national in the first half of the twentieth century, gradually broadened to include the European and then the global context. This is not to say that the national context is forgotten. In fact European and global issues tend to be discussed in the national context e.g. in Ireland (as in other countries) we discuss global or European issues in the context of what they mean to us living within the boundaries of this particular nation-state.

CONCLUSION

Efforts to revive the Irish language reflect wider ideological processes. Although there have been ideological shifts, and identity has changed (because it is always under construction), national identity has remained at the heart of justifications for reviving the Irish language. People learn Irish and support its promotion because of this sense of identity. Moreover, the Irish language is supported by the state to a degree to which other minority languages are not. In general the public supports (or at least tolerates) this level of commitment because of the perceived connection between the Irish language and Irishness. Identification with the nation, although not as 'hot' as it once was in Ireland, remains. The Irish language remains related to that identification.

It will be interesting to see if the relationship between the Irish language, culture and national identity continue to change gradually or if there will be a radical redefinition of that relationship. This is of particular interest given the dramatic changes to the ethnic composition of the population of Ireland over the past decade because of increased immigration. There are now many new ethnic groups in Ireland and many minority languages spoken by thousands of people. As Irish identity changes and is constructed in the presence of increasing diversity, it will be interesting to see if the symbolic significance of the Irish language for Irish identity will continue to be a factor in the survival of the language.

REFERENCES

Billig, M. 1995. *Banal nationalism*. London. Sage.

Breuilly, J. 1982. *Nationalism and the State*. Manchester. Manchester UP.

Cronin, M. 2005. *Irish in the new century*. Dublin. Cois Life.

Fishman, J.A. 1991. *Reversing language shift: Theoretical and empirical foundations of assistance to threatened languages*. Clevedon. Multiligual Matters.

Gellner, E. 1964. *Thought and change*. London. Weidenfeld & Nicholson.

Hamilton, H. 2006. *The sailor in the wardrobe*. London. Harper Perennial.

Kelly, A. 2002. *Compulsory Irish: Language and education in Ireland 1870s–1970s*. Dublin. Irish Academic Press.

McCloskey, J. 2001. *Voices silenced: Has Irish a future?* Dublin. Cois Life.

MORI Ireland. 2004. *Turning on and tuning in to Irish language radio in the 21st century: A research report prepared by MORI Ireland on behalf of the Broadcasting Commission of Ireland and Foras na Gaeilge*. BCI. Dublin.

O'Dowd, L. (ed). 1996. *On intellectuals and intellectual life in Ireland*. Belfast. Queen's University of Belfast, Institute of Irish Studies.

Ó hÉallaithe, D. 2004. 'From language revival to language survival' in Mac Murchaidh, C. (ed), *Who needs Irish?* Dublin. Veritas.

Reicher, S. & N. Hopkins. 2001. *Self and nation*. London. Sage.

Smith, A.D. 1981. *The ethnic revival*. Cambridge. CUP.

Smith, A.D. 1994. 'Gastronomy or geology? The role of nationalism in the reconstruction of nations' in *Nations and nationalism* 1(1): 3-23.

Thompson, J. B. 1994. 'Ideology and modern culture' in Giddens, A. et al (eds), *The Polity reader in social theory*. Cambridge. Polity.

Watson, I. 1996. 'The Irish language and television' in *The British journal of sociology* 47(2): 255-74.

Watson, I. 2003. *Broadcasting in Irish: Minority language, radio, television and identity*. Dublin. Four Courts.

Watson, I. 2007a. 'Identity, language and nationality' in O'Sullivan, S. (ed), *Contemporary Ireland: A sociological map*. Dublin. UCD.

Watson, I. 2007b. 'Recent and current trends in Irish-language broadcasting' in Horgan, J. et al (eds), *Mapping Irish media*. Dublin. UCD.

www.aikenpromotions.com/component/option,com_gigcal/task,details/gigcal_bands_id,47/Itemid,68 (accessed 26 September 2007).

Linguistic Change and Standardization

Liam Mac Mathúna

CONTEXT AND CONCEPTS

Languages of their nature are dynamic social constructs. Their dialects reflect community interaction based on region, occupation and class. However, the tendency towards variation is offset by a contrary impetus towards standardization for general or sectional purposes. Such a complex interplay of varieties was encountered in the Irish language prior to the English conquest of Ireland in the seventeenth century. The rigorously codified norm adhered to by the bardic poets in the Early Modern Irish period (1200-1650), is now known as Classical Irish. Nonetheless, increasing evidence of geographical diversity may be culled from Irish-language sources from 1200 on, and from the fossilization of sounds in forms borrowed into English as place-names. For instance, *Knock* which is to be found in place-names throughout the country, predates the sound change from /kn-/ to /kr-/ within Irish, which is reflected in the development from *cnoc* to *croc* in northern dialects, although the form *cnoc* remained in use in the south (O'Rahilly 1972: 22-3). Indeed, by 1577 the Old English in Dublin were aware of the regional variation in spoken Irish, as is clear from Richard Stanihurst's account of the differences between the dialects in each of the four provinces: 'Vlster hath the right Irishe phrase, but not the true pronunciation: Mounster hath the true pronunciation, but not the phrase: Leinster is deuoyde of the right phrase, and true pronunciation, Connaght hath both the right phrase and true pronunciation' (Miller and Power 1979: 19-20).

The exclusion of Irish from public life and the shift of vernacular to English, which gained momentum from the mid-eighteenth century on meant that Irish had become marginalized by the end of the nineteenth century. Although not exclusively confined to the oral sphere, it was spoken best by those on the lowest social rungs and in the remotest areas. It was almost totally bereft of social class distinctions. Most importantly perhaps, almost all of those recorded as speaking Irish in the 1881 census had acquired Irish socially and informally, the vast majority as a first language through intergenerational transmission in family settings. Revival efforts reintroduced Irish to the higher tiers of social interaction and function differentiation which it would have enjoyed without break had the English conquest not taken place.

Success, even partial success, brings its own challenges, as is clear from the mixed fortunes of the Irish language since the last quarter of the nineteenth century, when the revival of the language began to muster popular support. Concentrating much of their efforts on education and the creation of a modern literature, the Society for the Preservation of the Irish Language (founded in 1876), The Gaelic Union (founded in 1880) and in particular the Gaelic League (founded in 1893) campaigned effectively to reverse the marginalization of the language in the hedge schools and the antagonism of the national school system, established in 1831. Modern journalism and literature were fostered by the bilingual monthly *The Gaelic Journal / Irisleabhar na Gaedhilge*, founded in 1882, which began to publish *Séadna* by An tAthair Peadar Ua Laoghaire, the first novel of the revival, in 1894. Short stories and poetry consonant with contemporary literary taste in western Europe were increasingly cultivated from the turn of the twentieth century. Viewed from a linguistic perspective, one can see that Irish was extending its range of registers beyond those to which it had become constricted throughout 300 years of domain attrition and language shift. However, the differing impact of the revival movement in the Gaeltacht and the rest of the country was to complicate this scenario beyond measure.

IDEOLOGY, COMMUNITY AND STANDARDIZATION

The central and underlying challenge for the standardization of Irish in the various spheres of font, orthography, grammar and pronunciation has been the social and community nature of language, and the difficulty therefore presented by the limited progress made in the maintenance, regeneration and creation of Irish-speaking communities in the country. The communities in the traditionally Irish-speaking areas of the Gaeltacht were beset by emigration of good Irish-speakers, by immigration of non-Irish-speakers, by the inter-generational rise in the ability and willingness to speak English, by the demise of traditional and social settings in which Irish was established, with their developed vocabulary and terminology, and the extension of new social interactions and English-based terminology. These difficulties are compounded by the prevailing revival-cum-maintenance ideology, which sees Irish as an add-on for English-speakers rather than as an alternative or substitute. The tensions which have arisen in An Daingean (Dingle), Co. Kerry, over the designation of an Irish-language form of the town's name as the official one and over the use of Irish as the medium of second-level education show how difficult it is to motivate and sustain Irish as First Language and English as Second Language in a particular area, when the overall societal consensus is English as First Language and Irish as Second language, in a minimally differentiated state-wide entity.

The increased use of Irish in publishing from the end of the nineteenth century meant that many questions relating to standardization had to be addressed: issues that had taken other languages hundreds of years to resolve required urgent attention. The Irish which appeared in *The Gaelic Journal* was printed in the so-called Gaelic font or character and spelled according to the late Classical Irish conventions as practised by Geoffrey Keating and others in the seventeenth century. As writers strove to represent the various living dialects, variations in forms and grammar became increasingly apparent. With the extension in the use of Irish in education and literature pressure grew to present learners and readers with a unified form of language. Many of the questions proved highly contentious and took over half a century to resolve. Indeed, some have scarcely been brought to a satisfactory conclusion yet.

FROM GAELIC TO ROMAN FONT

Although the two typeface fonts, the so-called Gaelic and Roman fonts shared a common origin in the medieval scribal tradition of Western Europe, Irish-language manuscripts in Ireland were almost exclusively written in the Gaelic script. Following the provision of a print font based on this manuscript style by Queen Elizabeth I in 1571 for the printing of the first book in the Irish language, *Aibidil Gaoidheilge & Caiticiosma* (Ó Cuív 1994), it continued to be the font of choice for printing Irish. Apart from the shape of the letters, the main feature distinguishing the two fonts is the use of 'h' in the Roman font to indicate aspiration, a change shown in the Gaelic font by placing a dot over the letter, thus *ch, fh, gh,* for *ċ, ḟ, ġ,* for example. The principal arguments advanced in favour of switching to the Roman script were pragmatic, it not being necessary to have separate typewriters and typecasting for Irish. Furthermore, learners of both Irish and English would not need to learn how to read and write two different scripts (see Ó Conchubhair 2003). The Roman font ultimately prevailed, but the changeover was slow, as most of those who learned to read in the first generations of the revival had become attached to the Gaelic script. The 1931 decision under Earnán de Blaghd as Minister for Finance in the Cumann na nGaedheal government to adopt the Roman font was reversed under the Fianna Fáil government the following year. The constitution of 1937 was in the Gaelic font. Rannóg an Aistriúcháin, the Translation Section of the Houses of the Oireachtas, favoured the Roman font. On the other hand the Department of Education only made it mandatory for the Leaving Certificate from 1972 onwards (Ó Riain 1994: 63-7). Nowadays, with very few exceptions – the official version of *Bunreacht na hÉireann* ('The Constitution of Ireland') is maintained in this font – the Gaelic font is confined to formal contexts, where the emphasis is on design and ornamentation rather than information. It may be noted that a parallel debate took place in Germany and the Scandinavian countries concerning the relative merits of Gothic and Roman fonts, with a similar pragmatic outcome in favour of the Roman font.

SIMPLIFYING THE ORTHOGRAPHY

As regards orthography, the spelling system employed at the beginning of the revival was essentially the seventeenth-century usage, based on Classical Irish. This system undoubtedly had a number of practical advantages. The publication of Robert Atkinson's edition of Séathrún Céitinn's *Trí Bior-Ghaoithe an Bháis* in 1890 had made an appropriate example readily available. The system was consistent and provided general continuity with all writing in Irish since about 1200. In effect, it served as a sort of deep structure from which the living regional dialects of Munster, Connacht and Ulster could be derived. Its central weaknesses were perhaps twofold. It contained many intervocalic aspirated guttural consonants (*-dh-, -gh-*) which were no longer pronounced in any dialect, e.g. *filidheacht* (nowadays *filíocht* 'poetry') and *críochnughadh* (*críochnú* 'completing'). However, the dropping of fricative consonants such as *-bh-* between vowels in speech had given rise to varying realizations in the different regions, e.g. in the case of *leabhar* ('book'), *tabhair* ('give'). The pressure to represent the phonetic reality and the actual forms of contemporary dialectal speech placed the 300-year-old standard under increasing strain.

However, the system based on the works of Céitinn was challenged by the championing of *caint na ndaoine* 'the language of the people' as the basis of a new norm by An tAthair Peadar Ua Laoghaire, who practised what he preached with a persuasive felicity of style and a prodigious output of a publication a fortnight from 1893 until his death in 1920, over 500 works in all. The Ua Laoghaire position won the day with the result that the variations in the living dialects had to be reconciled if an agreed norm was to emerge. However, the realization of a standard orthography owed more to the exigencies of administration and political direction than the input of Irish-language scholars. Éamon de Valera gave the following account of the process in the Dáil on 7 March 1946, when the question of the spelling employed in *Bunreacht na hÉireann* was debated:

> The standard spelling was the result of several years' examination of the question. In 1941, I set up a committee to examine the whole problem of Irish spelling and to make recommendations for a system as simple as possible and suitable for adoption as a standard for general use. This committee found itself unable to make progress. I then entrusted the task to the chief translator on the Oireachtas Staff [Liam Ó Rinn] and, after his death, to his successor [Tomás Page] who, with the assistance of the whole translation section, re-examined the question in the greatest detail and, after some years of study, finally submitted the recommendations now incorporated in the booklet published under the title *Litriú na Gaeilge: An Caighdeán Oifigiúil.* (Ó Cearúil 2003: xv)

Originally set out in 1945, a second, expanded edition entitled *Litriú na Gaeilge: Lámhleabhar an Chaighdeáin Oifigiúil* ('The Spelling of Irish: The Handbook of the Official Standard') was issued by *Rannóg an Aistriúcháin* in 1947. In their Introduction the authors wryly advert to the impossibility of getting any two people to agree on the gamut of its recommendations but state that they were encouraged by the general public interest and response to their first edition.

A few of the rules are set out below, followed by a number of examples of the effect of the changes involved in the new standard, by way of illustration:

sg, sb, sd > sc, sp, st (e.g. *sgéal > scéal* 'story'; *sbéir > spéir* 'sky'; *ceisd > ceist* 'question')

dl > ll (e.g. *Nodlaig > Nollaig* 'Christmas'; exception: *codladh* 'sleep')

bhth, thbh, mhth, thmh > f (e.g. *lobhtha > lofa* 'rotten'; *uathbhás > uafás* 'horror'; *naomhtha > naofa* 'holy'; *lúthmhar > lúfar* 'agile')

Dropping of dh [dha, dhe, (a)idhe(a), (o)idhe(a)] (*bunadhas > bunús* 'origin'; *buidhe > buí* 'yellow'; *Gaedhilge > Gaeilge* 'Irish')

Dropping of gh [(i)ghe, ighea, ighi, gha, (u)ghadh] (e.g. *saoghal > saol* 'life'; *deimhniughadh > deimhniú* 'affirming'; *inghean > iníon* 'daughter')

Dropping of mh: amha > ú (*ceathramha > ceathrú* 'quarter'; *leanamhaint > leanúint* 'following'; *fearamhail > fearúil* 'manly').

Although changes such as **amha > ú** led to greater use of the *síneadh fada* or length mark, it was eliminated where its presence could be predicted from a consonant cluster, e.g. *árd > ard* 'high'; *bórd > bord* 'table'; and also in *beó > beo* 'alive'.

GRAMMAR: FORMS

Litriú na Gaeilge: Lámhleabhar an Chaighdeáin Oifigiúil, setting out a standardized spelling, was followed in 1958 by a larger volume combining regulations on grammar and spelling, *Gramadach na Gaeilge agus Litriú na Gaeilge: An Caighdeán Oifigiúil* ('The Grammar and Spelling of Irish: The Official Standard'), also prepared by Rannóg an Aistriúcháin. With regard to nouns, this work followed earlier grammars in recognizing five declensions, with up to five cases in singular and plural. The cases are differentiated by variation in their endings. But in fact this template gives the impression of a far greater number of forms than are actually to be found in most declensions. The plural for example generally falls into just two categories, one termed 'strong', in which the same form is used for all five cases throughout (e.g. *dochtúirí* 'doctors'), the other 'weak', in which the genitive is the same as the nominative singular, all other cases normally having one form (thus nominative/accusative/dative/vocative plural *fuinneoga*, genitive plural *fuinneog*).

The Introduction to *An Caighdeán Oifigiúil* states that it is based on the following principles:

1.   So far as possible not to accept any form or rule which does not have authority in the living language of the Gaeltacht;

2. To make a choice from the forms which are most commonly in use in the Gaeltacht;
3. To assign the importance due to the history and literature of Irish;
4. To seek for regularity and simplicity.

However, the volume also points out that it was frequently necessary to effect a compromise between these basic directions (Rannóg an Aistriúcháin 1958: viii). Although the Introduction clearly states that the Official Standard gives special recognition to certain forms and rules, it also affirms that it does not invalidate any other correct forms, and that there is nothing to prevent their use. It has to be said, though, that the Official Standard was interpreted quite narrowly prior to the publication of *Foclóir Gaeilge-Béarla* (Irish-English Dictionary), the most recent major dictionary (Ó Dónaill 1977).

With regard to the verb, *An Caighdeán Oifigiúil* prescribed so-called separate forms (*foirmeacha scartha*) rather than coalesced forms (*foirmeacha táite*), but not in the first person plural past tense, where *mholamar* 'we praised' was included, rather than *mhol muid* (Connacht) or *mhol muidinne* (Donegal). *An Caighdeán Oifigiúil* also chose one set of forms for the irregular verbs, which vary greatly from area to area. In the cases where simple prepositions are combined with the definite article and a noun the Standard uncharacteristically explicitly permits two systems, eclipsis of the noun (e.g. *ar an gcathaoir* 'on the chair', as in Munster and Conamara, *ar an chathaoir*, as in Co. Donegal). The complex systems of numerals to be found in the various regions is generally regarded as having defeated the best efforts of the framers of *An Caighdeán Oifigiúil*.

GRAMMAR: SYNTAX
Despite the place of *Gramadach na Gaeilge* in the title, the standardizing of the grammar really only relates to morphology or forms, little or no guidance being given as regards syntax, that is how words, phrases, clauses and sentences are put together. This omission was set to rights to a considerable extent by another, far more comprehensive, work which appeared soon afterwards, namely *Graiméar Gaeilge na mBráithre Críostaí* (The Christian Brothers' Irish Grammar), published in 1960. This invaluable book deals comprehensively with a range of clause types, in particular the relative clause and the adverbial clause, but many others are touched on lightly, sometimes

inadequately. A recent assessment of the strengths and shortcomings of the traditional approach followed in this Grammar is to be found in Ó Baoill (1996). He notes that many elements are wanting, including an appreciation of the registers of language which need to be adverted to and distinguished (e.g. writing, broadcasting, colloquial speech, education, administration), and the overall sociolinguistic situation of the language. Ó Baoill argues that while the link between meaning and syntactical forms benefits already from a number of studies drawing on the insights of contemporary linguistic theory, these need to be honed to suit the particular configurations of Irish as it is currently spoken. Other desiderata noted by Ó Baoill are the uses of the tenses and an account of how compound words and phrases containing a number of nouns are best formed in Irish.

PRONUNCIATION

The promotion of a standard form of the spoken language, which would be used in domains such as broadcasting and education, has been advocated at various times. A variety known as *An Lárchanúint* (The Central Dialect) was prepared as a pronunciation guide by a committee headed by Dónall P. Ó Baoill. This committee was charged with indicating a single realization for every headword in *Foclóir Póca: English-Irish/Irish-English Dictionary*, a pocket dictionary published by An Gúm and the Department of Education in 1986 whose aim was 'to meet the ordinary needs of school-goers and of the general public' (An Gúm 1986: vii). To this end we are told 'A thesaurus of rules and examples was compiled covering various aspects of Irish pronunciation including the basic sounds, stress patterns, deletions and assimilation of particular sounds and word inflection' (An Gúm 1986: xii). This system of pronunciation contains all the essential contrasts found in the three main dialects. While it does not correspond in every detail to any one dialect, it contains a core common to all three. The ultimate inspiration for this undertaking came from Máirtín Ó Murchú's ground-breaking article 'Common Core and Underlying Forms' (1969; see also Ó Baoill 1988: 123-4). While a conference held in 1988 brought together a number of speakers who were favourably disposed to such a spoken standard (Ó Baoill 1990), it has to be said that the initiative has not yet attracted widespread support, an exception being *Gasaitéar na hÉireann / Gazetteer of Ireland* (Brainse Logainmneacha na Suirbhéireachta Ordanáis 1989), which gives the names of centres of population and physical features. Ó Baoill argues that the prestige associated with such a spoken standard is essential if the future of Irish is to be assured. On the other hand, Ó Baoill himself has identified well the nature and origin of the

> prevailing tendency amongst academics, native speakers and those who have acquired Irish as a second language to adhere sternly to one dialectal pronunciation. This tendency has been cultivated over a long period due to historical and geographical reasons and has been eagerly promoted throughout our educational system and particularly so in universities and in third level institutions (Ó Baoill 1990: 99-100).

GAELTACHT SPEECH

Descriptions of the Irish spoken in the Gaeltacht tend to concentrate on the language of older speakers, those least influenced by English. The otherwise wide-ranging accounts of the three major regional dialects in *Stair na Gaeilge* (McCone et al 1994) limit themselves for the most part to comments on the increasing lexical pressure of English. In the case of Munster, Seán Ua Súilleabháin notes that, since the vast majority of Gaeltacht Irish-speakers are fully competent in English as well, that one hears English expressions and half-sentences in natural Gaeltacht Irish (Ua Súilleabháin 1994: 536). Among the examples he gives are *táim breoite dho* < 'I am sick of it', *'bhfuil sé a' teacht fíor?* < 'is it coming true?', *thug sé suas an tobac* ('he gave up the tobacco'). He also alludes to the influence of other types of Irish by way of the school system and Raidió na Gaeltachta, without citing specific instances (Ua Súilleabháin 1994: 537-8).

As regards Connacht, Ruairí Ó hUiginn observes that stylistic factors, rather than any easily discernible vocabulary need, seem to prompt lexical borrowings in many cases. He cites *sight, misfortune, sorry*. Exclamations and adverbs such as *bhoil, even (e'n), back, now, anyway(s)* were noted over fifty years ago. Similarly, there is a strong tendency to preface answers in Irish with English *no* and *yeah/yes*, thus: *beidh tú ag goil ann? Nó ní bheidh/ní bheidhead* ('you'll be going there? No, I won't'). Ó hUiginn too adverts to direct English influence on Irish expressions such as *tá sé suas duit féin* 'it is up to you', *bhí sé ag crochadh thart* 'he was hanging around' *fuair sé deireanach* 'it got late'. Another factor which Ó hUiginn alludes to is the influence of Irish learners who have not yet got a good grasp of the language, but points out that this awaits investigation (Ó hUiginn 1994: 608-9).

With regard to contemporary developments in Ulster Irish, Art Hughes associates the increased use of the substantive verb at the expense of the copula and a variety of other syntactical features, such as the loss of the vocative form (e.g. *Art*, instead of *a Airt*) with reduced use of Irish by bilingual speakers. He also quotes a number of particularly arresting examples of direct English infiltration of Irish: *bhí infection ar mo khidneys* ('my kidneys had an infection'), *cé d'organaisáil an weekend seo?* ('who organized this weekend?'), *Ar enjoyáil tú do holidays?* ('Did you enjoy your holidays?') (Hughes 1994: 659-60).

As against this, Peadar Mac an Iomaire (1983) provides evidence of some inner-Irish regeneration. Mac an Iomaire examined some of the linguistic impact of the new social interactions in factories and offices brought about by industrialization in the south Conamara Gaeltacht area. This showed considerable variation. The Irish used by a factory-worker showed no difference from that of someone not so engaged, all technical words associated with the work being simply taken over from English and incorporated in the Irish (e.g. *oven, plastic, quality*). On the other hand, a person working in the head office of *Údarás na Gaeltachta* freely used newly coined Irish words and expressions (e.g. *inneall deachtaithe* alongside *dictaphone machine, clóscríobhán* 'type-writer'). However, this speaker said she would use the English words with other speakers when at home. Two other speakers, both working in co-ops, show a mixture of new Irish coinings and English terminology. One of these speakers demonstrated a sophisticated appreciation of sociolinguistic reality when asked whether Irish or English terms would be more acceptable among people of her own age in the area. She replied that if the other speaker was from the area, English would be more acceptable. To do otherwise would be seen as trying to set oneself apart: *cheapfaidís go raibh tú saghas ardnósach i do chuid Gaeilge nó nach shin an saghas Gaeilge a labhraíonn siad fhéin, you know. B'fhearr leo roinnt téarmaí Béarla a úsáid ná a bheith ag cur focal Gaeilge ar chuile shórt.* ('they would think you were kind of pompous with your Irish or that that was not the kind of Irish they themselves speak, you know. They would prefer to use some English terms than to be putting Irish words on everything'). The fragile nature of the inter-relationship between economic development and linguistic well-being in Gaeltacht areas continues to be explored, it being the subject of the 1999 conference on '*An Ghaeltacht ar Thairseach na Mílaoise*' (Mac Mathúna et al 2000), and a steady stream of later publications (including Walsh 2004, 2006).

Nancy Stenson's re-examination of Marie Sjoestedt's 1928 study in Dún Chaoin, Co. Kerry, is particularly insightful (Stenson 1993). Sjoestedt had identified the lexicon as the sphere of language most open to borrowing. Grammar, phonology and morphology were less affected. Stenson's study is largely based on her own observations in Ráth Chairn, Co. Meath, and Dublin some sixty years later, and states that there was not much difference between the Irish of the two areas. Stenson notes a wide extension in the semantic fields in which lexical borrowings occur. Sjoestedt had found English influence on idiom to be relatively rare, citing as examples *táim briste* ('I'm broke') and *dulta chun an phota* ('gone to pot'). Two generations later Stenson found this phenomenon to be more frequent. Among the examples she gives are: *go gcoolfaidh rudaí síos* ('until things cool down'); *Téann [sé] síos go maith* ('it goes down well'); *Ní bhfaighidh sibh off chomh héasca sin* ('You won't get off that easily'). With regard to phonology she summarizes, saying 'some increase in influence on the phonological system can be identified, but it remains minor, with little resulting reanalysis in the native vocabulary' (Stenson 1993: 114). Similarly, morphological borrowings are limited. However, Stenson points to the continued productivity of *-áil* tacked on to English verbs: *Faintáil sí* ('She fainted'); *Emigratáil uilig siad* ('They all emigrated'). She further notes the rarer, and apparently more recent, occurrence of wholly English verbal morphology: *Decided Aer Lingus go . . .* ('Aer Lingus decided that . . .'); *Cén chaoi a bhfuil tú feeling?* ('How are you feeling?'). Stenson also gives some arresting examples of code-mixing:

'*I have to make the bank in Athboy before 3:00 because if I don't, ní bheidh airgead ar bith agam le haghaidh an deireadh seachtaine.*'
('I have to make the bank in Athboy before 3:00 because if I don't, I won't have any money for the weekend.')
Shíl mé go mbeadh leathuair an chloig oibre agam; as it turned out, ní raibh tada le déanamh agam.

('I thought I'd have half an hour of work; as it turned out I had nothing to do.')

Stenson observes that this phenomenon of code-mixing is becoming increasingly widespread, particularly among younger speakers, a phenomenon she links to the near total bilingualism that marks Irish and its speakers (Stenson 1993). At an equally fundamental syntactic level, Brian Ó Curnáin records the progression in Conamara from *é a shroicheadh* via *é a reacháil* to *reacháil é* ('to reach it') where English influence has progressed from the vocabulary to word order (Ó Curnáin 2007: I, 36). Similar expressions, such as *ag déanamh é* ('doing it'), are of course to be heard quite frequently outside the Gaeltacht. Confusion between categories is also evident from the increasing use in the Gaeltacht of the noun *difríocht* ('difference') rather than the adjective *difriúil* ('different') in phrases such as *rud éigin difríocht* instead of the normal *rud éigin difriúil* ('something different').

VARIETIES OF IRISH OUTSIDE THE GAELTACHT

Most of those living outside the Gaeltacht who speak Irish regularly have tended to choose one or other of the regional dialects as a model, so that Cathair Ó Dochartaigh speaks of there being 'several areal koines, based on Donegal, South West Connacht, and several Munster dialects, as learners from outside the Gaeltacht accommodated their pronunciations towards norms representing a common core for each of the three Gaeltacht areas in which they had acquired their Irish, and few learners achieved a high level of native-like accuracy in any local variety' (Ó Dochartaigh 2000: 22). This approach has been fostered by third-level institutions such as the universities and Colleges of Education. However, this tendency is placed under strain when rapid expansion takes place in the numbers of those opting to use Irish regularly, be it in the Shaw's Road community in Belfast (see Maguire 1990) or in Irish-medium schools, *gaelscoileanna*. This latter has given rise to a variety of Irish, which is heavily influenced by English, and rather disapprovingly referred to as *Gaelscoilis*. However, there is more to this variety than simple failure to attain an agreed goal. Its emergence involves at least an implicit questioning of what the ideal form should be. Most non-native speakers of Irish outside the Gaeltacht converse almost exclusively with other non-native speakers of the language, interaction with the Gaeltacht community being peripheral to their social and economic needs and interests.

Some of the more extreme kinds of English permeation of urban

Second Language speaking of Irish have been provided by Caoilfhionn Nic Pháidín (2003). Her examples include the following:

> *Cad a bhfuil sé mar?* ('What is it like?');
> *Tá chomh méid acu ann.* ('There are so many of them (there)');
> *Sin cad i gcónaí a dhéanann tusa.* ('That's what you do always.').

The traditional system of conjugated prepositional pronouns is under sustained pressure from the English system, evidenced by examples such as *do é* (for *dó*, 'to him'), *ag iad* (for *acu*, 'at them'), *le í* (for *léi* 'with her') and *faoi muid* (for *fúinn*, 'under us'). Nic Pháidín also cites this redoubtable turn-taking dialogue:

> *Cén fáth nach?* ('Why not?')
> *Mar!* ('Because!')
> *A deireann cén duine?* ('Says who?')
> *Mise, má chaitheann tú know!* ('Me, if you must know!') (Nic Pháidín 2003: 124-6)

Of course only context and time will tell whether these are transient features, or will become longer term speech elements of individuals, networks or communities.

Confusion between initial changes seems to be common to Gaeltacht and non-Gaeltacht areas. Nowadays, for instance, one often hears *an aire* ('the minister') and *ag an t-aire* ('at the minister'), rather than *an t-aire* and *ag an aire*, which indicates systemic confusion. More common are the extension of colloquial terms such as *go raibh míle* for *go raibh míle maith agat/agaibh* ('thank you (sg./plur.)), *fadhb ar bith* ('no problem'), *ná habair é* ('don't mention it'), which may have spread from Gaelscoileanna through Gaeltacht summer colleges to younger speakers in the Gaeltacht. In other cases, a phrase can become particularly popular on radio and television, e.g. *críochnú suas* ('to finish up') rather than *críochnú* ('to finish'), *díriú isteach ar rud* (lit. 'to focus in on something') rather than simply *díriú ar rud* ('to focus on something') and *sin é díreach é* ('that's exactly it'), rather than *sin é* ('that's it'). A colourful phrase such as *an gabhar á róstadh* (lit. 'the goat being roasted', meaning 'where the fun/action is') first became frequent on radio programmes from Corca Dhuibhne, Co. Kerry, before extending its reach to Co. Cork. Originally met with in Munster, *fadhb* ('problem') is now to be heard from Donegal speakers, just as northern *díospóireacht* ('debate') and *reáchtáil* ('run, organize') are in use in

Munster and the rest of the country. In principle, changes such as these are signs of language vitality, no matter how much the individual instances may grate on the ear initially.

CONCLUSION

In sum, one can say that the written Standard is now set out explicitly and most comprehensively in *Graiméar Gaeilge na mBráithre Críostaí*. It also underpins de Bhaldraithe's *English-Irish Dictionary* (1959; due to be superseded by the current Foras na Gaeilge dictionary project) and Ó Dónaill's *Foclóir Gaeilge-Béarla*, which includes a number of implicit revisions of the Standard, but leaves many issues unresolved. These are complemented by a host of terminological dictionaries and lists prepared and published by An Coiste Téarmaíochta ('The Terminological Committee'), now part of Foras na Gaeilge. Fiontar, Dublin City University, has produced terminological work in the areas of computing and finance, and provided the internet database www.focal.ie. Indeed database resources such as this and www.acmhainn.ie are playing an increasing role in contemporary Irish usage. It is vitally important, however, that issues relating to underlying principles and potential applications continue to attract professional and scholarly exchange (see, for instance, Nic Eoin and Mac Mathúna 1997). It is also essential that this debate be situated in its international context, as happened at the seminar on 'Minority Languages and Terminology Policies', held by the European Association for Terminology in Foras na Gaeilge's headquarters in Dublin in July 2007.

Many challenges lie ahead. The relative weakness of the Gaeltacht means that the Irish spoken in other areas of the country and broadcast in the media will be of increasing importance in the future. Ideological questions such as an appropriate goal for speakers into the twenty-first century, be it either a new spoken standard or *lárchanúint*, or continued approximation to regional dialects, would benefit from Irish-language scholars becoming more *engagé* in debate and delivery. The educational and administrative systems will continue to be crucial in the provision and dissemination of language models. Many genres of modern literature in Irish are robust enough both to continue to provide first-rate linguistic exemplars, where appropriate, and to interact effectively with the sociolinguistic dynamics of Irish and English inside and outside the Gaeltacht (see Nic Eoin 2005).

Ultimately, if Irish is to prosper, it must not only be used but used well. All speakers can improve their competence and hone their performance. However, given their central role in modern life, much of the onus for putting theory into good practice will inevitably fall on the practitioners of the broadcast and print media. Viewed from this language perspective, news, current affairs and documentary features are of crucial importance as they are in the vanguard when it comes to crystallizing terminology and idiom into a language appropriate for the up-to-the-minute actions and thoughts of our times. The future well-being and form of the Irish language is largely, if not exclusively, in their hands.

References

An Gúm, Brainse na bhFoilseachán, An Roinn Oideachais. 1986. *Foclóir póca: English-Irish/Irish-English dictionary.* Baile Átha Cliath. An Gúm i gcomhar le hOifig an tSoláthair.

Brainse Logainmneacha na Suirbhéireachta Ordanáis. 1989. *Gasaitéar na hÉireann / Gazetteer of Ireland.* Baile Átha Cliath. Oifig an tSoláthair.

de Bhaldraithe, T. 1959. *English-Irish dictionary.* Baile Átha Cliath. Oifig an tSoláthair.

Hughes, A. 1994. 'Gaeilge Uladh', in McCone, K. et al (eds), *Stair na Gaeilge.*

Mac an Iomaire, P. 1983. 'Tionchar na tionsclaíochta ar Ghaeilge Chonamara Theas' in *Teangeolas* 16: 9-18.

Mac Mathúna, L., C. Mac Murchaidh & M. Nic Eoin. 2000. *Teanga, pobal agus réigiún: Aistí ar chultúr na Gaeltachta inniu.* Baile Átha Cliath. Coiscéim.

Maguire, G. 1990. *Our own language: An Irish initiative.* Clevedon. Multilingual Matters.

McCone, K., D. McManus, C. Ó Háinle, N. Williams & L. Breatnach (eds). 1994. *Stair na Gaeilge: In ómós do Pádraig Ó Fiannachta.* Maigh Nuad. Roinn na Sean-Ghaeilge, Coláiste Phádraig.

Miller, L. & E. Power. 1979. *Holinshed's Irish Chronicle.* Dublin. Dolmen Editions.

Na Bráithre Críostaí. 1960. *Graiméar Gaeilge na mBráithre Críostaí.* Baile Átha Cliath. M. H. Mac an Ghoill & a Mhac.

Nic Eoin, M. 2005. *Trén bhfearann breac: An dílaithriú cultúir agus nualitríocht na Gaeilge.* Baile Átha Cliath. Cois Life.

Nic Eoin, M. & L. Mac Mathúna (eds). 1997. *Ar thóir an fhocail chruinn: Iriseoirí, téarmeolaithe agus fadhbanna an aistriúcháin.* Baile Átha Cliath. Coiscéim.

Nic Pháidín, C. 2003. '"Cén fáth nach?" – Ó chanúint go críól', in Ní Mhianáin, R. (ed), *Idir lúibíní.*

Ní Mhianáin, R. (ed). 2003. *Idir lúibíní: Aistí ar an léitheoireacht agus ar an litearthacht*. Baile Átha Cliath. Cois Life.

Ó Baoill, D.P. 1986. *Lárchanúint don Ghaeilge*. Baile Átha Cliath. Institiúid Teangeolaíochta Éireann.

Ó Baoill, D.P. 1988. 'Language planning in Ireland: The standardisation of Irish' in *The international journal of the sociology of language* 70: 109-26.

Ó Baoill, D.P. 1990. 'A standard pronunciation for Irish: Problems and implications' in *Teanga* 10: 93-102.

Ó Baoill, D.P. (ed). 1990. *Úsáid agus forbairt na lárchanúna*. Baile Átha Cliath. Institiúid Teangeolaíochta Éireann and Bord na Gaeilge.

Ó Baoill, D.P. 1996. 'Gramadach na Gaeilge agus na Bráithre Críostaí' in Ó Cearúil, M. (ed), *Gníomhartha na mBráithre*.

Ó Cearúil, M. (ed). 1996. *Gníomhartha na mBráithre*. Baile Átha Cliath. Coiscéim.

Ó Cearúil, M. 2003. *Bunreacht na hÉireann: An téacs Gaeilge arna chaighdeánú*. Baile Átha Cliath. Coiscéim.

Ó Conchubhair, B. 2003. 'The Gaelic font controversy: The Gaelic League's (post-colonial) crux' in *The Irish University Review* 33(1): 46-63.

Ó Cuív, B. (ed). 1994. *Aibidil Gaoidheilge & caiticiosma: Seán Ó Cearnaigh's Irish primer of religion published in 1571*. Dublin. School of Celtic Studies, Dublin Institute for Advanced Studies.

Ó Curnáin, B. 2007. *The Irish of Iorras Aithneach County Galway*. Dublin. School of Celtic Studies, Dublin Institute for Advanced Studies.

Ó Dochartaigh, C. 2000. 'Irish in Ireland', in Price, G. (ed.), *Languages in Britain & Ireland*.

Ó Dónaill, N. 1977. *Foclóir Gaeilge-Béarla*. Baile Átha Cliath. Oifig an tSoláthair.

Ó hUiginn, R. 1994. 'Gaeilge Chonnacht' in McCone. K. et al (eds), *Stair na Gaeilge*.

Ó Murchú, M. 1969. 'Common core and underlying forms' in *Ériu* 21: 42-75.

O'Rahilly, T.F. 1972. *Irish dialects past and present*. Dublin. Dublin Institute for Advanced Studies.

Ó Riain, S. 1994. *Pleanáil teanga in Éirinn: 1919-1985*. Baile Átha Cliath. Carbad.

Price, G. (ed). 2000. *Languages in Britain & Ireland*. Oxford: Blackwell.

Rannóg an Aistriúcháin. 1947. *Litriú na Gaeilge: Lámhleabhar an Chaighdeáin Oifigiúil*. Baile Átha Cliath. Oifig an tSoláthair.

Rannóg an Aistriúcháin. 1958. *Gramadach na Gaeilge agus litriú na Gaeilge: An Caighdeán Oifigiúil*. Baile Átha Cliath. Oifig an tSoláthair.

Sjoestedt, M.L. 1928. 'L'influence de la langue Anglaise sur un parler local irlandais', in *Étrenne de linguistiques offertes par quelques amis à Émile Benveniste*. Paris. Librairie Orientaliste Paul Geuthner, 81-122.

Stenson, N. 1993, 'English influence on Irish: The last 100 years' in *The journal of Celtic linguistics* 2: 107-28.

Ua Súilleabháin, S. 1994. 'Gaeilge na Mumhan' in McCone, K. et al (eds), *Stair na Gaeilge*.

Walsh, J. 2004. *An teanga, an cultúr agus an fhorbairt: Cás na hÉireann agus cás na Gaeilge*. Baile Átha Cliath. Coiscéim.

Walsh, J. 2006. 'Language and socio-economic development: Towards a theoretical framework' in *Language problems and language planning* 30(2): 127-48.

Corpus Planning for Irish – Dictionaries and Terminology

Caoilfhionn Nic Pháidín

HISTORICAL BACKGROUND AND INTERNATIONAL CONTEXT

The Irish language and its fortunes have changed considerably since 750 AD, when an anonymous Irish student in Germany made his contribution to lexicography in the Würzburg Glosses. This article describes the evolution and current situation of corpus planning for Irish, which includes dictionaries, terminology and corpora.

Writing in Irish was still partially transmitted through the manuscript tradition until the late nineteenth century. In just over a hundred years, the language has embraced large-scale print transmission and more recently the internet. Lexicographical methodologies everywhere have also been transformed by new technologies. From the middle ages until the late 1980s, the old craft of dictionary-making was centred in the power of tradition and rarely innovative. It involved excerpting extracts by hand from printed and manuscript sources, recording on paper slips in massive archives, and laborious drafting of dictionary entries manually for print publication.

In just over twenty years, a metamorphosis has taken place in dictionary design, production and use. Lone scholars have been replaced by project teams working with corpora and computational linguistics software for publication in print, CD, and the internet. The success of dictionary projects today depends on project management, matched with technological and linguistic expertise in multidisciplinary teams. Some of the individual enthusiasm for the imaginative creativity of words and their uses has invariably been lost in this process, as on-line databases are queried by quick-clicking translators working to deadlines on reports required by language legislation.

Once used extensively as a language of literary and spiritual expression, Irish under colonialism during the seventeenth to nineteenth centuries became primarily an oral language, albeit with a rich lexicon of oral literature and song, in rural and maritime communities. When the inevitability of irreversible language loss became ever more clear in the late nineteenth century the new revivalists grappled with determining written forms, and how script, dialects, orthography, and a written standard and grammar, might be moulded for modern use. Alongside this came the challenges of developing lexicography and terminology for a new age. The revival process provided the impetus for new literature, journalism and publishing, and established a literacy base.

Starkly contrasting trends emerged which affected development of the lexicon. The Gaeltacht heartlands have continued to contract, although revival policies and incentives have slowed the pace of decline. The ever-decreasing native-speaker base throughout the twentieth century and the accelerated modernization of the Irish economy and society, have resulted in major domain loss in Irish in its heartland, where the language was strongest and best able to develop new forms and expressions and assimilate borrowings. In parallel with this, revival policies expanded the learner base through education, which in turn generated development of communications, literature and use of Irish in legislation and public administration.

The literacy base expanded considerably as each cohort progressed through school and readership peaked around the late 1960s, if sales figures of newspapers and periodicals can be taken as evidence. Since the 1970s, the main emphasis in education has shifted to speaking the language and acquiring the most basic skills in reading and writing it. The literary texts studied become fewer and less challenging linguistically as each decade passes with a consequent decline in written standards. The sustainability of any meaningful literacy is now in question.

In quantity if not quality, learners gradually overtook the native speakers and this gap continues to widen. As the revival programme ran parallel to a process of language loss in Gaeltacht areas, the native-speaker base diminished, accompanied by loss of irreplaceable domains in everyday speech. In contrast with this, Irish was being introduced to a huge range of new domains though the media and education, and the need for modern dictionaries and terminology increased exponentially.

Meaningful implementation of the Official Languages Act 2003 and the status of Irish as an official working language of the European Union from January 2007 is directly dependent on provision of adequate lexicographical and terminological resources. This requires a long-term strategy, looking ahead at likely needs over two to three decades, and providing for both electronic and printed resources, probably in this order from now on.

Dictionary and terminology development in Irish must be seen in its own historical context and in comparison with other languages. Despite the weakened political, economic and social status of Irish under colonial rule, a series of scholarly individuals made distinctive contributions to lexicography in Irish, both in manuscript and in print since Ó Cléirigh's glossary was published in 1643. Several of the following displayed in their work a knowledge of their predecessors' contributions: Pluincéad (ms.1662); Lhuyd (1707); Ó Beaglaoich and Mac Cuirtín (1732); Ó Neachtain (ms.1739); Ó Briain (1768); Connellan (1814); O'Reilly (1817, 1821, 1864); Ó Conaill (ms. 1826); Coneys (1849); Mac Ádhaimh (ms. c.1850); Foley (1855); Albe (1903); and O'Neill Lane (1904, 1918). This work constitutes a substantial contribution to Irish lexicography before the foundation of the state.

It is no historical accident that the era of great dictionary-making in late nineteenth-century Europe coincided with the height of colonial ambition. Dictionaries were statements by great nations about the supremacy of their languages and cultures. The *Oxford English Dictionary* (1858-1928) was established in direct response to the *Deutsches Worterbuch* of the brothers Grimm (1838-1961) and Emile Littré's *Dictionnaire de la langue Française* (1841-73).

When Irish is positioned in this landscape we see the burgeoning of literacy and lexicography across Europe at the weakest period in usage of the language outside the traditional heartlands. When Irish readers and writers could be counted in dozens, the OED could boast in 1880 of 754 readers on its voluntary reading programme, who had recently read 924 books and returned 361,670 quotations. Great national dictionary projects which commenced as ambitious and pioneering scholarly ventures became more relevant and commercially viable over time as mass literacy became a reality in major European languages. We also see the scale of commitment necessary over generations to sustain and complete lexicographical work.

The remainder of this paper examines the range of activity undertaken since the foundation of the Irish State in 1922 and the current position of corpus planning for lexicography, corpora and terminology in Irish. We begin with the monolingual historical dictionary, followed by dialect lexicons, bilingual dictionaries, corpora and terminology work.

IRISH DICTIONARIES OF THE TWENTIETH CENTURY

Monolingual historical dictionaries form the corner-stone of dictionary provision in all established languages, where the art of lexicography is nurtured and transmitted over generations despite changes in work-place technologies. An English dictionary to most people means a monolingual one, probably a concise version extracted, even if indirectly, from the *Oxford English Dictionary*. However, an Irish dictionary invariably means a bilingual dictionary, usually English-Irish as translation is predominantly into, rather that out of, Irish. This perception arises because we have never had an historical dictionary of modern Irish, and we are now unlikely to see one.

Upon completion of its *Dictionary of the Irish Language* (1913-76) based mainly on Old and Middle Irish materials, the Royal Irish Academy embarked in 1976 on Foclóir na Nua-Ghaeilge, an historical dictionary of modern Irish for the period 1600-2000, based on two quite different strands. The first of these comprised literary and linguistic sources for the period 1600-1882 prior to the revival movement when general publishing and modern language applications began. The second encompassed language sources from the revival period onwards, including works by writers in all dialects and various forms of official publications and print media. Tomás de Bhaldraithe was General Editor until his retirement in 1994. To date this project has produced a CD-ROM and booklet (2004) entitled *Corpas na Gaeilge / The Irish Language Corpus 1600-1882*, which contains some 7.2 million words. Eight volumes of dialect lexicons by individual scholars were also published by the project between 1981 and 1989.

Two major external factors militated against completion of this dictionary as envisaged. Economic recession in the 1980s prohibited recruitment on the scale required for any meaningful progress. A strategic decision at that time would have recognized the impossibility of completion under these circumstances. The second external factor inhibiting progress was the arrival of computing technologies and the revolution in lexicographic methods as corpora displaced mountains of paper slips, over a million records in the case of Irish. Dictionaries in early to mid-cycle with no publication stream in flow, were particularly affected as new skills and mindsets were needed to implement radical changes and lead modern technological projects. Many of the old scholarly institutions across Europe which housed creaking national dictionary projects found themselves in difficulty. Progress became bogged down in many instances, particularly where management structures more appropriate to an era of individual scholarship failed to implement the radical change management required for forging dynamic interdisciplinary teams.

Irish is not alone in its lack of an historical dictionary. Similarly troubled histories affected the Norwegian and Romanian dictionaries, commenced in 1930 and 1959 respectively, and not yet completed. By comparison, the Danish dictionary, established in the new corpus-based era took just twelve years to complete and appeared in 2003. When national dictionaries run into difficulty, however, governments are reluctant to reform or abandon them.

Upon de Bhaldraithe's retirement in 1994, and eighteen years into the Irish-dictionary project, the Royal Irish Academy redefined the objectives as 'the creation within the next seven years of a computerized dictionary archive of Modern Irish.' The outcome was published ten years later as the CD-ROM and booklet discussed above, in which reference to future outputs is vague.

Work on general bilingual dictionaries, dialect lexicons and terminological dictionaries, was undertaken throughout the twentieth century to service real needs. Besides the large native-speaker base of some half million in early century, users were predominantly teachers and learners in the education system. These students were concerned with broadening their vocabulary and deepening their grasp of the native idiom in hope of acquiring a near-native competence in their chosen dialect, while striving to understand and appreciate the highly textured language of Irish literary texts. Several dialect lexicons like *Caint an Chláir* (Mac Clúin 1940), and *An Béal Beo* (Ó Máille 1936), although seldom used today, were once studied assiduously by generations of students.

Two names stand tall above all others in twentieth-century Irish-language lexicography, Pádraig Ó Duinnín and Tomás de Bhaldraithe. The former published the main edition of his dictionary, *Foclóir Gaedhilge agus Béarla*, in 1927. It is interesting to note that it was the poetry of Aogán Ó Rathaille which first awakened his interest in words and lexicography. In 1901 he inherited 12,000 dictionary slips from the Irish Texts Society to form the basis of an Irish-English Dictionary which was intended to be 'a cheap handy pocket dictionary for use of students of the modern tongue' and the first edition was published in 1904. His much expanded 1927 edition, discussed by de Bhaldraithe (1983), is a testament to lexicography as art, a respository of literature, learning and native traditions, drawing as he claims in his preface on 'the folklore, habits and beliefs, the songs and tales, the arts and crafts of the people.' Much satirized in the work of Myles na gCopaleen, he captured as none other before or since the capacity for figurative expression in Irish, listing as he does several hundred headwords for types of people for example, like these three from a short section beginning with st-:

> *stipéar*, one standing a long time;
> *storc*, the corpse of one who dies in an upright position;
> *stocalach*, a person standing like a pillar in the road.

The incongruity of his listings juxtaposed with his own comments and his use of all verbs in the first person, can be just as unintentionally humorous:

> *sagairtín*, a small priest, a small inedible periwinkle, *préachán (faochán) dubh* is the edible variety;
> *coin-riocht*, a werwolf, wolf-shape, *teighim i gcoin-riocht*, I become a wer-wolf.

Apart from Lane's *Larger English-Irish Dictionary* (1916), only two further English-Irish dictionaries appeared in the twentieth century, McKenna (1935) and de Bhaldraithe (1959), and both bearing the title *English-Irish Dictionary*. With English as source-language, their purpose was to find Irish equivalents for current English expressions, and the opportunities for presenting the rull range of Irish idiom were limited. De Bhaldraithe's work gained him international status as a lexicographer and his dictionary is significant in prioritizing standard above dialect forms and in undertaking large-scale development and integration of new terminology, to which subject he devoted over half his short preface (1959: v):

> But with the inception of the movement for the preservation of the Irish Language, and more particularly with the founding of the State, the need for the extension of the vocabulary became more urgent, in order to meet the new demands made on the language, in fields in which it had been formerly neglected.

> ... The ways in which these demands have been met, during a period of abnormal development of the language, have created certain problems for the lexicographer. A new word has sometimes been coined where an equivalent (here placed in brackets) was already well established in traditional speech, e.g., *ciabhdhealg,* hairpin *(biorán gruaige); tuailmeá,* spring balance *(ainsiléad); forionar,* pullover *(geansaí); seilbhscríbhinn,* lease *(léas); gnáthcheannaitheoir,* customer *(custaiméir)....*

> Modern technical terms have been coined by different authorities and individuals, with the result that, in some fields there existed a superabundance of conflicting terms.

De Bhaldraithe's dictionary served the needs of mid-century Ireland very well. It is no reflection on his work that it became the mainstay of teachers and students for far too long as, incredibly, no action was taken to replace it until Foras na Gaeilge embarked on its New English-Irish Dictionary (NEID) in 2002.

Lexicography in Irish is a testament to the dedication and achievement of individuals operating in a policy vacuum. Dictionaries have been commissioned much too late considering the timescale invariably required to complete them. The decision to place statutory responsibility for dictionaries and terminology on one body, Foras na Gaeilge, in 1999, was clearly a step forward, although clarification of the relationships with the Royal Irish Academy (historical dictionary/corpus) and the Translation Section of the Houses of the Oireachtas (official standard) was unfortunately not specified.

One occasional paper on corpus planning (Nic Pháidín et al, 1999) was published by Bord na Gaeilge at this time, and the decision to press ahead immediately with the most urgent task, the NEID, is to be commended. However, individual dictionaries and projects are best planned and executed within a published national strategy. A full programme of cyclical bilingual dictionary renewal, both English-Irish and Irish-English, including pocket and school-dictionary derivatives, updated or replaced each fifteen to twenty years, in both electronic and print formats, is the essential minimum requirement for a language whose status is guaranteed by legislation both in Ireland and the European Union. Individual dictionary projects, however commendable, do not constitute a strategy for corpus planning which includes lexicographical resources, corpora and terminology. A clear policy for links and interactions between these strands is essential, bearing in mind that synergies are not easily achieved when resources are owned and managed by different organizations.

Given the profound changes in lexicographic practice and poor transmission of editorial skills in Irish, a gap of almost sixty years may well occur between de Bhaldraithe's dictionary (1959) and publication of its replacement. Ironically we see the biggest gap between dictionaries under native government.

One commendable strategic decision was the preparation of an Irish-English dictionary immediately after publication of de Bhaldraithe (1959), thus enabling valuable skills to be retained and developed. This comprehensive modern dictionary appeared as *Foclóir Gaeilge-Béarla* by Niall Ó Dónaill (1978). This effectively replaced Dineen's work for the general user and presented the modern language in the Roman script. A cursory glance at Dineen's dictionary today, however, reveals the sad extent of domain loss in our own time, as very few Irish-speakers now would have even a passive knowledge of most of the vocabulary contained there.

Ó Dónaill's dictionary contained a great deal of new terminology, and wore well, as dictionaries do, for a period of twenty years or so. It too is now showing its age, and its scope for use in education is becoming limited, considering the explosion in new terminology which has entered everyday use in newspapers and the classroom in the three decades since it appeared. Considering the lack of expansion in other aspects of the native lexicon since 1978, a case could be made for updating the existing dictionary by a process of revision and inclusion of all new terminology in current use in schools and the general media. This work could be completed in the short term over five years or so. The strategic vacuum and the project-by-project focus in lexicographical planning is once again apparent. The fact that this dictionary is overdue for revision has passed without comment due to the more urgent and pressing need for an English-Irish dictionary.

DEVELOPMENT OF CORPORA FOR LEXICOGRAPHY

Modern dictionaries are corpus-based, and future Irish dictionaries will be as comprehensive and reliable as the corpora on which they are based. The historical language as it existed up to 1882 in published and manuscript sources has been captured in the Royal Irish Academy corpus (2004), which can be drawn on for lexicography, particularly when Irish is the source language of the dictionary. A more user-friendly interface would make this a more attractive tool, but this could easily be rectified.

Provision for the period post-1882 is more complex. When the NEID project commenced Foras na Gaeilge acquired existing corpus materials from the EU PAROLE project carried out by ITÉ (Institiúid Teangeolaíochta Éireann) before its abolition, including additional material amounting in total to some eighteen million words, at various stages of processing. This was incorporated into the New Corpus for Ireland (NCI) for the new dictionary.

NCI contains two strands, one is Irish and the second is Irish-English, or English as used in Ireland. Space does not permit a detailed discussion here of corpus design and compilation and this has already been published (Kilgariff et al 2006). Although this corpus is not currently available to the public, it is a major resource for lexicography in Irish. The Irish-language strand contains thirty million words drawn from:

> books imaginative 7.6m
> books informative 8.4m
> newspapers 4.5m
> periodicals 2.6m
> official publications 1.2m
> broadcast material .4m
> websites 5.5m.

It is therefore an excellent source for examples of contemporary Irish and terminology in use. Most of the material, however, was clearly produced by learners of Irish, non-native speakers. Since even the imaginative books section is restricted to works available electronically from publishers, including a few recent texts by Gaeltacht authors, the bulk of native-speaker materials created by the giants of twentieth-century literature is not represented and not yet available in any corpus as a resource for lexicography. This is regrettable and will need to be rectified particularly before any new Irish-English dictionary is undertaken. It highlights once again the need for a national strategy for corpus planning for the language.

TERMINOLOGY

The major area of expansion in Irish since the revival project commenced over a century ago was terminology, and its growth has masked to some extent the huge domain loss in the traditional lexicon of native speakers. Creation of new terms became a social pastime and a preoccupation of the early print media in Irish in the late nineteenth century. Coinages appeared in the weekly newspaper *Fáinne an Lae* (1898-1900) like *leictiú*r (lecture), *feadán cainte* (telephone), and *ardscoil* (university), and well-known authors contributed lists of terms for parts of the bicycle and other modern inventions.

Under native government, the education system became the main driver of term creation, and for many years it was envisaged that the general bilingual dictionary could continue to be the main organ of dissemination. Term creation and usage remained quite random and uncoordinated for decades, as de Bhaldraithe states in his preface (1959: v)

> For example, the prefix hydro was variously Gaelicized as follows (all examples are from text-books or examination papers): *hydro-, hídro-, hidro-, hudro-, íor-, íodhro-, -udar, údró-, udró-, udra-, uidr-*. Apart from these, use was made of native prefixes, e.g., dobhar-, bual-, uisce-, fliuch-, leacht-. 'Telescope' was variously rendered: *cianarcán, cianamharcán, ciannarcán, ciandarcán, ciandearcán, cianradharcán, ciandracán, fadradharcán, fadamhrcán, faidearcán, radharcghloine, súilghloine, súil-fhiodán, gloine fadradhairc, gloine fhéachaint, telescóp, tealoscóp, teileascóip.*

Responsibility for the development of the written standard and orthography as well as the creation of legal and statutory terminology in Irish has been in the Translation Section of the Houses of the Oireachtas since it was established in 1922. The definitive work establishing standard spelling and grammar *Gramadach na Gaeilge agus Litriú na Gaeilge: An Caighdeán Oifigiúil* was published in 1958, with very minor revisions in the 1960 and 1979 editions. This remains the written standard for Irish. The Acts translated by the Section are now available on www.achtanna.ie and constitute a valuable linguistic resource. A databank of terms and other phrases used in legislation is contained as an ancilliary resource on www.focal.ie.

A strategic issue has arisen from the division of responsibility which placed lexicography and terminology in Foras na Gaeilge, while Rannóg an Aistriúcháin retained custodianship of the written standard and grammar. Several minor but significant differences have emerged in practice, particularly in the use of aspiration, or *séimhiú*, and modern dictionaries as far back as Ó Dónaill (1978) are not entirely in line with *An Caighdeán Oifigiúil*. This emerging divergence has been extensively discussed by several researchers, such as Ní Mhurchú (1981), Ó Baoill (1999) and Ó Ruairc (2007). Criticism has been coupled with calls for a revision of the written standard to also take account of changes and simplification of forms used in contemporary native speech.

Although these concerns impact only marginally on the general public or the education system, this anomaly needs to be strategically addressed as a matter of urgency, because of its obvious implications for all corpus resources produced. As indicated in the *Irish Times* (13 October 2007), implementation of EU status is now proving to be a catalyst for decision-making, and progress on revising the written standard, while contentious, is now awaited with interest.

External pressures arising from international status should not be underestimated. Under accession arrangements for Ireland to the EEC in 1973, Irish was granted treaty status only and a restricted number of documents were therefore translated into Irish. The principal work generating term creation in other languages, the *Acquis Communautaire*, was never translated into Irish, and the number of Irish terms in the publicly accessible EU database IATE (iate.europa.eu), is consequently only 13,427, on a scale spanning from 2,859 in Maltese to 1.5 million in English at time of writing, in September 2007. Delivery of translation and interpreting services as required under the status provision requires a radical increase in the provision of terminology in Irish in this database, work currently being undertaken by Fiontar, Dublin City University.

Unlike other aspects of corpus planning in Irish, development of terminology in Irish has derived major benefit from interaction with international bodies formulating best practice. The merits of compliance with ISO requirements and UNESCO guidelines in this field are invaluable, and create an international framework for development of resources.

Earlier in the twentieth century, terminology in Irish was developed in response to demand from education, the media and creative writing. A massive corpus of translated material was generated by the literary translation scheme of An Gúm, the government publishing branch, established in 1926. By 1939, some ninety-nine novels mainly of English literature, had been translated by Irish-language authors including such works as *The War of the Worlds* by H.G. Wells, with a consequent use of new terminology.

The broadcast media have also contributed enormously to the creation and dissemination of new terms in Irish, with its impact increasing steadily throughout the twentieth century as new media came on stream and the number of active broadcasters and journalists increased to several hundred in recent years. It is unfortunate that no on-line live support service exists for the media in Irish where terms could be created immediately, validated and circulated on-line throughout the sector.

Official structures were established quite early to support terminology work. A terminological committee was set up by the Department of Education in 1927. Interrupted by World War II, it functioned again on an *ad hoc* basis until 1968. During this period some thirteen domain-specific dictionaries or lists were compiled. A new syllabus for post-primary schools, requiring new terminology, was due for introduction in 1968 and the Terminology Committee was then established by the government on a permanent basis. Structures and practices have remained largely unchanged since, with committees meeting on a voluntary basis, supported by a small full-time secretariat. Dozens of dictionaries and lists were published ranging from Astronomy to Telecommunications to Biology. Many other domains were provided for by typewritten or handwritten lists. As terms were largely created in response to specific demand, principally in education, communications or public administration, the balance of terms in particular domains is different from that in languages where terms emerge through usage *in vivo*. Subjects studied in school tend to be strongly represented while poor provision is made for sport and other leisure activities, medical and related domains, or industrial manufacturing.

Terminology development in Irish embraced the technological revolution very late. Canadian terminologists in Montreal, for example, had embarked on this route in 1969. Digitization of Irish terminological data had been discussed by the Terminological Committee on several occasions since 1971 but had not resulted in any definitive action of benefit to the user. In the new century, and under the galvinizing influence of impending language legislation, some dictionaries and lists were made available on www.acmhainn.ie.

The practical difficulty of querying several sources for a term and the absence of an English-Irish dictionary became increasingly problematic for translators and professionals who needed to write Irish daily, following the enactment of the Official Languages Act 2003.

At this time, Fiontar, Dublin City University, requested INTERREG funding from the EU for the creation of a national database for Irish terminology 2004–7. The project was undertaken with the collaboration of Foras na Gaeilge, which partially funded the work. The result can be seen at www.focal.ie which contains 287,000 terms, previously available in fifty-four dictionaries and lists. The database is one of the largest of its kind in the world. The work has continued since, in partnership with Foras na Gaeilge, as new domains and terms are added to the database, and data cleaning progresses.

The electronic solution has liberated Irish terminology from the constraints of printed lists, invariably out of date. The on-line resource can be expanded and updated daily, and inconsistencies removed. More valuably, it allows for dialogue and interaction with users worldwide, and new terms can be requested on an on-line form. The positive feedback since launching the resource in September 2006 has been overwhelming and the database has transformed the working environmnent of the Irish-language translator. Over 3.2 million searches had been recorded on the site by September 2007 ranging from Norlisk in Siberia to Dunedin in New Zealand. The editorial interface serves as a terminology management system for the Terminology Committee and has facilitated the transition of work practices from paper to screen.

Focal.ie is queried most frequently (62 per cent) from English to Irish. The most frequently sought items are not highly specialized terms but words which may be translated in different ways depending on context: *performance, potential* and *project* featuring consistently on top of the list. Unfortunately, the resource is also used by many in lieu of a full English-Irish dictionary, a function for which it was not intended and is only partially suited. If learners and writers are restricted in their searches to terminological words and phrases, opportunities for enrichment of expression may be seriously curtailed.

Creation of the database focal.ie has brought corpus resources for Irish to a new threshold. It is a dynamic tool capable of further innovation and development, and is accessible without charge to users of Irish worldwide. Fiontar has adapted this technical solution for the national database of place-names to be published later in 2008 on www.logainm.ie.

CONCLUSIONS

However innovative, terminology databases do not replace the need for a full suite of general bilingual dictionaries in both print and electronic formats. Teachers, translators, writers and linguists need access to corpora and to full dictionary-length entries to enable creative use of the existing rich lexicon.

Corpus planning on the basis of invidual dictionaries is no longer appropriate. Considering the long-term nature of investment, the strategy must look ahead and forecast needs two decades hence, providing for corpora and databases from which a suite of complementary outputs can be derived cost-effectively, and presented to the public in user-friendly formats. Coordination and integration of all these resources will bear the optimum result, where dictionaries, termbanks and corpora are developed in tandem. Development of electronic resources is maximized when the constraints of the print mindset are abandoned. We must bear in mind that data created now is not for human use initially, and must be capable of being retrieved by computers and converted in data management systems. Synergies must be achieved, where terminological, corpus and lexicographical data can be easily imported from one system to another.

The national and international status of Irish creates new opportunities for the language. It has sharpened the focus on planning for deficits in our corpus resources. It provides an incentive for young people to invest in acquiring high level linguistic and literacy skills, while highlighting the challenge in meeting the current professional skills deficits in translation and interpreting.

We are witnessing a huge shift in the type of writing activity taking place in Irish now. Translation of official documents may become disproportionate to other areas. We must ensure that production of functional text does not become an end in itself to the detriment of creative and critical work.

Focal.ie is promoted as 'the Irish you need at speed', which indeed it is, if a term is required at a click. We must ensure, however, that the prophecy of Yeats (Kiberd 1979: 221) remains unfulfilled, 'It may be the language of a nation, and yet losing all that has made it worthy of a revival.' Colonial powers and nations have come and gone, but a dictionary is still a statement by a society about itself, as each new word and meaning in its language documents a change. Corpus planning is only worthwhile in a language in which poetry is still possible.

REFERENCES
(not including dictionaries, dialect lexicons and corpora cited above with dates)

------- 1958. *Gramadach na Gaeilge agus Litriú na Gaeilge: An Caighdeán Oifigiúil.* Baile Átha Cliath. Oifig an tSoláthair.
de Bhaldraithe, T. 1982. 'Aisling an Duinnínigh' in *Comhar* Aibreán 16-25.
Kiberd, D. 1979. *Synge and the Irish language. London.* Macmillan.
Kilgarriff, A., M. Rundell & E. Uí Dhonnchadha. 2006. 'Efficient corpus development for lexicography: building the New Corpus for Ireland' in *Language resources and evaluation journal* 40(2): 127-152.
Nic Pháidín, C., F. Ní Ghallchobhair & D. Ó Baoill. 1999. *Ar thóir na bhfocal.* Baile Átha Cliath. Bord na Gaeilge.
Ní Mhurchú, C. 1981. 'Cad d'éirigh don Chaighdeán?' in *Comhar* Márta 12-15.
Ó Baoill, D. 1999. 'Litriú agus Gramadach' in Nic Pháidín et al, 1999.
Ó Ruairc, M. 2007. *Aistrigh Leat.* Baile Átha Cliath. Cois Life.

The Gaeltacht Today

Conchúr Ó Giollagáin and Seosamh Mac Donnacha

INTRODUCTION

The first attempt to provide an 'official' definition of the geographical extent of the Gaeltacht and to estimate the number of Irish-speakers within it was made by *Coimisiún na Gaeltachta* (Gaeltacht Comm-ission), which was established by the government in 1925. The Commission was asked to advise what proportion of a district should be Irish-speaking to allow it to be prescribed as:

> (a) an Irish Speaking District or (b) a Partly Irish Speaking District, and to indicate the present extent and location of such districts. (Coimisiún na Gaeltachta, 1926)

The Commission recommended that two categories of Gaeltacht be recognized: districts in which 80 per cent or more of the community could speak Irish should be regarded as a *Fíor-Ghaeltacht* (Irish-speaking District), and districts in which between 25 and 79 per cent of the community could speak Irish should be regarded as a *Breac-Ghaeltacht* (Partly Irish-speaking District). Based on a special enumeration carried out for it by An Garda Síochána (Ó Riagáin 1997: 51), the Commission reported that *Fíor-Ghaeltacht* districts, with a total population of 164,774 persons (of which 146,821 were Irish-speakers), were to be found in the counties of Donegal, Mayo, Galway, Clare, Kerry, Cork and Waterford. *Breac-Ghaeltacht* districts with a total population of 294,890 persons (of which 110,585 were Irish-speakers), were also to be found in the above counties, and in the counties of Sligo and Tipperary.

In the years between 1926 and 1956 government departments remained inconsistent in their definition of the Gaeltacht. While the Central Statistics Office consistently used the boundaries as proposed by the Gaeltacht Commission (Ó Riagáin 1997: 53), other government agencies continued to adopt their own definitions of the Gaeltacht for the various schemes under their aegis, rather than using the definition proposed by the Gaeltacht Commission. This inconsistency was rectified in 1956 with the enactment of the Ministers and Secretaries (Amendment) Act, which established the Department of the Gaeltacht and included a provision allowing the Minister for the Gaeltacht to place a parliamentary order before the Houses of the Oireachtas defining the extent of the Gaeltacht and to make changes to this definition if necessary. The first such order, the Gaeltacht Areas Order, 1956, designated 85 District Electoral Divisions (DEDs) in full, and parts of a further 57 DEDs in the counties of Donegal, Mayo, Galway, Kerry, Cork and Waterford as being in the Gaeltacht. Since 1956, three further parliamentary orders have been placed before the Houses of the Oireachtas which have extended the boundaries of the Gaeltacht. The most significant of these was the 1967 order which included the Gaeltacht colonies of Ráth Chairn and Baile Ghib in County Meath as part of the officially designated Gaeltacht. No changes have been made to the boundaries of the Gaeltacht since 1982, and it is now estimated that the Gaeltacht as designated under the provisions of the 1956 Act constitutes approximately 7 per cent of the state's landmass (Commins 1988).

Despite the fact that the Gaeltacht as officially designated in 1956 and including the areas that have been included in the revisions of 1967, 1974 and 1982, represents a more realistic picture of the geographical extent of the Gaeltacht than that proposed by the Gaeltacht Commission of 1926, it is generally accepted that the boundaries even as set out in 1956 overextended the true representation of the Gaeltacht as it then stood. As early as 1975 the CILAR (Committee on Irish-language Attitudes Research 1975: 347) referred to research done by An Foras Forbartha in 1970 which indicated that: 'the extent of Irish speaking communities is considerably smaller than the officially designated Gaeltacht boundaries suggest'. Based on an analysis of earlier research on the Gaeltacht in the early 1970s (Ó Riagáin 1971; Mac Aodha 1971) and the CILAR Report (1975), Ó Riagáin (1982/1997: 77) concluded that only:

> 30 per cent of Gaeltacht communities were predominantly Irish-speaking and stable and another 25 per cent were almost entirely English-speaking. The remainder were bilingual but were unstable and showing evidence of a shift towards English.

He goes on to say that: 'It was only in the two largest Gaeltacht areas of Donegal and Galway that bilingual core areas of any significant size were to be found.' Subsequently, however, Ó Gliasáin's analysis of the Department of the Gaeltacht's data for the period 1974-1984 in relation to the number of children qualifying as Irish-speaking children under one of its schemes (Scéim Labhairt na Gaeilge) suggested that the process of language shift occurring in the Gaeltacht was such that 'even the core areas were becoming unstable' (Ó Gliasáin 1990: 74).

SOCIAL DYNAMICS AND DEMOGRAPHIC CHANGES

Evidence from the research referred to above, from Ó Giollagáin (2002, 2004 and 2005), Mac Donnacha et al (2005), and Ó Giollagáin and Mac Donnacha et al (2007, hereafter referred to as CLSUIG), indicates that language shift away from Irish is being driven by social dynamics. Gaeltacht communities are linked into regional, national and international networks which gradually influence their linguistic composition. Additionally, the linguistic composition of some Gaeltacht areas has been transformed due to their location: their physical proximity to developing urban centres makes them attractive for suburban settlement. As a result of these social dynamics and demographic movements, a significant number of people of non-Gaeltacht origin have moved into statutory Gaeltacht areas. Although some of them may speak Irish, it is reasonable to assume that the vast majority of them are not active Irish-speakers. Notably, there is evidence to show that English-speaking in-migrants form a large proportion of young Gaeltacht-based parents, a fact which has serious implications for future sociolinguistic trends in the Gaeltacht. As the proportion of English-speaking young parents increases, their influence impacts more significantly not just on the proportion of Irish-speakers in their own age cohorts, but on the proportion of Irish-speakers in future Gaeltacht generations as well.

Mac Donnacha et al (2005) provide data on the number of schoolchildren attending Gaeltacht schools who were born outside the Gaeltacht or who lived outside the Gaeltacht for a period of time before attending school in the Gaeltacht: 26 per cent in the case of primary pupils (p. 28) and 23 per cent in the case of post-primary pupils (p. 78).

The effect of this mixed linguistic intake of pupils on language usage patterns in Gaeltacht schools is clear, with only 46 per cent of primary schools and 26 per cent of secondary schools reporting that their pupils

used 'more Irish than English' in their everyday social interactions
while in the environs of the school, the study concluded that although
the school system in the Gaeltacht plays a pivotal role in providing the
institutional support necessary to assist children coming from a non-
Irish speaking background to achieve a significant increase in their
level of competence in Irish, they were not succeeding in transmitting
what CILAR (1975: 254) refers to as 'the propensity for use of the
language'.

LINGUISTIC COMPLEXITY IN GAELTACHT SCHOOLS
Ó Giollagáin (2002, 2004 and 2005) in his studies of the Gaeltacht
communities of Ráth Chairn, Ceathrú Thaidhg and Ros Muc presents a
typology of language speakers that exist in such communities (see Table
1) and argues that in order to understand the processes of language shift
consideration must be given to the ways in which each type of speaker
impacts on the patterns of language acquisition and usage of other
speakers.

Category	Description
Native speaker	An individual from the Gaeltacht who has been brought up through the medium of Irish.
Neo-native speaker	Individuals who are brought up through the medium of Irish by parents who are not native speakers of the language themselves, i.e. the children of second-language speakers.
Semi-native speaker	An individual who is brought up in a setting which provides exposure to more than one language, i.e. where one parent speaks Irish and the other speaks English, or where both parents speaks English, but the child is exposed to Irish through his/her interactions and the interactions of the parents with other members of the family / community.
Second-language speaker	Individuals who have acquired the language in an institutional (as distinct from a home) setting and who are able to participate effectively in the social interactions of the community through the medium of Irish.

| Learner | There are two categories of learner: ***competent learners*** i.e. learners who can be expected to achieve a level of competence in the language that will allow them to eventually participate effectively in the social interactions of the community through the medium of Irish and ***non-competent learners*** i.e. learners who for various reasons are unlikely to overcome the initial hurdles and discouragements which are part and parcel of the process of second language acquisition and whose efforts at language learning are likely to come to an unfruitful end. |
| English-speaker | An English-speaker who cannot converse in Irish and is not actively learning the language. |

Table 1: Categories of Irish-Speakers (translated from Ó Giollagáin 2002)

There is evidence from Harris (2006) that students in Irish-medium schools outside the Gaeltacht outperform Gaeltacht students in some of the language ability tests detailed in his research. It seems that the teaching of Irish to students as a second language in the Gaeltacht and the linguistic complexity present in such schools has negative implications for the ultimate academic outcomes which relate to linguistic attainment for children raised through Irish. Many parents who are raising their children through Irish at home reported that their children are not succeeding in reaching expected levels of ability in their native language (Mac Donnacha 2005 and CLSUIG). In other words, Irish-speaking children are not evidencing the full range of linguistic competencies expected of native speakers. Research undertaken by Harris (2006) raises critical linguistic questions in relation to the educational aims and practices currently implemented in Gaeltacht schools, particularly in light of parental assessment of the linguistic ability of their own children and the assessment the young people make of their own ability in Irish (CLSUIG). Thus, it would appear that those participants in the Gaeltacht education process who learn Irish outside the home setting exert a stronger effect on both language ability and language-use patterns of native speakers of Irish than native speakers have on learners of the language

This analysis suggests that even when Gaeltacht parents opt to bring up their children through the medium of Irish, the likelihood is that once their children enter the school system they are entering a socialization process which operates partly in English at primary level and mainly in English at post-primary level. Thus as young adults they are more likely to be predisposed to speaking English within peer social networks, even if Irish remains their primary home language.

DEMOGRAPHIC FRAGILITY OF THE IRISH-SPEAKING COMMUNITIES

A clear implication of contemporary research is that the Gaeltacht as a linguistic entity is under enormous pressure. It confirms what has been indicated in the language data of recent Census returns (2002 and 2006) and in the latest sets of results of Scéim Labhairt na Gaeilge (a support scheme for Irish-speaking families resident in the Gaeltacht administered by the Department of Community, Rural and Gaeltacht Affairs), that less than a quarter of the contemporary Gaeltacht population live in districts where Irish rather than English is spoken as the predominant communal language. The results from the 2006 Census show that the Gaeltacht population numbers 95,503, a rise of 6 per cent from the 90,048 Gaeltacht population reported in the 2002 Census; the language data in the Census pertains to the population of 3-year olds and over, which number 91,862 and 86,517 in the 2006 and 2002 Censuses respectively.

A matter of even more serious concern, however, can be found in an examination of the language data in the recent surveys which indicate that only about half of the children in the strongest Gaeltacht areas are acquiring their ability in Irish in a home setting primarily (CLSUIG; Mac Donnacha et al 2005 and Ó Giollagáin 2005).

In turn, the language-use patterns of the younger speakers of Irish, even in the strongest Irish-speaking districts, are exhibiting the indicators of a minority language community that is succumbing to the pressures of language shift as a result of contact with a majority language community. Academic examination of language contact and fragility issues has given rise to a sociolinguistic discourse which has unearthed many universal traits and trends in the language dynamics between a majority and minority linguistic community, but the Gaeltacht experience is a sobering example of the failure of state and communal interventions to manage this contact in a manner that is not detrimental to the linguistic integrity of the minority community. The research to date demonstrates that the social dynamics which are driving the language shift away from Irish are a consequence of the failure of institutional and communal support structures to empower communities to engage proactively with these contact issues in a manner that does not fundamentally alter the linguistic composition of the community.

It is in this challenging linguistic scenario of demographic fragility combined with a complex and mixed sociolinguistic context that the current generation of Irish-speakers is being reared in the Gaeltacht. This in turn has critical implications for the capacity of Irish-speaking families and communities to create the context in which the linguistic development of native speakers of Irish can be fostered. The contrasting nature of the language acquisition processes which occur in Gaeltacht communities has fundamentally hampered the ability of young Irish-speakers to form Irish-speaking networks among their own peer group because the proportion of home-based speakers is not sufficiently high to buttress the use of the minority language against the pressures to conform with the language use norms in this age cohort. These pressures are evident even in the strongest Irish-speaking areas where the home transmission of Irish, the mixed transmission of Irish and English in the home and increasingly the reliance on the school system to acquire Irish all compete with one another and contribute to the sociolinguistic complexity of these areas.

INCOMPLETE ACQUISITION
Comparisons with the language acquisition processes pertaining to previous generations suggest that the limited social and communal reinforcements of the initial home acquisition of Irish among the current younger age cohorts in the Gaeltacht is precipitating the emergence of pervasive non-traditional language acquisition patterns. Younger speakers are now evidencing higher levels of ability in the majority language than in their native language. It is becoming increasingly clear that the home transmission of a language, especially in a minority context, merely fulfils a foundational role in our linguistic development and that language acquisition happens via a complementary process of peer-group reinforcement of language use in both social and institutional/educational settings. In other words, the home transmission of a language lays the initial acquisitional framework, but the younger speakers complete the process themselves by using and developing their linguistic capacities within their own social and institutional networks. As the Irish-speaking networks among the young become

more marginalized and disrupted in their own community, their ability to complete the acquisition process becomes increasingly compromised by the introduction of English into these networks, replacing Irish as the *lingua franca* of the young.

The pervasive nature of non-traditional or incomplete acquisition is both a serious challenge and a by-product of the Gaeltacht educational system, in that the Gaeltacht schools provided the *locus* where the English-dominated peer-group networks could proliferate and thus dislocate the peer-group socialization processes from the communal and familial context from which these young speakers initially emerged. As a result of this linguistic irony, Gaeltacht schools are faced with the daunting challenge of providing Irish-medium education to bilingual speakers of Irish and English whose capacity to fully acquire the target language, i.e. Irish, is being severely compromised and hindered by the lack of social reinforcement of its use within the schools themselves.

Indicators of the fragile nature of both the demographic profile of the speaker community and of variations in language-use norms across the generations are also now evident in the variety of Irish spoken by the young. Aspects of the linguistic fragility of Irish can be identified in the following features:

• The phonetic influence of English on Irish
• Pervasive irregularities in the morphology and syntax of Irish
• Extensive use of code-switching in registers not associated with advanced or specialized language use
• Deficiencies in ability to use Irish in contexts and registers associated with native speaker competency
• Preponderance of learner grammar and use patterns in the speech of native speakers.

These linguistic features and difficulties are not surprising when one considers the enormous social and linguistic pressure that is being exerted on young native speakers of Irish: even in the strongest Gaeltacht districts, the proportion of young people who speak Irish at home has seen a significant reduction in recent years. The precarious nature of this demographic scenario, combined with the predatory aspects of the majority-minority language dynamics which govern the social norms by which language contact between speakers of Irish and

English is negotiated, is drastically limiting the opportunities for the social use of Irish among young people beyond the institutional settings of home and classroom.

When viewed from a young person's perspective, is it hardly an astonishing insight that they associate the use of their minority language, i.e. Irish, predominantly with institutional functions. For a significant proportion of young Gaeltacht speakers of Irish, whether home-based or learners (L2 Irish-speakers), speaking Irish manifests itself as conforming or yielding to the language choice of an authority figure (parents, teacher, community leader, etc) rather than acting in accordance with social and linguistic norms which their own age cohort has established, as part of the process of establishing the social conditions for its linguistic reproduction. We are currently witnessing the emergence of a non-traditional sociolinguistic configuration in the Gaeltacht which has the communal and institutional capacity to transmit a passive ability in Irish to a significant proportion of the young age cohort, but which exhibits only limited success in fostering the active or socially productive use of Irish among the young. It is clear that the passive or reactive nature of the younger generation's ability in Irish will fundamentally undermine the linguistic productivity of the Gaeltacht community in its desire and efforts to reproduce another generation of home-based speakers of Irish unless the issues which are causing the erosion of the social use of Irish are adequately addressed.

It is in this social context that the issues relating to the phenomenon of the incomplete acquisition of Irish should be addressed. If state and Gaeltacht community interventions are incapable of fostering the linguistic development of native speakers, it will become increasingly unrealistic, from a sociolinguistic perspective, for them to become fully active and productive users of the Irish language in the same way their parents did. The lack of social reinforcements of Irish-language use among the current younger generation, as opposed to that of previous generations, is resulting in the emergence of an interlanguage. Younger speakers do not exhibit a level of fluency in Irish which would enable them to develop their narrative abilities and creative use of language in order for them to employ wit, sarcasm, mockery, irony etc. in their social contacts with their own age-group. For the vast majority of competent speakers of Irish these narrative and creative abilities have been acquired to a higher degree in English because of the social reinforcements afforded to English in the networks in which the young people operate. Their weaker competence in the minority language means that Irish is not in a position to compete in an effective way in the social domains which are determined by the young people themselves. They are merely therefore opting for the linguistic instrument most fit for purpose in relevant social contexts.

The sociolinguistic disadvantage with which Irish-speaking families and communities must contend cannot be more clearly illustrated than by a comparison between the level of linguistic attainment by native speakers of Irish and other speakers of Irish in the Gaeltacht who have acquired Irish in school: in many cases the level of fluency of the learners after several years of schooling is not substantively different from that attained by native speakers. Rather than being an example of dynamic and progressive pedagogy, the sociolinguistically mixed educational context is creating a subtractive linguistic dynamic which is undermining the linguistic, and quite possibly the educational, development of native speakers of Irish. Ó Curnáin (2007: 59) has pointed out in his authoritative linguistic study of the Irish of Iorras Aithneach in Co. Galway that: 'Nontraditional peer groups tend to exert an influence of lowest common denominator on the members so that the most extreme instances of reduction or nontraditional usage become prominent; in contrast with norm-enforcement within traditional vernacular.'

CONCLUSION

It is clear that concerted action and decisive policies are required in order to engage in a serious manner with the challenges, delineated above, to the linguistic vitality of the Gaeltacht. Priority should be given, as a matter of utmost urgency, to strategic initiatives which seek to proactively reinforce the acquisition and socialization of Irish in the following sectors and contexts:

- Implementing policies aimed at protecting the remaining communities to maintain the proportion of active speakers above the vitality threshold required to support the social use of Irish across the generations
- Increasing the proportion of home speakers of Irish, especially in districts which still support the communal use of Irish

- Encouraging and promoting the language socialization of Irish among the young
- Administering and operating community and educational institutions in a manner that ensures the social use of Irish
- Supporting proactively the language choice and efforts of parents to raise their children as speakers of Irish, by integrating into school objectives a fostering of the social, rather than merely the educational, use of Irish
- Developing linguistically-literate educational policies that are capable of addressing, and differentiating between, the educational and linguistic requirements of native speakers as opposed to the learner community of Irish in the Gaeltacht
- The need for various state and communal institutions to clarify their language aims and policies and to indicate how their strategies will benefit the language maintenance aims of the linguistic minority (given that a *laissez-faire* approach will facilitate the ongoing language shift to English)
- Developing a proactive approach to counteract issues associated with language fragility; in other words, that state and communal organizations with administrative responsibilities in the Gaeltacht would choose the institutional option for the weaker language community.

An essay by its nature only affords authors the opportunity to set out their thesis in a preliminary fashion. However, the issues which have given rise to the emergence of pervasive incomplete acquisition of Irish, even among the most competent young speakers in Gaeltacht communities, are not merely complex themes worthy of further academic investigation: they also highlight the language planning initiatives and interventions necessary to support the continuing transmission and socialization of Irish and address the educational strategies that would further these aims in the fragile linguistic context in which Irish still survives. Gaeltacht policy makers should facilitate further research in this field as a matter of priority.

Recent research serves to highlight what is readily evident to Gaeltacht inhabitants: the Gaeltacht as a linguistic entity is in crisis and struggling with the pressures of an advanced stage of language shift. The approach to date has served to implicate our communal and educational institutions in this process of language shift rather than providing proactive support to resist the pressures of this sociolinguistic endgame. As the use of English becomes more embedded in the social networks of the young, the clear challenge of educational and communal institutions in the Gaeltacht is to empower young speakers of Irish to counteract the pressures of the majority language in a manner that fosters the socialization of Irish in the social networks of the young living in the Gaeltacht. The obvious outcome of an inadequate response to this stark challenge is the completion of the language shift from Irish to English in the remaining Gaeltacht districts where the use of Irish still predominates as the communal language.

REFERENCES

Central Statistics Office. 2003. *Census 2002, Principal demographic results* and *Volume 11, The Irish language*. Dublin. Stationery Office.

Central Statistics Office. 2007. *Census 2006, Principal demographic results* and *Volume 9, The Irish language*. Dublin. Stationery Office.

CILAR – Committee on Irish-language Attitudes Research. 1975. *Report*. Dublin. Stationery Office.

Coimisiún na Gaeltachta. 1926. *Gaeltacht Commission: Report*. Dublin. Stationery Office.

Commins, P. 1988. 'Socio-Economic Development and Language Maintenance in the Gaeltacht'. *The international journal of the sociology of language*, 70:11-28.

Department of Community, Rural and Gaeltacht Affairs (2002/3-2005/6). Scéim Labhairt na Gaeilge: Results.

Harris, J. 2006. *Irish in Primary Schools: Long-term national trends in achievement*. Dublin. The Department of Education and Science.

Mac Aodha, B. 1971. *Galway Gaeltacht survey*. Galway. Social Sciences Research Centre, University College Galway.

Mac Donnacha, S., F. Ní Chualáin, A. Ní Shéaghdha & T. Ní Mhainín. 2005. *Staid reatha na scoileanna Gaeltachta*. Dublin. An Chomhairle um Oideachas Gaeltachta agus Gaelscolaíochta.

Ó Curnáin, B. 2007. *The Irish of Iorras Aithneach, County Galway*. Dublin. School of Celtic Studies, The Dublin Institute for Advanced Studies.

Ó Giollagáin, C. 2002. 'Scagadh ar rannú cainteoirí comhaimseartha Gaeltachta: gnéithe d'antraipeolaíocht teangeolaíochta phobal Ráth Chairn', in *The Irish journal of anthropology* 6:25-56. Maynooth. The National University of Ireland, Maynooth.

Ó Giollagáin, C. 2004. 'Dinimicí teanga phobal Cheathrú Thaidhg', conference paper for Dáil Thuamhan: Teanga agus Saíocht na Gaeilge. Mary Immaculate College, Limerick, 13 November 2004.

Ó Giollagáin, C. 2005. 'Gnéithe d'antraipeolaíocht theangeolaíoch phobal Ros Muc, Co. na Gaillimhe', in Kirk, J. & D. Ó Baoill (eds), *Legislation, literature and sociolinguistics: Northern Ireland, the Republic of Ireland, and Scotland.* Belfast Studies in Language, Culture and Politics 13:138-62. Belfast. Cló Ollscoil na Banríona.

Ó Giollagáin, C., S. Mac Donnacha. et al. 2007. *Staidéar cuimsitheach teangeolaíoch ar úsáid na Gaeilge sa Ghaeltacht / Comprehensive linguistic study of the use of Irish in the Gaeltacht.* (Abbreviated as CLSUIG here.) Dublin. Stationery Office.

Ó Gliasáin, M. 1990. *Language shift among schoolchildren in Gaeltacht areas 1974-1984: An analysis of the distribution of £10 grant qualifiers.* Dublin: Institiúid Teangeolaíochta Éireann.

Ó Riagáin, P. 1971. *The Gaeltacht studies: A development plan for the Gaeltacht.* Dublin: An Foras Forbartha.

Ó Riagáin, P. 1982. 'Athrú agus buanú teanga sa Ghaeltacht' in *Taighde sochtheangeolaíochta agus teangeolaíochta sa Ghaeltacht.* Dublin: Institiúid Teangeolaíochta Éireann.

Ó Riagáin, P. 1997. *Language policy and social reproduction: Ireland 1893–1993.* Oxford: Clarendon Press.

Territories of Desire:
Words and Music in the Irish Language

Lillis Ó Laoire

AIRS AND GRACE

Gabhtar fonn le fonn agus le mífhonn, states the proverb, a subtle play on varying meanings of the word *fonn*, an Irish word that may mean 'desire,' 'wish,' or 'urge,' but which can also signify 'song air,' among other interesting referents. Ó Dónaill's dictionary translates into comprehensible English, 'things are done with good or bad grace.' The phrase is thus elegantly rendered, and *fonn* in the process acquires another amplification of sense, 'grace,' which, though implied, is not explicitly stated in Irish. Another way of translating this well-known sentence more literally might be 'Songs may be sung with good feeling and with bad feeling.' Equating a *fonn,* a song air, with feelings, desire, urges, inclinations, and indeed grace itself presents ways of understanding the culture from which this interconnected semantic web emerges, associations complicated by the addition of still other layers of meaning, specifically, 'base,' 'foundation,' 'land,' 'territory'. Other words for desire and singing in Irish augment the significative network such as *dúil,* 'desire,' and *guth* 'voice,' or again 'song air'. The human voice and its singing faculty are thus, in some senses at least, synonyms and such meanings may also be closely linked to feeling, grace, foundations and even land and territory. We might think of far and exotic locations such as aboriginal Australia where, as the late Bruce Chatwin so memorably showed, songs act as maps, that in performance 'sing up the land' re-enacting the deeds and stories of the ancestors in the Dreamtime, through music communicating embodied, articulate, memory: history, law, identity, and boundaries both moral and geographical for their present day singers and listeners.

However, it is salutary to remind ourselves that it is the Irish language that carries these meanings for us here and that they arguably reveal attitudes that might even be considered to encapsulate a conceptual framework, if not an ideology of melded words and music. Recognizing such connections can make us contemplate the idea of 'air' as a term for the melody or tune of a song in English as well as the term for the atmosphere that we must necessarily breathe every moment of our lives. Although this identification may be disputed by etymologists, the connection is intriguing and striking, especially when regarded across the two most historically important languages in Ireland. Consequently, when taken together in Irish and in English, it is perhaps possible to consider music and language combined in song as rather an important element of human experience and culture. The ubiquity of music and of song in particular in our lives, whether encountered on our MP3 players or in the supermarket, reveals multifarious soundscapes that underscore a structure or form deeply embedded in the human body and imagination. The very banality of much of the music that surrounds us is a tell-tale sign of how ingrained this phenomenon is in the mind.

OPPORTUNITY IN EXCLUSION

The Irish language and its associated poetic and musical traditions might be said to have existed apart from mainstream musical developments in Europe from the seventeenth century on. The removal of the Irish-speaking elite in that period meant to some degree that Irish languished. If there is any merit in exclusion, it lies in the notion that Irish may sometimes remember more clearly what English and other languages have forgotten, discarded, suppressed or simply ignored. Music and language are universals in human culture, and, consequently, important markers of what constitute humanity as John Blacking famously discovered among the Venda, a South African people. Gaelic song is among the foremost cultural resources in the Irish language, one that has frequently been availed of productively. The advertisement promoting the Eircom shares when the company went public in 1999 remains a memorable example of how identity (using the song 'Dúlamán na Binne Buí') and marketing were effectively combined through the use of music and language. Sung poetry has drawn many learners to the language. Even a suggestion of Irish in a musical piece has the potential to draw the curious listener to discover more. Many people have mentioned the excitement at hearing songs as one of their first encounters with the Irish language, and give this as a reason for stimulating them to go on to become fluent speakers.

Mainstream poetry in English today is not considered to have any direct relationship to music although many poets would dispute this. For many people, a yawning chasm exists between the oral and the literate. Although there are exceptions, song does not form the core of the material studied in conventional poetry classes in universities. The musical dimension is somehow regarded with suspicion. However, great artists such as Bob Dylan, Bob Marley or Joni Mitchell might be considered poets as much as they are musicians and singers. In the past, and to some extent still in Irish, poetry and music formed complementary parts of a single whole, that to be fully realized must be recited, sung, performed, heard and listened to. This communicative dynamic lies at the heart of the experience of music and language in Irish, and may be the very element that some find so tantalizingly alluring. Singing songs in Irish has been accorded a high value in the cultural canon of our island and, we may add, in that of our sister Gaelic language in Scotland.

VOICING VERSES

Early poets set their poems to music although we do not know today exactly what kind. It may have been like that of many traditions, what to uninitiated ears might not sound particularly attractive or musical. We have some evidence for this in our archives. Micheál Ó hIghne from Teileann, Co. Donegal, for example, performed a poem about Fionn and the Fianna for the Irish Folklore Commission in the 1940s. Although sonically, it aspires to being music, few listeners today would consider it truly so. The tune is monotonously chant-like in structure with a strong accent and is reminiscent in some ways of music to which the famous epic poems of the Balkans are sung. Because musical tastes have changed over the centuries we cannot be sure what such a musical structure might have meant to its original hearers. For us, because the tune is not particularly melodic, we do not easily relate to it.

Séamas Ó hIghne, a storyteller and singer from Mín na Saileach in Gleann Cholm Cille also sang a poem about Fionn and Oisín for the Irish Folklore Commission in the 1940s. His version of the music was much more melodic than his namesake's and, significantly, I believe, was the one chosen for publication in the 1980s. For us today, Séamas' version is considered the 'better' one because to us it seems more musical.

Such links with the past provide clues that early poets may very well have understood 'music' in a radically different manner to the ways in which modern listeners do. In Scotland, where the tradition of singing the poems of Fionn and Oisín (or Oisean) continues productively until today, the tunes for these poems, as in Ireland, are considerably less elaborate than those used for other kinds of songs. However, it is the more elaborate melodies that enjoy the esteem of contemporary listeners, a development which can be firmly associated with eighteenth- and nineteenth-century European Romantic movements. An acclaimed Scottish singer I know once sang for an assembled audience of French and German tourists. At their request, she sang what she considered to be the oldest pieces from her repertoire, some Ossianic lays, but her listeners pronounced themselves unsatisfied with this and requested melodic songs with more embellishment. Their longing for an authentic experience of Gaelic song and music in their own terms differed vastly from the singer's understanding. The fact that the singer's judgement of her own repertoire was sound counted for nothing for the listeners who, unable to appreciate the poetry of these heroic verses to any great extent, longed only to experience the melodies and the embellishments so that they could literally be enchanted.

The tunes of the older poetry often had a more chant-like sound than we are used to today, perhaps because music was principally thought of as one more *aide memoire* from an array of devices used to retain material in a predominantly oral culture. It is difficult to believe, however, that the poet's *reacaire,* his reciter, to whom the performance of the work was entrusted, would not have followed aesthetic conventions considered pleasing by his listeners. We do not know what these were although certainly, it would seem odd that in works where the words were of utmost importance, and in which the poets spent their time constructing intricate rhymes to set metrical patterns, that such points were not to be emphasized in delivery. Reading bardic poems in the strict *dán díreach* metre, even today, reveals a highly developed sonic aesthetic that live performance with musical accompaniment could only have served to enhance. The musical instrument of the elite in those days was the harp, a robust instrument with metal alloy strings (bronze or brass) and played with the finger nails. The harpers themselves were members of the *aos ealadhna,* the artistic class, part of the poet's professional *dámh* or retinue. The descriptions of the music of some harps show how bewitching this music was intended to be:

a núall ban sídhe a Síth Lir	Call of the fairy women of the Mound of Lir
'S gan ceol do chor at aighidh	No music can surpass you
Ód threoir as téidbhinn gach teach	Your direction makes each house sweet-stringed
a chéidrinn cheóil na gcláirsioch.	Pinnacle of music among harps.

Thus music is associated with the fairy otherworld, the world of magic and enchantment, and this association has continued to the present day. To have one's music or singing described as *ceol sí* is one of the highest possible compliments. Indeed, there has been a resurgence of interest in the Irish wire strung harp in recent years, so that it is possible to experience modern interpretations of this older tradition. Perhaps indeed, as Martin Hayes has claimed, the best of the tradition is yet to come. As a sign of this, some interesting and appealing recordings of songs have been produced by the collaboration of the harper Siobhán Armstrong with *sean-nós* singers such as Róisín Elsafty and Bríd Ní Mhaoilchiaráin from Carna. These collaborations reveal the strength and depth of the musical and poetic resources of the Irish song tradition in innovative, creative ways that simultaneously connect 'tradition' with a completely contemporary sensibility. To my ears, these excellent recordings fall within the bounds of 'ceol sí' and deserve to be widely heard.

SOMETHING OLD, SOMETHING NEW

Most people interested in music in Ireland today are familiar with the term *sean-nós*. Usually, the term encompasses a number of regional traditions of singing in Irish. The most renowned of all of these is that of Co. Galway, whose singers have dominated the competitive arena at Oireachtas na Gaeilge for over forty years, taking the gold medal and *Corn Uí Riada* time and again. Interest in traditional song in Irish as an art form in its own right began in earnest during the first Oireachtas festivals held from 1897. Gradually, from a disparate collection of regional styles, a new, highly prestigious style of singing emerged. Because of the *sean* element in the term *sean-nós*, its newness is frequently not emphasized, and people involved in its circles are at pains to emphasize its authenticity, so that its venerable antiquity is frequently stressed. But *sean-nós* song and the venues in which it is performed have changed as Irish society and culture have changed.

Although singing still occurs in people's houses at informal gatherings, nowhere is evening visiting the institution it formerly was, so that more organized gatherings have become a more usual forum for the performance of unaccompanied song in Irish in traditional style. Some of these try to reproduce the informality of the home, while others, such as the Oireachtas competitions, are more formal and, frequently, highly pressurized events that reflect their late Victorian romantic nationalist origins. The Oireachtas competitions require stamina and endurance of both performers and audiences, as they can go on for up to three hours without a break. Such intensity was unusual in community performance where song performance tended to be interspersed with conversation, storytelling and dancing, providing a more variegated and dynamic format.

Today, however, song follows song until all the competitors have had their turn. Then the adjudicators decide to recall a reduced number from among those they have heard. In the second round, singers are required to sing a different kind of song to the one they have sung in the first. The tendency has always been for singers to perform a slow song first and to follow with a more rhythmical upbeat item in the second round. The tacit understanding was that the slow songs show off a singer's ability more than the faster paced ones. The skill involved in singing a faster item is felt to be easier and does not generally earn the same respect. There was, however, some discretion and competitors sometimes performed their fast item first in the hope that the variety might give them an edge. This discretion has now been ruled out and now, it is explicitly stated in the rules that slow songs must be sung in the first round and fast songs in the second. The skill involved in singing a faster item is felt to be easier and does not generally earn the same respect. This, indeed, is another of the changes brought about by competitive singing and the ideologies that underpin it, and differs considerably from the concerns suggested in the semantic outline at the beginning.

In traditional performance situations, however, it is part of the singer's aesthetic and social judgement what song will suit a particular moment at an event. In a context where slow songs have previously been sung, the singer might deliberately avoid singing another and choose instead a light-hearted, amusing, and often ribald item that could relieve and uplift the mood (or *fonn*) of the gathering. By choosing the right song, and by performing it well both technically and emotionally, *i gceart* in Irish, the singer's prestige and reputation as a performer are enhanced. Such choices require attention and a complete understanding of the dynamics of performance and community interaction. The singer performs a service for his or her companions, steering the entertainment in the right direction and hence sustaining its quality and standards, bringing what may indeed be termed a form of grace to the company. It is a gift, part of a cycle of reciprocal exchange at a symbolic level that goes to the heart of the role that culture plays in a community. Thus, unlike in Oireachtas competitions where the focus is squarely on the decontextualized item and the style of performance, in other settings, the focus is more holistic and slow and fast songs are valued according to how they are chosen and when they are sung – each complementing the other.

Context is crucial so that words and music together may be properly heard. In the non-competitive contexts that I am referring to, then, there is another kind of unspoken contest, a desire to say the words (*abair amhrán, an t-amhrán a rá*) properly; to execute the music in a like manner in order to embellish and heighten the theme of the song. In a society where strict parental control was the norm and indeed where marriages were often made matches, it is not too surprising that the love theme under various guises is the most popular in traditional Gaelic song. The picture emerging from a study of these texts shows a patriarchal society, where a double standard obtained, one for men and another for women. Women had to guard their honour assiduously against the gossip common to small communities where everyone was known, and some of most plangent songs of Irish are meditations on the theme of a woman deserted by her male lover. 'Dónall Óg' is the best known of these and exists also in English versions that have been translated from Irish. Other perennials include 'An Droighneán Donn,' 'Tiocfaidh an Samhradh' or 'An Sagairtín' and 'Caisleán Uí Néill'. These are the songs where the dramas of unhappy love are played out in a truly desolate manner.

These songs were first written down at the end of the eighteenth century and cannot have been new songs then. In a society where psychotherapy and counselling were far in the future, these songs, like much of the narrative legend and folktale repertoire, provided distanced or controlled insights into thorny personal problems, distraught mental states that were otherwise difficult to discuss, and through performance, listening and 'oral literary criticism' a partial mode of processing such problems. The songs seem to protest against the ideology of the small community while at the same time they act as a warning to those who are caught out by it. Thus, paradoxically, they confirm the supremacy of patriarchy by highlighting its injustice and inconsistencies. They do this in a language which recalls aristocratic splendour and luxury, mentioning gold and silver, silk and other items hardly available to the singers of the past. Lady Gregory once remarked on the contrast between the riches to be found in the songs and tales of the storytellers and the poverty of their everyday surroundings. This language, for all its references to wealth and affluence is direct and simple and readily comprehensible today. In fact, the formulaic nature of the language provides another compelling mnemonic aid to listeners with lines and half-lines recurring in several different songs that set off shimmering echoes of each other in the listeners' mind. Anyone who has seen Baz Lurhman's 2001 film *Moulin Rouge,* and who enjoyed the feast of mid- to late-twentieth century pop songs that is such a memorable feature of it, will immediately empathize with those who become entranced by the words and music of *sean-nós.* As in the film, the response elicited by the familiar sounds of the past, repeated anew in the present, may create a delicious transformation allowing insight into the tragedy and comedy of life, a trait sometimes called *cumha* in Irish. The feeling of *cumha* is usually considered one of longing and pining for an absent place or person, but perhaps it might also be thought of as a desire for peace, tranquillity and rest. Listening to *sean-nós* songs performed by those who know how to sing them in an audience who knows how to listen, can sometimes fleetingly satisfy such a yearning wish.

POPS AND CLASSICS

Sean-nós today has acquired classical or high-art status; it has become a cultural artefact that is deemed highly worthy if not necessarily always enjoyable. The formulaic language and the modally based melodies of the songs, together with the ornate simplicity of the performance style, put it in a special category of its own. It holds up a golden standard of authenticity for Irish traditional music in general according to some commentators. Consequently, it is often regarded as a pure form that should not be tampered with, although in practice Irish melodies have been popularized since Roibeard Mac Eoin's (Robert Owenson) time, who sang Irish songs in the Crow Street theatre in Dublin to great acclaim in the late eighteenth century. This public debut for Irish-language songs on stage was short-lived. Owenson's daughter, Lady Morgan, and those who followed her, most notably Thomas Moore, used the melodies, but supplied lyrics in English instead of Irish words. In modern times, as I have mentioned, songs and singing have proved to be highly effective pedagogical strategies, pressed into service regardless of their high cultural aura. Perhaps this aura has been formed in opposition to such popularizations, which many would regard as contamination.

The composite of modal melody and lyrics that forms *sean-nós* singing seems to resist appropriation by market forces. Although *sean-nós* is produced on commercial albums nowadays, it remains very much a minority interest, notwithstanding the heartening number of young singers that continues to emerge. In recent years however, a new form of combining poetry and music has emerged and grown significantly, largely though not exclusively through the support of Raidió na Gaeltachta. Over a hundred songs have been composed in the Galway Gaeltacht since the late 1970s, many of them composed by poets such as Tom an tSeoighigh and Seán Ó Ceoinín in *amhrán* metres that would seem perfectly at home in eighteenth-century poems. These are sung in the *sean-nós* but also in a new contemporary style by such great performers as John Beag Ó Flaithearta.

The Irish-language pop song may seem an anomaly, somewhat like a singing duck, but this only reveals how entrenched certain attitudes remain about the possibilities of the Irish language. Regardless of such limitations, the modest growth in the production of truly popular material is highly encouraging. Some of the best of this material comes from a duo giving themselves the daring title of 'The Gaelic Hit Factory.' Louis de Paor, the lyricist, is an acclaimed poet in Irish, and his song-writing reveals a highly developed linguistic imagination at work. His *reacaire*, John Spillane, a professional singer, song-writer and broadcaster himself, supplies the tunes to these lyrics. These are unusual and highly sophisticated creations and contain some hard-hitting social commentary on Celtic Tiger Ireland – such commentary being a time-honoured role of the poet. The song 'Bata is Bóthar' carries a particularly mordant edge in this respect. Kila is another group that has produced interesting and compelling material in Irish, as has Máire Breatnach, whose wonderful 'Éist a Stór' continues to be one of the most popular items on Irish-language radio. Another song writer, Seán Monaghan, from Tuam in Co. Galway, composed the famous 'Ó mo Dhreoilín' incorporating hip hop in Gaelic style into his work.

All in all, the current situation of music and language in Irish is a moderately healthy one. This is not to discount the huge pressure felt daily from the English language and from monoglot English-speaking Ireland, which, with some honourable and notable exceptions, manages to singularly ignore most of this vibrant activity. But perhaps it is enough to be still here, *yma o hyd,* as the Welsh phrase puts it. We haven't gone away, you know. Come join us.

Prose Writing in Irish Today

Máirín Nic Eoin

Few writers or readers in 1969 (when Brian Ó Cuív's *A View of the Irish Language* was published) could have predicted the developments in Irish-language writing which have occurred over the last forty years. While it is sometimes argued that lyric poetry may thrive in conditions of linguistic minoritization, the health of prose composition is often a more accurate indicator of the creative strength of a language and the cultural force of a language group. The sheer volume of prose works published in recent years is in itself remarkable, but more remarkable still – and cause for a certain amount of linguistic optimism – is the high standard of the works produced, both in terms of aesthetic quality and in terms of general design and production standards. This is all the more surprising when one takes into account that literary publication in Irish is carried out by small publishing houses, which rely on state subvention and much dedicated voluntary editorial effort.

While a literary genre such as the autobiography, which has been one of the most prevalent prose forms in Irish since the 1920s, is still prominent on Irish-language publishers' lists, the range of prose genres has increased considerably in recent years, encompassing everything from realist teen-lit with its emphasis on dramatic and engaging story-lines to highly literary non-populist works, often produced in an academic environment. In the hope of increasing literacy levels in the language, both publishers and funding sources, such as Bord na Leabhar Gaeilge, are keen to develop the more popular genres, and writers are encouraged to produce fiction for 'an gnáthléitheoir' (the ordinary reader). The result has been an increase in particular kinds of genre writing, including romantic novels, detective stories, and travel journals. In the context of the Irish language, however, the concept of 'an gnáthléitheoir' is a rather nebulous one, as a young or adult learner of Irish is more likely to read regularly in the language than a non-academic adult native speaker.

Publishing houses have different approaches to the diverse nature of the Irish-language book market. While they all strive to promote high quality literary works, and Irish-language publishers in general have always been supportive of literary experimentation, certain differences can be discerned in their approach to their core Irish-speaking readership. Some publishers promote writing with a Gaeltacht focus, whether generically traditional (autobiography, realist fiction with a regional focus) or experimental (magic realism, fantasy, metafiction). Others have encouraged genre writing and popular fiction for teen or adult learners of Irish. Certain very small publishing companies have developed as literary art houses, seemingly oblivious to the marketability of their publications. Some try to do it all, and publish relatively large volumes of works with little attempt to niche-market them. To survive at all, all Irish-language publishers rely heavily on the third-level student market, but in recent years the more challenging literary works have come to be replaced by the more popular books as core texts on third-level courses. This has not discouraged authors, however, and a significant strand in prose writing in Irish today is still the non-realist experimental work which tends to be both linguistically and stylistically challenging. The rest of this article will foreground the critical issues raised by contemporary prose writing by focusing on the dominant genres and on the work of a number of the most successful authors.

The creation of a body of realist fiction was a central objective of the Irish literary revival from the outset. In recent years, this objective has resulted in a body of writing which includes popular adult fiction often with a regional thrust (such as is to be found in the work of Pádraig Standún, Maidhc Dainín Ó Sé, Joe Steve Ó Neachtain and Máirtín Ó Muilleoir), romantic fiction (especially by female authors such as Siobhán Ní Shúilleabháin, Nóirín Ní Mhaoilaoi and Tina Nic Éinrí), fiction for adult learners (by authors such as Pól Ó Muirí, Colmán Ó Drisceoil and, more recently, Anna Heussaff), and teenage fiction (by authors such as Muireann Ní Bhrolcháin, Mícheál Ó Ruairc and Ré Ó Laighléis). Particularly successful titles include, for the adult reader, *Sobalsaol* (2005) by Pádraig Standún (about a scriptwriter for a television soap opera whose own life resembles that of the genre he practises) and, for the young teen, *An bhfaca éinne agaibh Roy Keane*

(2003) and its sequel *I bhfad ó bhaile* (2004) by Mícheál Ó Ruairc. While Joe Steve Ó Neachtain and Maidhc Dainín Ó Sé attract loyal local audiences in Conamara and Kerry respectively, one of the most successful authors of popular fiction in Irish is Dublin-born bilingual writer Éilís Ní Dhuibhne, whose novels *Dúnmharú sa Daingean* (2000), *Cailíní Beaga Ghleann na mBláth* (2003) and *Hurlamaboc* (2006) have proved attractive both to teenage and to young adult readers.

Popular fiction in Irish today is cool and contemporary, and doesn't shy away from dealing with youth culture or with societal problems such as family breakdown, bullying or consumerism. Certain authors, such as Ciarán Ó Coigligh, Tomás Mac Síomóin and Aodh Ó Canainn, use fiction to explore cultural and political issues and there is also a tendency for some realist writers to draw on traumatic biographical or sociological material. Déirdre Ní Ghrianna's short-story collection *An Gnáthrud* (1999) is an example of what could be termed 'miserable realism' in its stark depiction of depression and domestic and sectarian violence. Another tendency, recognized by a number of critics, is for novelists to employ first-person narration or internal monologue as narrative techniques, thus avoiding some of the technical difficulties of depicting non-Irish-speaking situations through Irish.

All Irish-language prose writers must grapple with the question of linguistic credibility and many of them incorporate issues of language into the plot. In the case of the central character in two very entertaining who-dunnits, *Crann Smola* (2001) and *Rí na gCearrbhach* (2003), by Belfast writer Seán Ó Dúrois, for example, we are informed that he learned Irish from his maternal grandparents. Set in late-nineteenth-century Belfast and environs, detective William Watters and side-kick Cameron are presented naturally as negotiating historical layers of sectarian and class hatred to discover the perpetrator of ferocious crimes. Reader interest is sustained also through the development of a compelling romantic sub-plot with an inter-religious, inter-class and interlingual dimension, the woman in question being a native speaker of Irish.

In stark contrast to the work of the realists and genre writers is a growing body of non-realist and experimental fiction. This strand always existed in Irish, but it is now so prevalent that one is tempted to suggest that the minoritized state of the language is a shaping force behind it. Are

Irish-language writers looking to genres 'which make a strength of
what appear to be disabilities', as suggested by one critic (Ó Drisceoil
1989). Are they demonstrating genuine freedom of expression or are
they merely exploiting the freedom of the margins and discounting
the possibility of communicating with a recognisable interpretative
community?

One of the most interesting writers of non-realist fiction to emerge in
recent years is short-story writer Dáithí Ó Muirí whose lyrical prose
combines the real and the super-real, the material and the imaginative
in finely wrought tales of modern (often urban) life. His best books
to date are his thematic collections on the subject of war and death,
Cogaí (2002) and *Uaigheanna agus Scéalta Eile* (2002), both of which
appear to be heavily influenced by Latin American magic realism. The
Irish language has often produced unusual once-offs, such as Dáibhí
Ó Cróinín's novel *An Cúigiú Díochlaonadh* (1994), one of those
unclassifiable novels which reads like a folktale, until the narrator
is brought to an otherworldly location where his encounter with a
community of Irish-language revivalists becomes a hilarious send-up
of Irish literary and scholarly activity.

Certain contemporary writers stand out for the range and versatility
of their work. Micheál Ó Conghaile's fictional writings, for example,
range in style from the realist to the absurd, from the mundane to
the fantastic. His novel of homosexual youth *Sna Fir* (1999), though
marred by its stereotypically tragic denouement, is as honest and as
explicit a depiction of a young man's initiation and integration into gay
community life as one is likely to find in any language. Ó Conghaile's
best work is to be found in his short story collections, however, and in
the collections *An Fear a Phléasc* (1997) and *An Fear nach nDéanann
Gáire* (2003), in particular, he moves from the real to the surreal with
a great ease and fluidity of language. Seán Mac Mathúna's quirky
short stories, as exemplified in the collections *Banana* (1999) and
Úlla (2005), are dramatic masterpieces, which range from the comic
to the tragic, often combining both in the one story. Novelist Liam
Mac Cóil has moved from the philosophical, in *An Dochtúir Áthas*
(1994), to the historical, in *Fontenoy* (2005), via a contemporary novel
of cultural critique *An Claíomh Solais* (1998). Mac Cóil's fiction is a
world of ideas as much as plot. His metafictional *An Dochtúir Áthas* is

a dramatic exploration of Freudian theory, and in particular of the role of narrative in personal identity. The work of Liam Prút should also be alluded to here. His first novel *Désirée* (1989) is a lyric meditation on the role of desire in identity formation. Prút explores the inner world of a speechless disabled individual in *Geineasas* (1991), while *An Leanbh sa Lamborghini* (1996) is a subtle psychological study of human attachment and detachment.

Other writers who have eschewed the realist mode in some or all of their work include Dara Ó Conaola and Lorcán S. Ó Treasaigh. Ó Conaola's surreal stories, as exemplified in *Mo Chathair Ghríobháin* (1981) and *Amuigh Liom Féin* (1988), are rooted in the oral tradition of the Gaeltacht, but are not at all folkloristic in subject matter or outlook. Ó Treasaigh has experimented with surreal and realist modes of narration. Having produced two highly experimental episodic novels, Ó Treasaigh's third book, *Bás san Oirthear* (1992), was an allegorical exploration of the psychological pressures associated with an Irish-speaking upbringing in a non-Gaeltacht environment, a theme he has subsequently developed in a realist fashion in his bildungsroman *Céard é English?* (2002). Ó Treasaigh's latest work, *Cnoc na Lobhar* (2007), is a combination of real and dream worlds, which draws on the strengths of his earlier work.

Of all contemporary prose writers in Irish, the work of Alan Titley demonstrates the greatest versatility and freedom of expression. Capable of spinning a yarn out of any material at all, his short stories and fables, as illustrated in the collections *Eiriceachtaí agus Scéalta Eile* (1987), *Leabhar Nóra Ní Anluain* (1998) and *Fabhalscéalta* (1995), develop pet themes and press home political points with a combination of linguistic panache and earthy humour. His most accomplished work to date, however, is arguably his historical novel *An Fear Dána* (1993), based on the scattered biographical references to thirteenth-century Gaelic poet Muireadhach Albanach Ó Dálaigh. Playful intertextuality is integral to this novel's technique, and such intertextuality (particularly with reference to the Irish textual tradition) is also a feature in the prose work of other contemporary writers such as Pádraig Ó Siadhail, Pádraig Ó Cíobháin and, recently, Biddy Jenkinson. Ó Siadhail is of particular interest as his first two novels were realist in style and theme and his third was a thriller with a political edge. His latest work of fiction, however, the short story collection *Na Seacht gCineál Meisce agus Finscéalta Eile* (2001) contains stories which are firmly embedded in the Irish literary or folk tradition and would make little sense to a reader unfamiliar with that tradition. Pádraig Ó Cíobháin, a successful realist writer in his earlier work, has moved gradually, and most notably in his latest novel *Ré an Charbaid* (2005), towards a form of self-reflexive – and ultimately self-indulgent – intertextuality. Similarly, poet Biddy Jenkinson, in her first foray into the realm of the short story in *An Grá Riabhach* (2000), employs an ironic intertextuality in comic stories which rework motifs or story-lines from the Irish literary canon.

Autobiography is still a popular Irish-language genre, but the classic twentieth-century Gaeltacht autobiography, with its graphic descriptions of the hardship of life on the western seaboard, is being replaced by the travel journal as the dominant autobiographical mode. There has been a steady stream of travel writing in Irish in recent years, as Irish-language writers now describe intercultural encounters on several continents. Recent examples of the genre include two exceptional travel journals by Irish-language poets. Gabriel Rosenstock's *Ólann mo Mhiúil as an nGainséis* (2003) describes a journey through Dubai, India, Hong Kong, Japan, Australia, Chile and the United States, and Cathal Ó Searcaigh's *Seal i Neipeal* (2004) documents the Donegal poet's experiences as a visitor in Nepal. Both of these accounts demonstrate the authors' affiliation with cultures where physical poverty is compensated for by rich human and cultural resources. Other popular examples of the genre include Mícheál de Barra's account of his pilgrimage to Santiago de Compostela, *An Bóthar go Santiago* (2007) and mountaineer Dermot Somers' description of his climbing experiences in *Rince ar na Ballaí* (2002). Other noteworthy autobiographical works include Pádraig Standún's *Eaglais na gCatacómaí* (2004), where the priest-author exposes the political conviction and personal reality underlying his most controversial novels about the issue of priestly celibacy.

No description of contemporary prose writing could ignore the ever increasing body of non-fiction works in the language. Academic publishing house An Clóchomhar continues to publish scholarly and critical texts of the highest standard, with biography, literary and cultural history and literary criticism being the main fields of enquiry covered. Irish-language journals have always been an important outlet both for creative writers and for critics and journalists. The annual *Bliainiris* (2000-) takes up where the journal *Oghma* (1989-1998) left off in that it publishes both creative and critical prose writing and has broadened the range of Irish-language cultural critique to include visual art and media criticism, philosophy and politics. Similarly, the three volumes published to date of *An Aimsir Óg* (1999, and 2000 Vol 1 and Vol 2) illustrate the wide range of material now covered by Irish-language writing and scholarship, with articles on subjects as diverse as biotechnology, contemporary art, the Northern Ireland peace process, the Gaeltacht as construct, autobiography and memory, the relationship between poetry, folklore and the virtual reality of computer games, emigration, terminology, Michael Hartnett and translation, travel literature, and the list goes on and on. Such publications illustrate that the Irish language is now a sophisticated, versatile and creative medium of critical analysis.

Similarly, Irish-language journalism is also healthier than ever, with the Belfast-based newspaper *Lá Nua* providing a minimal daily news service and weekly newspaper *Foinse* a more extensive Irish-language view on current affairs. Journalists such as Cathal Mac Coille, Póilín Ní Chiaráin and Máirín Ní Ghadhra have contributed hugely not just to journalism but to the development of the language as a medium of contemporary political commentary and debate. The Irish-language opinion column in the *Irish Times* has been an important forum for writers over the decades, with Alan Titley currently occupying the chair. The recent publication of collections by former columnists such as Liam Ó Muirthile, and the critical analysis of the earlier journalistic work of Seán Ó Ríordáin in Stiofán Ó Cadhla's monograph *Cá bhfuil Éire? Guth an Ghaisce i bPrós Sheáin Uí Ríordáin* (1998), have rightly drawn attention to the cultural significance of this type of journalistic essay.

Writing for the theatre has always been a challenge for the Irish-language writer, and that is still the case, though television has provided a new context for playwrights and the success of television drama and soap operas, such as TG4's popular 'Ros na Rún', has had a spin-off effect in certain quarters. Conamara-born actor and script-writer Joe Steve Ó Neachtain has emerged as a significant dramatic presence, and has moved effortlessly from the role of scriptwriter of the Conamara-based radio soap 'Baile an Droichid' in the 1990s to acting for television and stage and writing a number of highly successful plays for the theatre. Interestingly enough, however, many of the most successful recent dramatic productions have been stage adaptations of prose classics, such as Myles na gCopaleen's *An Béal Bocht* and Máirtín Ó Cadhain's *Cré na Cille* (both produced by Taibhdhearc na Gaillimhe), or stage documentaries such as Diarmuid de Faoite's one-man-show *Pádraic Ó Conaire*. Television documentary is another important prose genre and scripts by Alan Titley – for documentaries on writers Liam Ó Flaithearta, Máirtín Ó Direáin and Máirtín Ó Cadhain – stand out as exceptionally accomplished examples of the genre.

Another recent phenomenon has been the publication of extended prose essays in the form of pamphlets, such as *Pobal, Féinmheas, Teanga* (2004) by Peadar Kirby. They range from the polemical to the analytical but have all been concerned with cultural politics and particularly with the present state and future prospects of the Irish language. While many of these pamphlets are directed at the Irish-language community only, dual-language publications such as *Guthanna in Éag: an Mairfidh an Ghaeilge Beo? / Voices Silenced: Has Irish a Future?* (2001) by linguist James McCloskey and *An Ghaeilge san Aois Nua / Irish in the New Century* (2005) by critic Michael Cronin, seek to place the Irish language in the context of international debates about cultural change and interculturalism in a globalized world.

There is no indication that the recent flowering of literary activity in Irish is going to cease. Indeed, the books written far outnumber those published and most literary competitions attract sizeable entries. There is concern about literacy levels, however, and attempts have been made to encourage reading in Irish through book clubs and literary festivals. The readership figures for monthly e-zine www.beo.ie (whose readers now far outnumber those of the long-established monthly magazines *Comhar* and *Feasta*) are, however, very encouraging and may signal a new direction for Irish-language writers and Irish-language writing in the future.

REFERENCES AND FURTHER READING

Nic Eoin, M. 2006. 'Contemporary prose and drama in Irish: 1940-2000' in Kelleher, M. & P. O'Leary (eds), *The Cambridge history of Irish literature Vol.2: 1890-2000*. Cambridge. CUP. 270-316.

Ní Dhonnchadha, A. (ed). 2006. *An prós comhaimseartha: Léachtaí Cholm Cille XXXVI*. Maigh Nuad. An Sagart.

Ó Drisceoil, P. 1989. 'Lead us not into shenanigans' in *The Irish Times* 14 January.

Offshore on Land — Poetry in Irish Now

Liam Ó Muirthile

If being a poet in Irish feels like living offshore on land, that feeling of offshoreness seems to be the undercurrent of a primary call: of journeying there in order to stay here. A paradox of course, but confirmed and sustained by experience. In the world of poetry in Irish – a compass without co-ordinates – each poet marks out an individual point without making the compass whole.

There have been and are enough poets working in Irish to box the compass – 'to know and to be able to recite the points and quarter points of the magnetic compass from north through south to north again, both clockwise and anti-clockwise. It is now a lost art....' *(The Oxford Companion to Ships and the Sea, 2006)*. In Irish now, each recites his or her own point outside the hearing range of the other. A strange journey indeed.

It was still possible in or about 1968, with Seán Ó Ríordáin's poems 'Adhlacadh mo Mháthar' (My Mother's Burial) and 'Saoirse' (Freedom) embedded in the Irish-language syllabus of second-level schools, for poems to have a far-reaching effect on a generation which was entering university. His first collection, *Eireaball Spideoige*, was published in 1952. The Irish language itself, as an entity, had a viable currency of thoughtful and coherent expression. Literacy in Irish among a generation of learners was peaking. Literature was still a gateway to the language, with television just gaining a foothold. There was a congruence between education, a first glimpse of economic ease, the community language of the Gaeltacht, and notions of national political aspirations and local cultural identities. The Northern Ireland 'troubles' were beginning to rock the South to its core. Paris had erupted. World events impinged. Protest was the new religion of the age.

Cork city was to become the main *locus* for the great burst of poetry in Irish through the poetry journal *Innti*. The city had an open backdoor to the southwest and the feeling of being a European crossroads-on-sea. It was possible, even in the late 1960s, to imagine an authentic Irish-language voice of the English-speaking city. Nowhere else in Ireland had the written text of the language been worked so late into the nineteenth century by dairy farmers, tradesmen, tailors, stonecutters, teachers, Catholic and some Protestant clergy, and professional scribes with commitment and playfulness, and with an enduring sense of regional and local identity. The remnants of a classical tradition had left their tidal mark. Frank O'Connor too, was a fluent Irish-speaker who had mediated the world of poetry in Irish through his translations. All this, the strong oral storytelling and *seanchas*, and much more had contributed to zones of feeling and thinking which could be construed as alternatives to the predominant culture.

The poet Seán Ó Ríordáin (1910–77) shuffled within that nexus, in his forays into the city and in his TB room on its outskirts in Iniscarra. The village of Iniscarra was not only a bus terminal for Sunday afternoon trips to the river Lee, but also a regional symbol of the economic regeneration of Sixties' Ireland. A new hydroelectric dam had been built there. Ó Ríordáin's work reflects that renewal, in the shadows cast by the candlelight at his bedside on his poems, and in his diary references to his brother's hopes for employment on the so-called Lee Scheme.

If we are to believe in any linear descent at all – and it may be doubtful – poetry in Irish became possible for the generation born in the early 1950s, when Seán Ó Ríordáin sat in a sunny apple orchard re-reading a letter from his dead mother. The Aran Island poet Máirtín Ó Direáin (1910-88), too, had attended a lecture on poetry in Dublin by the scholar and Revivalist Tadhg 'Torna' Ó Donnchadha from Carrignavar, in the late 1930s, which kickstarted his work.

The fact that Ó Ríordáin's mother's letter was in English, and the resulting poem 'Adhlacadh mo Mháthar' in Irish, is more than an underlying reality. It is integral to all contemporary poetry in the Irish language, which is a poetry of two languages, one on the page, the other crowding the stage. While the dead mother syndrome may be of more enduring interest to psychoanalysts than to poets, nevertheless, Ó Ríordáin's lifelong mining and sifting in his journals of an authentic language in pursuit of poetry in Irish is one of the most remarkable literary stories of Ireland in the twentieth century. Norman MacCaig's comment about his fellow Scottish poet Somhairle MacGill-Eain writing in Gaelic, firmly applies here: 'Nobody does that except for the deepest and most compulsive reasons.'

Those 'reasons' might well be a matter of interesting speculation, and revealing insight, especially around the whole area of mother tongue and father language, and what we now have come to understand by compulsion. Ó Ríordáin's poetry issues from his exploration of the unnavigated and terrifying depths of the unconscious. All authentic lives are subject to terror, as is clear from his diaries. It is the interpenetration of both languages, synergized in his work as two functioning lungs, which made all the difference.

Innti, the poetry journal first published in 1970 as a broadsheet, owes its title to an adverbial phrase from the speech of an individual in West Kerry. Through *Innti*, the *caint na ndaoine* slogan of early Revivalist writers was turned on its head to become *daoine ag caint*. Poems for the *Innti* generation would be grounded in living speech, following more Pound's – as in Ó Ríordáin's poem 'An Feairín' (The Maneen) – than Ezra Pound's advice. Both Máirtín Ó Direáin, that great dignified man, and Seán Ó Ríordáin, had poems in the first edition. Michael Davitt (1950-2005), the poet and founding editor of *Innti* with fellow-poet Gabriel Rosenstock and the musician Con Ó Drisceoil, was the main catalyst of change. He had been at school in the North Monastery, where Seán Ó Ríordáin too had attended. Charismatic, a showman and shaman, he had one foot planted firmly in West Kerry and the other, exploratory, on the campus of University College Cork.

Like many campus initiatives of its time, *Innti* turned the course of poetry in Irish toward the demotic and formal experimentation. It admitted a frank sexuality, and presented a brazen, youthful face to the world. In time, the Irish-language lyric poem would break open on its pages. The initial campus energy was sustained through fourteen editions until 1994, and the most important contemporary poets would be associated with it. Michael Davitt's editorial hand was always firmly on the tiller, but he engaged editorially with others besides Gabriel Rosenstock – Louis de Paor and Proinsias Ní Dhorchaí especially – to bring the journal forward as the national journal of poetry in Irish. It displaced the monthly literary magazine *Comhar*, as the main publishing conduit for new poetry, but not before *Comhar* itself had nurtured some of the emerging poets under the editorship of Eoghan Ó hAnluain and threw open its pages later with Proinsias Ní Dhorchaí as editor.

Michael Davitt's own poetry is marked throughout his work by a cinematic eye, filtered through a varying but intense focus, as if the manner of recording reality were the act of revealing the poetic insight itself. In a style of hyper-realism at times, it has all the elements of the wideshot panorama to the close-up, phrased in an uncompromising, contemporaneous language of the now, humorous, sometimes searing, always adjectivally unfrocked and with a tensile beauty in lines of his own tuning. That tuning is as much a matter of his own inner ear as his unerring instinct for calibrating newly-minted words and terms with the resonance of living speech. His conscious project of emulating Bob Dylan has yet to be examined in any meaningful way – his first collection *Gleann ar Ghleann* (1982) marks *Blonde on Blonde*, but his second collection, *Bligeard Sráide* (1983), which has the look at least of *Self-Portrait*, has an iconic status in contemporary Irish poetry. There is a metallic, lyrical tension at the core of his work, in the tone beneath his overlying style, which is mysterious – 'Meirg agus Lios Luachra' – and which is possibly never definitively resolved but from which there is a joyful, sensual and easeful respite in the later collections – *Fardoras* (2003) - and especially in the suite of poems which gives its title to his last collection, *Seiming Soir* (2004).

Innti was at its core, a non-academic initiative. While there are no absolute breaks with the past, *Innti* was in many respects *sui generis*. Gabriel Rosenstock's wide reading of literature, his editorial involvement with *Motus*, the English-language literary magazine, and his mediation of the world of English poetry through *Innti* had a major influence on *Innti's* initial development. But *Innti* owed more to Gaeltacht-speak, rock 'n roll and the Sixties' folk revival, the cinema and whatever-you're-having-yourself, than to any early reading of William Carlos Williams, Frank O'Hara or Robert Frost if not Eliot or E. E. Cummings and French poetry. *Sean-nós* too, an art form in itself at its best and brought alive by Seán Ó Riada both on disc and in his invitations to singers to perform on campus, was a further important point of entry into the language.

The Seáin Triumvirate in University College Cork – Ó Riada, Ó Ríordáin and Ó Tuama – created an atmosphere in which exhuberance, at least, could thrive. Seán Ó Tuama's *An Grá in Amhráin na nDaoine* (1960) and *Caoineadh Airt Uí Laoghaire* (1961) seemed to have a synchronicity with the age. But in many respects it was Ó Riada, like Hamlet's ghost, who had the most profound influence. As if he were playing not only the language of music, but the music of a language on a national and world stage. It was Ó Riada who had clasped the classical heritage of poetry and song of a language community, and it was he who forged his own vital linkage with a community which allows artistic work to truly come alive and thrive. It is through Ó Riada that poets in English and in Irish, can legitimately claim that heritage as their own. It was highly ironic that Seán Ó Riada, who travelled the world, had made his home in Cúil Aodha, while the 1960s generation of learners of Irish and their teachers from Cork city headed west past his door to Kerry.

Nuala Ní Dhomhnaill and the Donegal poet Cathal Ó Searcaigh, who is as much an *Innti* poet in spirit as any, have stayed close to their own language communities. Nuala Ní Dhomhnaill's voice is as much her own as ancestral, surging through the marvellous psychic drama of her poems especially in *An Dealg Droighin* (1981) and *Feis* (1991). Her outpourings on the page are seemingly unmediated by formal rigours as we knew them, before Nuala, or might have wished them, but are turbo-driven by a more immediate urgency. It is as if an ancestral community were not so much thinking through her as feeling through her, in the poem's present tense, with the authentic voices of *mná ag caint*. She, indeed, is the inheritor of *banseanchas* with the great heave of her poems washing up on the bare page. She achieved an untrammelled, almost industrial access to the unconscious through her hard work on folklore and storytelling and through her wide reading. She has great humour and handles the big themes as assuredly as the everyday, household traumas of suburbia which can also of course become big themes. She refeminized the territory, and swept away much of the aridity of the Revivalist spirit. The whiplash of some of her lines is her own making as much as the pickled variety of Corca Dhuibhne speech.

It is understandable that many contemporary poets in English would have wanted to translate her work, Michael Hartnett early on and Paul Muldoon later in *The Astrakhan Cloak* (1992). However, the handing over of the original work has major consequences, one of them being

John McInnes's quip, as quoted in *An Tuil* (1999), the anthology of twentieth-century Scottish Gaelic Poetry, by the editor Ronald Black: 'It loses something in the original'.

It is perhaps, a matter of how we believe a poem might live a life. Either in terms of its own integrity, hoping that it might make room for itself, or with the help of others. There is not much, now, to support the belief that an Irish-language poem might live a life through that natural flowing into a common stream. It is not entirely injudicious to think that it might be through translation into English that the original might bounce back in unexpected ways. However, translation into English of contemporary Irish-language poetry can selectively reduce the poem itself and undermine the possibilities of forms of further evolving life for the original poem. A recent commentator suggested, while reviewing a collection in Irish, that the originals might have been written in English and subsequently translated into Irish. This might well be true, but is a masquerade, a subterfuge too far for any intelligent engagement with real poems in Irish. Whatever our personal view, this is more than likely the path of future development of the poem in Irish, a mere palimpsest of the poem in English.

Gabriel Rosenstock is the great innovator of his generation, and his first collection *Suzanne sa Seomra Folctha* (1973) still has great charm – it already marks out the course that Gabriel's path through poetry would take, original work and translations forming part of the whole. It bridged the generations and brought the Irish-language poem into domains it had never known. His 'Laoi an Rua-Indiaigh Dhíbeartha' stands totemically on its own. 'Deireadh Seachtaine na Martinis Dry' still has that wonderful tone of world-weariness and urbanity of an underated *film noir*. His prodigious if not bewildering output can at times mask his achievements. He has translated from many languages into Irish and has developed the *haiku*. His poetry and books for children are often a collaboration with visual artists, and he more than anyone has actively sought to engage others in the world of the poem in Irish. He has a mordant wit and a scarifying lyricism. Inclined to the Gothic, his greatest gift to the Irish-language poem is his stance as outsider. He has turned the poem in Irish inside out, and outside in – *Conlán* (1989), a selection of Heaney poems – and has often left his contemporaries scorched in his slipstream. In many respects,

Rosenstock's achievements have exposed the threadbare texture of the range of writing in the Irish language. At times our hope for him would be that he would have more stamina in pursuing the possibilities of individual poems. It could well be that, in time, the language itself might catch up with him. It is more likely that, in some future domain, his work will be seen as how poems in Irish might have been.

The form of what constitutes a poem, whatever its mode, is of fundamental importance to the essential life of the poem. A poem must be able to hold its own ground. It is very difficult to see, now, how any poem in Irish might hold its ground. In Irish, because of a residual collective neurosis serving the cause of the language and active individual neuroses serving the cause of poetry, together with little or no critical judgement and uninspired academic performance, the health of the poem itself is indeed precarious. The first responsibility of the poet is to serve the poem itself. The matter of translation downwards, as in Seamus Deane's phrase in reference to Joyce, and translation *inwards* into the internal dynamics of the poem itself, is a process that can take a lifetime but it is what serves the poem. In an age which serves the poet more than the poem it is difficult to sustain the work which, in its own time, results in real poems.

Cathal Ó Searcaigh's joyous celebration of his own people and place in northwest Donegal, his buoyant homo-eroticism, is both convincing and infectious. He has a geographic range from Mucais to Nepal. Reading the bulk of his poems in the original *Ag Tnúth Leis an tSolas* (2000), something happens. A boyishness comes alive in his imaginative landscape, marvelling at the humanity of it all, which affirms a boyishness in ourselves. This can be easily and unjustifiably misconstrued. If there is harshness there – 'Gort na gCnámh' – it is in the suffering inflicted by human beings through an inability to love and receive love. His portraits of older people are superb, and awaken us to our own intimacy by our participation as listeners to, and readers of his own relationships. One of the consistent aspects of his work is his musical phrasing, broken in unexpected places to arrest the ear. His emotional range gathers us in with its unadulterated exhuberance, especially in his love poems. His earlier work struggled with the displacement to the city from his native Donegal Gaeltacht, in pursuit of his beloved beats. While he resolved the matter in his grounding of the work in his own place it has also kept the development of a broader emotional range in check. It is not merely an issue of sentimentality, but more of growing away from the fold, from being, literally, penned in.

The relationship between the poem in Irish and music has never been properly explored, due in no small measure to the scholarly obsession with the fractured text of the language and semantics. Language carries meaningfulness beyond semantics, perhaps into some area of the collective unconscious. The Gaelic poets of Scotland understood this far more clearly than their brothers and sisters in Ireland. In Ireland, we have nothing to rival 'Moladh Beinn Dobhrainn', 'Birlinn Chlann Raghnaill' or Somhairle Mac Gill-Eain.

The sounds of Irish poetry move us in mysterious ways. The language itself has a strange hold on us, beyond reasonableness. It is possible to view the vast panoply of Irish poetry, for example, as a language with an unwritten musical notation, the music of itself. One of the tasks in dealing with it is to absorb it aurally as much as to read it. The result of this is a translation into itself. In that way, the Irish language can become a 'foreign language' of unimagined richness.

Gréagóir Ó Dúill has pursued his own determined, single-handed course as a poet and *homme de lettres* with integrity, intelligence, and honesty. An important reviewer and teacher of poetry, his body of work – *Rogha Dánta 1965-2001* (2001) – demands and merits close reading. Born in Dublin, he grew up in Antrim and was educated in Belfast, and has lived both in Dublin and in Gort a' Choirce in the Donegal Gaeltacht. An outsider of both the Hobsbaum school in Queen's University, where he was a student at that period, and an *Innti* dissenter as it were, his work has been revitalized by his strong connections with the Donegal Gaeltacht community. He himself has acknowledged this as a matter of 'the music' of a language. While his earlier work might have benefited from a stricter editorial hand, rather than being too strict with the self, he has doggedly produced very fine poems of a different type from the *Innti* output – 'Turas Luaimh', 'Stowaway', 'Téim fá Chónaí', 'Bailitheoirí an Deannaigh', 'Ceacht', 'Don Chonstábla Taca Michael Williams' and, interestingly, has worked the sonnet form in Irish. The challenge for him, perhaps, is to let the metaphor find its inherent energy within his own self rather than overburden it with too much detail and meaning. His Northern perspective has allowed him into broad political domains where other Irish-language contemporaries have not gone. He has many memorable phrases – *'óglachas an ólacháin'* – and certainly has one of the most buoyant lines, at least, in a poem in contemporary Irish – *'Ag longadán ar ucht Mae West na n-aislingí dubh-is-bán'*/ 'Rocking on the black-and-white apparitions of Mae West's chest'.

One of the primary characteristics of poetry and song in the Irish language, as long as it has been produced on and off the island of Ireland has been a love of small things. It is as if the Irish always knew that it could never be otherwise, and then got on with fully inhabiting their imaginative world. Whether composed by named authors or anonymously, it has issued from a collective, intimate consciousness, earthed in the ground of collective values but often with an unearthly reach. Its unfailing appeal has always been to affirm humanity, the human dimension of our being in this world and more often than not of our being in an otherworld. The mainstay of the poem in Irish may not be to wear the world's cloak through whatever means, but to wear its own cloak as a loose garment. This is not an appeal for 'nativism' or even atavisim, merely a statement of belief in the intrinsic value of the poem itself.

Louis de Paor has reversed the usual relationship of the text in Irish with its translated version – *Ag Greadadh Bas sa Reilig / Clapping in the Cemetery* (2005) – by placing his original poem on the facing right page, and his collaborative English versions on the left. This is an important statement of intent. Interestingly, for an Irish-langauge reader the translations offer extended glosses on the originals. A 'second-wave' member of the *Innti* generation, together with Colm Breathnach, he has a painterly eye and an acute intelligence. His sensual imagery is easy on the eye – 'Aonach na dTorthaí' – and his poems are remarkable for their shadings and colours. His inversions, or new connections – 'Fabhalscéal' – release a whole new way of *seeing* through the Irish language. He, too, has undertaken his own filtration of home, spending time in Australia, and has further extended the range of the city in Irish-language poetry. His brilliance is, literally, dazzling. If that leads at times to what can seem like rhetoric or overstatement, it may be because the poem powers ahead leaving the original impetus stranded. But invariably, he manages to retrieve it – 'Corcach' – as if he knew best himself that he needed to take the long way around, home.

Colm Breathnach is the most grounded of the contemporary poets in the classical South-Munster mould. The beat and measure of his lines dance off the floor to tunes we think we know. While his imagination travels by shadow and often through undergrowth, there is an enduring solidity at the core of his work which is the true mark of a master craftsman. He is honest and direct, never an actor in his own poems. His tone is restrained, never pushing the decibel level beyond the limiter, and he delivers his work with what can seem like forensic detachment at times. A form of understatement, it is also the mark of true feeling. His collection *Scáthach* (1994) still reads like one seamless poem in many voices, both male and female. His organization of the collection would seem to wish it to be so. 'Fáschoill' is a poem of great integrity to return to, again and again. He, too, has journeyed towards that sublimation of the male and female form, mother and father, into the one form. *An Fear Marbh* (1998) is a heartbreaking collection for his dead father, full of regret, but a relationship resolved. Some of those poems, at least, *have* gone into the common stream. For a poet of great integrity who has stayed close-hauled to the original call, it is time for himself, perhaps, to allow versions in English translation to take him on a broader reach.

Much the same applies to Biddy Jenkinson, who draws together in her *fantasia entymologiae et zoologiae*, as it were, that offshoot stream of *Innti* and what could be called the textual literary tradition of Leinster and other territories. She too has resisted the pull of translation. Her poems can go off like fireworks, or ground us – 'Eanáir 1991'; '15 Eanáir 1991' – in the locally globalized inhumanity of the now. Biddy Jenkinson, for all her seemingly impromptu references to sexual organs, is a deeply *moral* poet, as, for example, was Eoghan Ó Tuairisc. In many respects, she is working out of that important literary branch of writing in Irish – represented by Ó Tuairisc, Rita Kelly, Conleth Ellis, Micheál Ó hUanacháin and others – which can be as difficult to reach as to fix in place. She is playful and has an exhuberant lightness of touch, with that specific humour of the poem as almost a found object. The Jenkinson *character* is as interesting in the poems as her flights of fancy and her close-up observations of the natural world. If the thinness of her lines is sometimes problematic, she mostly manages to bring off the poem with great panache and that leavening of the spirit which is the hallmark of her work.

Many others' poems need to be looked at, and addressed, especially Gearóid Mac Lochlainn's work. If there is a vibrant, new contemporary voice in Irish-language poetry, Gearóid's is it. Aifric Mac Aodha's first collection is also due, and much expected. Tomás Mac Síomóin was a very important presence during the early years of *Innti*, and his *Damhna agus Dánta Eile* (1974) especially, marked a strong new voice in Irish poetry. He also worked the longer and narrative poem, but in latter years has given his attention to prose. However, pressure of space will not allow such a review for now.

Much has been achieved in the poetry of the past forty years in Irish. It has seen much individual achievement, international performance and recognition. While the main English-language focus in that period has been on the poets of Northern Ireland, a coherent and highly significant body of work continued to evolve in Irish, giving voice to another very contemporary Irelandness. It would be interesting, too, to explore the range and nature of that voice through the poets who work out of that same Munster tradition in the English language.

Poetry itself has become marginalized, its status diminished on the outer edge of our field of vision. Much of our hopes for what the poem in Irish might achieve, in its further evolutionary forms, are groundless. The ground itself has shifted and even opened up under the poem. The poem in Irish is in freefall. Literacy in the language has all but collapsed in that same period since 1968.

Broadcasting and newspaper journalism are now working the oral and written text of the language to the degree that a public just about tolerates and enjoys, and the broadcasters are the contemporary storytellers and *seanchaithe*. In many respects, this is quite healthy. But there is little room for the real poem, that form of emotional and intellectual engagement with the world that can change our lives. A new home must be found for the poem in Irish. Translation outwards, is of course, a reality of our lives. But the poem in Irish now must be constructed out of thin air. Some of the best of the lyric poems in Old Irish, too, were also plucked out of the air. As the possibilities of a poetry in contemporary Irish have diminished completely, a new interest emerges in the soundscapes of the classical language, of unchanging forms. This is a sort of evolution backwards. The ancient vernacular has extraordinary endurance.

Even if the poem in Irish has become an anchronism, the original call still rings true. The Blasket Island writer Tomás Ó Criomhthain in *Allagar na hInise* (1928), a true offshore man and probably aware of the initial paradox in reverse, says on one of the days of his life:

> '*Tar éis dinnéir dom, buailim siar chun an ghoirt úd go mbraithim pé díth sláinte a bhí orm ag dul ann dom, ag scaradh liom le linn é fhágaint dom, buíochas mór le Dia.*' (After dinner I head back to that piece of ground where I feel any ill-health that I had going there lifting from me as I leave there, great thanks be to God.)

The ground of the poem has always been the key.

If heeding the call can seem, in hindsight, 'a need for legitimate foolishness', in a phrase of the psychoanalyst Otto Rank, it is sustained nevertheless by the ongoing revelation in poems of the truths of our lives. Why would we then, in further foolishness, not proceed further out of the original daze? The Anglican theologian, H. A. Williams, refers in his work *The Joy of God* to something very close to what happens in the world of the poem: 'The joy of God lies waiting with infinite patience for the appointed time, working continuously with every kind of recalcitrant raw material, until it deliver as golden what formerly was brazen.'

The original promise of the poem still rings true.

Irish and the Media

Breandán Delap

Mass media is often compared to a spoiled child – noisy, easily bored and tirelessly craving attention. If anything, the Irish-language media is needier still – a ginger-haired country cousin desperately wanting to be taken seriously, yet cut off from the majority of the Irish population by their own national language. But few minority language communities have it so good. The Irish language has its own national television and radio stations, a daily and a weekly newspaper, a lively internet magazine, part-time radio outlets in the country's two biggest cities, regular weekly columns in Ireland's paper of record, *The Irish Times*, and a plethora of magazines and periodicals of varying degrees of value and worth. Clearly if the volume and variety of material available is anything to go by the Irish-language media could be said to be entering something of a golden age.

Its global village is based firmly in Conamara, where it seems at times that every townland alternates as a film set, and locals tread carefully for fear of tripping over cable wires. Nowadays a visitor to this rural area is as likely to overhear a conversation about a screen test or a treatment for a documentary as one about REPs payments for agriculture or the latest EU fishing restrictions. The national Irish-language television station (TG4), radio station (RTÉ Raidió na Gaeltachta) and weekly newspaper (*Foinse*) are based within six miles of one another. Film companies like Telegael, Gael Media and TG4's flagship soap opera, *Ros na Rún*, are a short hop to the east. Altogether, there are over three hundred people employed in media-related projects in the South Conamara Gaeltacht. This figure is all the more remarkable when you consider that there are approximately eight doctors, ten Gardaí and fifteen priests operating in this same area.

On closer inspection, however, it could be argued that the growth of Irish-language media has resulted in the language's marginalization in mainstream outlets. The language is now firmly back in the media ghetto.

When TnaG (now TG4) was established in 1996 the then Minister for the Gaeltacht, Michael D. Higgins, insisted that it should not be used as an excuse for RTÉ to renege on its statutory obligation in relation to Irish-language programming. Yet most commentators would agree that the language has a more peripheral profile than ever on the national broadcaster. *The Irish Times* and *The Irish News* notwithstanding, few if any articles in Irish appear in the country's bestselling newspapers from one end of the year to the other.

But the Irish-language media has made considerable strides in the last few decades. It has grown from a cottage industry run by enthusiasts into something of a corporate enterprise, which services an active language community. Much about its character and purpose can be traced back, however, to very humble origins in a significantly different era. The narrative begins, over 130 years ago in Brooklyn, New York where Micheál Ó Lócháin established a bilingual monthly *An Gaodhal* in 1881. It was followed a year later by the establishment of *Irisleabhar na Gaedhilge* in Dublin. These early efforts reflected the zeal of the language activists who established them rather than providing an insight into contemporary society and its mores. The ensuing fifty years saw a slew of unsophisticated publications (*Fáinne an Lae*, *An Claidheamh Soluis*, *Misneach*, *An Tír* etc.) whose primary aim was the preservation of the Irish language rather than being a means for communicating news or a forum for debate. It goes without saying that this was a weak foundation on which to build a newspaper-reading tradition. Although there was the occasional tug of the forelock to the communities where the language was spoken on a daily basis, it was usually done as outsiders peering in rather than reflecting a genuine insider's perspective.

To some extent *An t-Éireannach* (1934-7) bucked that trend. It took a radical editorial line during a period of much social upheaval and was a bulwark against the rising tide of fascism, rural poverty and economic inequality. One third of its content was set aside for stories relating to Gaeltacht areas and as a result it succeeded where previous publications failed in establishing a dedicated readership of sorts within those areas.

Inniu (1943-84) surpassed all its predecessors in terms of longevity but retained a similar focus. Its monochromic layout and agitprop journalism were a throwback to the early efforts of the language enthusiasts – more viewspaper than newspaper. *Inniu* was the first all-Irish publication to target the schools market, though many feel that this had a detrimental effect on the standard of its news journalism. It was joined in 1980 by a re-jigged Conamara version of *Amárach*, which had previously been published by a language lobby group called 'Muintir na Gaeltachta.' *Amárach* achieved some of the street credibility of *An t-Éireannach* and reflected the growth of a radical community-based movement which demanded increased rights and recognition of their linguistic identity. In 1984, the Department of the Gaeltacht decided to end its funding of *Inniu* and *Amárach*, paving the way for one weekly newspaper with stronger state support. *Anois* started with a bang – with a reputed distribution of 17,000 copies per week at the height of its popularity – but soon fizzled out as its heady mix of tabloid values in a wordy design more suited to a broadsheet, failed to retain readers. It was also clear that the campaigning 'for the cause' journalism that shaped the Gaelic publication landscape for over a hundred years had now become redundant.

Anois was succeeded by *Foinse* in 1996 (under the ownership of Gaeltacht businessman Pádraig Ó Céidigh) as the main state-supported Irish newspaper. Based in An Cheathrú Rua, *Foinse* is the most westerly national newspaper in the European Union. It has certainly made a virtue out of its isolation. It set itself apart from its predeccesors in its scope and ambition by placing a greater emphasis on reportage than opinion. In 2003 the Belfast based *Lá*, which had been publishing since 1984 against every adversity and with little monetary support, re-invented itself as a daily newspaper. The failure of successive weekly newspapers to leave their mark on the Irish public might seem to be a thin basis for the establishment of a daily product, but it is a measure of the way in which *Lá* has set about its herculean task that it continues to reach its target of publishing five editions a week, albeit to a limited readership. It feeds off the growth and success of other linguistic projects in West Belfast, Irish-medium schooling in particular. As well as providing provocative comment and opinion, both *Foinse* and *Lá Nua* (as it is now titled) have a core focus of stories relating to the Irish language and the Gaeltacht but are not adverse to tackling major national issues either.

The traditional print format for Irish-language journalism is complemented by new media efforts like the eclectic internet magazine *Beo.ie* which receives up to 40,000 visits per month from all across the globe and operates effectively as a cyber-Gaeltacht. Other publications include *Saol,* a monthly freesheet, sponsored by Foras na Gaeilge to promote Irish-language events. Conradh na Gaeilge's publications *Feasta* and *An tUltach* focus on political and cultural issues as well as book and music reviews. *Comhar,* the foremost Irish-language literary magazine in its heyday, dwindled in content, readership and impact in its latter decades until Foras na Gaeilge's decision in September 2007 to cease funding it.

Irish-language periodicals have suffered in the past from their lack of cogency and have made it difficult for the current crop to penetrate the market and reach a wider readership.

The weight of this legacy has meant that, despite its long and at times distinguished history, the written word now has a subordinate status as a form of communication in Irish. Budding writers are deserting the print media for the more lucrative lure of television while loyal readers increasingly seem to find that their cultural diet is sufficiently satiated by TG4 and Raidió na Gaeltachta. This decline is likely to become more pronounced as the media landscape broadens.

Almost sixty years after an all Irish radio station was first mooted, it eventually become a reality. As far back as 30 November, 1926, the Minister for Post and Telegraph, James J. Walsh, announced that his department was to establish a Gaeltacht station. Nothing more became of it until 1943 when the Taoiseach of the time, Éamon de Valera, set up a committee to examine the matter. While its report was largely positive, it concluded that the proposal was unviable as 90 per cent of the people of the Gaeltacht didn't own a transistor. This was not an insurmountable obstacle according to de Valera who then proposed that free radios would be distributed in these areas. But the spending caution of civil servants prevailed and the idea was shelved for another three decades.

Then in March, 1969, a newly-formed radical Gaeltacht organization picketed the Teach Furbo hotel in Conamara where an episode of the popular TV quiz show *Quicksilver* was being recorded entirely through

English. The incident received much publicity and soon afterwards
Gluaiseacht Chearta Sibhialta na Gaeltachta (Gaeltacht Civil Rights
Movement) demanded a Gaeltacht-based radio station of their own to
cater for their specific cultural needs. A pirate station which broadcast
on a number of occasions from Ros Muc during the following year
added significantly to the pressure on the government and within six
months Minister George Colley announced that he was to establish
an all-Irish station. The red light was lit on Easter Sunday 1972 and
Raidió na Gaeltachta began broadcasting on a part-time basis initially,
gradually extending its schedule over the years. It is available now
twenty four hours a day on VHF throughout Ireland, on the Astra digital
satellite platform in Europe as well as on the internet throughout the
world. It has studios in Kerry, Donegal, Dublin and Mayo as well as
its headquarters in Casla, Conamara and employs over eighty people,
between staff members and part-time workers.

RnaG can be said to have laid down a gold standard of quality for
spoken Irish, a standard to which it has adhered since its foundation.
Its formula of local news and regional magazine programmes has
carved out a loyal listenership in the Gaeltacht areas and it gives good
coverage to local GAA matches, Oireachtas competitions as well as
music and singing festivals. A shift in policy came in 1996 when it
attempted to broaden its listenership by focusing on material of more
national appeal.

But there were signs that the station was suffering a mid-life crisis,
particularly when it came to catering for the needs of a younger
generation of Irish-speakers. Central to this debate was the station's
rule that no songs in English could be broadcast. This produced the
bizarre situation in 1988 when you could listen to the Cocteau Twins
from Grangemouth, Scotland, singing in Esperanto but were banned
from hearing *Orinico Flow* by Enya, who was born and bred in the
Donegal Gaeltacht, even though it had reached number one in the
British and Irish charts. This rule was amended in 2005 with the launch
of ANOCHT FM, a segment of programming within the standard
schedule aimed primarily at younger listeners. During its operating
hours of 9pm to 1am, programmes are presented through the medium
of Irish but restrictions on songs with English lyrics are waived. No
reliable scientific data has yet been made available, however, to suggest

that the service is making any huge impact in this very competitive slice of the market. As in any trade, it is of the utmost importance to capture consumers when they are forming their buying habits and tackling generational change will remain a key issue in the future development of Raidió na Gaeltachta.

Apart from RnaG, there are two all-Irish stations operating on a part-time basis: *Raidió na Life*, established in Dublin in 1993, and *Raidió Fáilte* which has been broadcasting under licence from Belfast since 2006. As you would expect from stations serviced largely by volunteer broadcasters, the standard of programming varies greatly from presenter to presenter. Both stations have proved to be invaluable training grounds and nurseries for the development of new broadcasting talent, however.

The growth of Irish-language television has followed a similar trajectory to that of the radio. It was first mooted at a meeting of Fianna Fáil's Coiste na Gaeilge in May 1969 when the then Taoiseach, Jack Lynch, voiced his support for the establishment of an all-Irish TV station. It would take another twenty-seven years, however, before Teilifís na Gaeilge would haul the old language into its own exclusive place in Ireland's sitting rooms. Encouraged by the success of Raidió na Gaeltachta and of the Welsh language television station S4C, a campaign was set in motion in the late 1980s and early 1990s for the establishment of an all-Irish service. The story has far outgrown the event, however, and it sometimes seems that as many people claim to have been instrumental in the campaign as those who claimed to have been in the GPO in 1916. Some members of Conradh na Gaeilge and other campaigners went to jail, however, for refusing to pay their television licences as a protest for the lack of Irish-language programming on the national broadcaster. As was the case with Raidió na Gaeltachta, a pirate station was set up to highlight the issue. Once again, the western redoubt of Ros Muc was the venue and it broadcast for several hours during the weekend of Oireachtas na Gaeilge in 1987. Having bravely defied the authorities for several days the pirate broadcast finally came unstuck when a sharp gust of wind felled the makeshift transmitter on Cnoc Mordáin.

Although the campaign received support from across the political divide, there was still a credibilty gap to be bridged. A report commissioned by Údarás na Gaeltachta from KPMG Stokes Kennedy

Crowley in 1989 went some way towards providing a scientific analysis and costing of the project, and thereby allaying some of the concerns of sceptics. Both the Minister of Communications at the time, Máire Geoghegan Quinn, and her immediate successor, Michael D Higgins, voiced their support for the station but there was still disquiet that it would be difficult to obtain the €14m required from the state coffers to erect the required broadcasting network. At this point the future Deputy Head of the station, Pádhraic Ó Ciardha, who had been working as a ministerial consultant on the issue, recommended that revenue could be used from a frozen account which had been set up in 1990 when a controversial cap had been put on the amount of revenue RTÉ could generate from advertisements. This discovery provided the impetus for the government to give the project the green light. The campaign had succeeded in the teeth of sustained and at times vindictive opposition. *Irish Times* columnist, Kevin Myers, referred to the station as 'Teilifís de Lorean' (after the ill-fated car manufacturer) and described it as a life-support machine for a language that was already clinically dead. Its main purpose, according to Myers, was to provide 'State-subsidized jobs in the few reservations where it lingers like lichen.' The level of invective was best summed up by this vitriolic rant from Eamon Dunphy:

> Telefis na Gaeilge is a sick, expensive folly. Set up in Galway, staffed by Irish-speaking 'nutters', to feed fantasies about cultural purity to a constituency that won't register on the TAMs, this monument to political conceit will cost £20m A YEAR. Until it is closed. *(The Sunday Independent, 7 April 1996).*

On 31 October, 1996, *Teilifís na Gaeilge* was launched amongst much fanfare and not a little scepticism. Some difficult years lay ahead as the station struggled to find its feet in a highly competitive environment that was undergoing rapid change. In 1999 the station changed its name to TG4, to ensure that it maintained its fourth slot in the Irish cable system. It gradually went from strength to strength in its vitality and range, reaching a critical respectability amongst Irish audiences – not quite essential viewing but an integral part of Irish television entertainment nonetheless. On 1 April, 2007, TG4 cut its umbilical cord with RTÉ and started to operate as a fully fledged independent television station. The separation was far from amicable, however. Some argued that the station could never fully be expected to leave its mark on Irish broadcasting without striking out on its own while others thought that the costs it would incur in the future for the use of RTÉ facilities and archive material could be better used on the production of new programmes.

But the station has had many successes, and its bright and breezy approach has been credited with the new sexy image that the language now enjoys. TG4 is largely a commissioning house which means that most of the programmes are produced by independent film companies off-site, though there has been a tentative move towards in-house current affairs programming and chat shows in recent years. Despite its independent status, RTÉ is still required by legislation to provide an hour of programming per day for TG4, which currently includes its news service. About seventy-five people are directly employed by TG4 but it is estimated that it provides work for some 350 others between actors, producers, directors, subtitlers and allied media professionals.

Not surprisingly, considering its origins, most committed Irish-speakers feel they have a stake in their language media. They apply rigorous standards of judgement amongst themselves but will stoutly defend it in public. In a multi-channel environment where aggregators recommend content and customize news intake, and in an era where newspapers come in polybags, this sense of ownership takes on added importance. The mantra of public-service broadcasting as laid down by the BBC – to make the popular good and the good popular – is of particular relevance to the Irish-language media as it can never compete on a commericial basis with its rivals. Its integrity therefore is its core purpose. But the distinction between hardcore journalism and factual entertainment has become blurred and the Irish-language media is as much a hostage to the whims of fickle viewers and listeners and their fidgety fingers as media outlets in more widely-spoken languages. After all, programmes about Kerry pensioners like *na Bibeanna* and *na Caipíní* may not have the same rock n' roll appeal as *The Osbournes* or *The Simpsons* but they still have to compete with them.

TG4's slogan 'Súil eile' (a different outlook) works as both a rallying cry and a mission statement for the Irish-language media as a whole. It is also fast becoming an article of faith. The received wisdom runs that the Irish-language media's values are not just different to other publications and channels, but diametrically opposed. As most of its outlets are in the west of the country far from the influence of the chattering classes of Donnybrook, it naturally follows that it should have a different set of priorities and news values. This works best when it highlights issues unique to its constituency (Shell's proposed gas terminal that caused much controveresy in the Mayo Gaeltacht, for example, or the ban on drift-net fishing of salmon which had a devastating effect on small communities along the Atlantic seaboard). It also works well when major national and international stories are refracted through the lens of small Gaeltacht communities, living on the edge of Europe. After the carnage of 9/11, for example, the Irish-language media highlighted the implications for illegal immigrants in America, while not ignoring the global picture. Who would have thought either that the death of Yasser Arafat could affect the lives of people in the Conamara Gaeltacht? On the occasion of his death in 2004, Nuacht RTÉ/TG4 ran a story on how his family and the Palestinian Authority had taken out shares in the Canadian parent company of Bioniche in Indreabhán. It is not so much a question of reading, watching, or listening to the Irish-language media, therefore, as finding yourself in a different mental and cultural space.

Such an approach has its pitfalls, however. To view events through the almost exclusive lens of a language community is to run the risk of becoming myopic and failing to focus on a world beyond ourselves. This means that the Irish-language media often makes much of little and occasionally little of much. Put simply, some news items carried by the Irish-language media are so local you can see your own house in them. One of the challenges it faces in the future is to strike a balance between catering for the needs of its core target audience while at the same time providing material of sufficient interest to attract a wider audience and readership. Failure to achieve this could see the Irish-language media becoming an exclusive club for members only.

There is also a question of connectivity. Irish-language media organizations inhabit a shared space – some would say a comfort zone – where people think the same and follow similar agendas, but its priorities are not always relevant to its core audience and indeed are sometimes entirely at variance with their needs. They are wedded to their target audience by linguistic fluke but may be estranged by so much more. Despite almost 130 years of existence, for example, there is little evidence that the Irish-language print media has established a firm foothold amongst Irish-speakers, particularly those in the Gaeltacht. Moreover, no Irish-language media outlet exists as a commercial entity, independent of state subvention. There may be a gap in the market but it would appear that there is no market in the gap.

There is no doubt that most Irish-language media organizations punch above their weight and gain maximum impact from limited resources. But that is not to say that they have been untainted by mediocrity. 'More is better,' seems to be the guiding philosophy of the Irish-language media – broadcast hours are regularly increased and pages are added to publications – but this is not always matched by an increase in quality control. It can also be said with some justification that a culture of investigative journalism has yet to take root. In a small language community with a sense of shared unity (and a limited pool of interviewees) there is a temptation not to rock the boat. But one man's analytical timidity is another man's smugness. Irish-language media organizations can be faulted for rarely pushing people beyond complacency or offering a voice to the forgotten.

But the Irish-language media cannot be judged in isolation from the wider context of the fortunes of the language in general. A major report on the usage of Irish in the Gaeltacht (see the article by Ó Giollagáin and Mac Donnacha for more detail) has stated that Irish will cease to become the primary language of home and community in the Gaeltacht within fifteen to twenty years unless something radical is done to stem the decline. Even if the language manages to prove the direst predictions wrong, where will the fluent broadcasters and writers of tomorrow come from?

Nor is the Irish-language media exempt from the pressures faced by mainstream media concerning the speed and durability of journalism in the competitive environment created by multi-channel, rolling news and on-line services. The advent of blogs, digital photography, mobile phones and other portable devices, means that almost anybody can produce and disseminate text, video and audio. As more and more people acquire the necessary technology, the role of the public is being transformed from a passive consumer of information to that of an active producer. Broadcasting and publishing therefore are becoming less of a dictation from trained professionals and more of an open-mike session with audience participation. Like many other outlets, however, the Irish-language media has been slow to embrace the digital age and its more participatory formats. But the success of Nuacht Pobail in 2006 – when the Gaeltacht community of Baile an Sceilg, Co Kerry researched and presented its own news bulletin on TG4 – is an example of what can be achieved when the newly-amplified voice of citizen journalist is harnessed to good effect. For the tools of new media provide as many opportunities for Irish as threats. Blogs, for example, are an invaluable source of background information for journalists though their provenance need to be properly vetted and their accuracy tested. Likewise, podcasts offer a great opportunity for learners of the language who can listen to the pronounciation of the words they are reading in their Irish newspapers. Web TV and Radio enable emigrants and learners alike to watch and listen to events unfolding in real time through the medium of Irish.

Although the interactivity of the internet opens up many possibilities for the Irish language, content rather than technology must still be the master in this brave new world of choice. As sources of news and comment proliferate, the demand for authoritive, well-informed articles and programmes increases rather than diminishes. Moreover, cyberspace is a largely lawless domain that knows no visual, aural or written boundaries. This exposes it to all kinds of manipulations and abuse. Such was the torrent of abuse and poisonous venom anonymously posted on Irish-language chatrooms like www.cumasc.ie and www.beo.ie that they had to impose stict regulations on their usage and close their portals to all-comers. Legal implications alone will delay the traditional media's engagment with the tools of new media. The challenge for the Irish-language media is to integrate these on-line activities into their newsrooms as a means of serving quality and commitment to the public interest while at the same time ensuring that there is no lowering of standards.

For if it is to survive and flourish in the twenty-first century the Irish language must adapt its content and style to reflect cultural, political and technological changes. The media landscape in ten years time will be fundamentally different from that which prevails today. The Gaeltacht and language community target audience is also a society in motion and constant flux and this must be matched and reflected in its media outlets. It is worth noting, for example, that there is no social networking site operating exclusively through Irish. The Irish-language media must change with the times therefore, or it could find itself hurtling aimlessly down Conamara boreens toward destinations of receding worth, suspended between the brilliant and the mediocre, between self-acclaim and self-doubt.

Placenames Policy and its Implementation

Dónall Mac Giolla Easpaig

Placenames are an integral part of our everyday language and are an indispensable component in defining our relationship with our physical environment. Communication without placenames is almost inconceivable. Placenames also carry with them an important cultural resonance in that they are constant reminders of the dominance of the Irish language in the country over the last two millennia. Placenames are the products of language, formed from, and according to, the rules of the language of the community that creates them. Placenames are intelligible to the speakers of the language at the time of their formation. Once formed, however, a placename takes on a life of its own and its function as a name, denoting a particular place, becomes independent of its lexical meaning over a period of time. A name such as Milltown will be immediately intelligible to a speaker of English just as Baile an Mhuilinn is to a speaker of Irish, although neither speaker will be conscious of the lexical meaning every time he uses the respective name. A name such as Binn Éadair is as unintelligible to an Irish speaker as the name Howth is to his English-speaking counterpart. The opaqueness of these two examples does not diminish their function as names. It is this capacity to function independently of its original lexical meaning that allows a placename to survive for centuries, or over a millennium in the case of the last names mentioned. Just as importantly, it is this independence from its original lexical meaning that allows a name to be borrowed into languages other than that in which it was coined.

ANGLICIZATION OF PLACENAMES

Ireland has been described as one of the most densely named countries in Europe. The country is divided into some 65,000 administrative units, in an historical hierarchical structure of four provinces, 32 counties, about 275 baronies, 2,400 civil parishes and some 62,000 townlands, all bearing their own names. The most common unit of civil administration in use today, however, is the (district) electoral division, of which there are approximately 3,500 in the state. The latter unit is a nineteenth-century creation, consisting of clusters of townlands, which generally derives its name from a pre-existing placename. In addition to administrative names, the large-scale maps of the Ordnance Survey contain thousands of other placenames, including names of centres of population (towns, villages and districts), those of physical features (lakes, rivers, streams, bays, headlands, islands, mountains, hills), and of man-made features (ringforts, churches, monasteries, graveyards, bridges, crossroads). Of a somewhat different category from traditional placenames, and of much more recent origin, are the thousands of streetnames, at least 45,000 of them, in cities and towns throughout the country.

The great majority of the placenames of Ireland have their origin in the Irish language, particularly the names of the baronies, civil parishes, townlands and major geographical features. Most of the names were coined before the seventeenth century and a significant number are at least a thousand years older than that. All of these have come down to us in anglicized form and only a small proportion have been recorded in the Irish language, whether in the corpus of native sources in Irish and Latin, dating from the sixth century to the nineteenth, or in the traditional spoken language of the twentieth.

The process of phonetic adaptation of Irish-language placenames into neighbouring languages has a long history; there is evidence to show that the Roman Britons, Anglo-Saxons and Welsh all borrowed Irish placenames into their respective languages. The Scandinavian settlers in Ireland from the ninth century coined a small number of placenames in their own language some of which such as Lambay and Waterford have survived to this day. The evidence would suggest, however, that this group simply borrowed existing Irish placenames into Norse on a large scale; we have references for a small number of these in the Icelandic Sagas, notably Dyflyn (Dublin), and Hlymreks (Limerick).

The Anglo-Norman colonization of the twelfth and thirteenth centuries brought with it a wave of English-speaking settlers to most parts of the country, along with a highly efficient centralised administrative system. For the first time, we have documentary evidence for the wholesale anglicization of Irish-language placenames, a process that was to continue down to the nineteenth century and, arguably, to the present day. By the late seventeenth century, the placenames of every part of the country were being written down according to the spelling conventions of the English language by all arms of the establishment, central and local civil administration, the Established Church, and by the newly-ascendant landowners. Although the original Irish-language versions of the placenames were still being used by the vast majority of the population at this time, official documents provide no evidence that this was the case.

The Ordnance Survey and the standardization of placename forms

By the early nineteenth century the spelling of the names of the principal towns of the country had become standardized. This was not true of townland and minor feature names, for which a variety of different versions were used by different bodies, notably, the Grand Jury, who were in charge of local government, landowners, the Established Church, the Catholic Church, and local inhabitants. This situation created a dilemma for the Ordnance Survey when it undertook its first large-scale survey of the country in 1824, as only one version of a name could appear on the map. In response to this, the officer in charge, Thomas Colby, issued instructions on the treatment of placenames in which it was stated that 'Persons employed on the survey are to endeavour to obtain the correct orthography of the names of places diligently consulting best authorities within their reach.' When it was realized that the British Army officers conducting the survey could not satisfactorily undertake this task, a team of Irish civilians, competent in the Irish language, was employed by the Survey to collect and examine the evidence in order to decide a standardized English-language spelling for each name. Foremost of this group was John O'Donovan, a native of County Kilkenny, who was later to achieve fame as the great Irish scholar, and who was to become the first Professor of Celtic in Queen's College, Belfast (now Queen's University). He was ably assisted by others, by Clare-born Eugene Curry in particular, another noted scholar who was to become Professor of Archaeology and Irish History in the Catholic University of Ireland (now University College, Dublin).

Captain Thomas Larcom, Colby's second-in-command in Ireland, has left a concise description of the methodology followed by O'Donovan and his assistants in an official document published in 1844. He states:

In order to ascertain the correct names of places for the engravings, that they might become a standard of orthography as well as topography, numerous maps, records, and ancient documents were examined, and copious extracts made from them. In this manner a certain amount of antiquarian information has been collected relating to every place, parish, and townland in Ireland – more than 60,000; and various modes of spelling them at different times has (sic) been recorded. When these investigations were complete, it was usual to send a person thoroughly versed in the Irish language to ascertain from the old people who still speak the language, what was the original vernacular name, and we then adopted that one most consistent with the ancient orthography, not venturing to restore the original and often obsolete name, but approaching as near to correctness as was practicable.

During the course of his work, O'Donovan travelled throughout the country, from Donegal to Wexford, consulting with Irish-language speakers wherever he could, in order to ascertain 'the original vernacular name.' The Irish form of each name, with a translation, was added to the other forms in the Ordnance Survey Name Book. O'Donovan recommended a standardized English spelling of the name based on all the accrued evidence, including the Irish form and its meaning, and this form was then engraved on the Ordnance Survey's series of maps at the scale of six inches to one mile, or 1:10,560. The Ordnance Survey spelling of the placenames has served as the official standard spelling since.

Although it was never intended that they should be engraved on the maps, the Irish forms collected by O'Donovan and his colleagues constitute one of the most important sources of Irish-language placenames ever assembled. Most serious work on the placenames of the country has drawn on the Irish name-forms in the Ordnance Survey Name Books, including that of the leading authority on Irish placenames in the late nineteenth and early twentieth century, Patrick Weston Joyce (1829-1914), author of the great series *Irish Names of Places*, I-III (1869-1913).

While the results of the toponymic work of the Ordnance Survey received a general welcome at the time, dissenting voices were heard. In a review of the work of the Ordnance Survey in *The Nation* in 1844, the Young Ireland leader, Thomas Davis, expressed the hope that 'Whenever those maps are re-engraved, the Irish words, will, we trust, be spelled in an Irish and civilised orthography, and not barbarously,

as at present.' Almost fifty years later Douglas Hyde expressed
much the same sentiment. In his famous lecture, 'The Necessity for
De-Anglicising Ireland,' which he delivered in 1892, Hyde had the
following to say about the placenames of the country:

> On the whole, our place names have been treated with about the same
> respect as if they were the names of a savage tribe which had never
> before been reduced to writing, and with about the same intelligence and
> contempt as vulgar English squatters treat the topographical nomenclature
> of the Red Indians. .... I hope and trust a native Irish Government will be
> induced to provide for the restoration of our place-names on something like
> a rational basis.

By 'a rational basis' was meant that the placenames should be restored
to their Irish-language forms. Hyde's wish was partially fulfilled some
years before the establishment of a native government. Twelve years
after its founding by Hyde and others, the Gaelic League published
Post-Sheanchas Cuid I. – Sacsbhéarla-Gaedhilg by the Irish scholar,
Seosamh Laoide, in 1905. This book gave Irish-language forms for all
the post-offices in the country, based on the author's own researches.
While remarkable for its time, *Post-Sheanchas* had many flaws, the
most serious of which derived from Laoide's rejection on ideological
grounds of the foreign imposed county system, as he saw it, in favour of
earlier native territorial divisions. This approach led to the creation of
the many unhistorical placename forms in the publication, names such
as Brí Cualann for Bray, County Wicklow, and Brí Uí Cheinnsealaigh
for Bree, County Wexford, for which absolutely no evidence exists.
Despite these defects, however, *Post-Sheanchas* was to have a lasting
influence down to the present day.

THE PLACENAMES COMMISSION
Following the establishment of the Irish Free State in 1922 with a native
government whose policy was to promote the use of Irish in various
areas of public life, there was particular urgency for authoritative
work on Irish placenames, since Irish forms of those names would
be required for regular use by both government departments and the
general public. The Department of Post and Telegraphs adopted most
of the Irish-language forms of the post-offices that had been published
in *Post-Sheanchas* and these were in turn used by other government
departments in a semi-official capacity. Many scholars working in
the placenames field disagreed with the forms that had been proposed

by Seosamh Laoide, in particular, Risteard Ó Foghludha ('Fiachra Éilgeach'), who published his own Irish versions of some 7,000 placenames in *Logainmneacha .i. Dictionary of Irish Placenames* in 1935.

The urgency for authoritative Irish-language names was increased with the coming into force of Bunreacht na hÉireann (The Constitution of Ireland) in 1937 which gave a special status to the Irish language as first official language. In 1945 the Taoiseach at the time, Éamon de Valera, recommended that a booklet giving the correct Irish form of the names of the post-offices be published. The following year, An Coimisiún Logainmneacha (The Placenames Commission) was established by warrant of the Minister for Finance and was composed of private scholars of toponymy and related disciplines under the chairmanship of the Irish scholar An Seanadóir Pádraig Ó Siochfhradha (An Seabhac). The terms of reference of the Commission were:

1. To examine the placenames of Ireland ...and to search for the correct original Irish versions of those placenames insofar as they had Irish forms and those forms can be established.
2. To prepare for publication and for official use lists of those names, in their Irish forms.

For the purpose of the Commission's work, placenames were defined as names of 'townlands, parishes, baronies, districts and other geographical areas, postal towns, villages, towns and cities, and other principal denominations.'

In order to fulfil these aims, the members of the Commission were expected to undertake the necessary research, aided by a small number of researchers provided by the Civil Service. It was eventually recognized that the task of researching all the placenames was beyond the efforts of private individuals. Consequently, in 1955, the terms of reference of the Commission were amended making their duties that of advising the Government on Irish-language placename matters and the actual research was left to a permanent research staff, The Placenames Branch, which was attached to the Ordnance Survey in 1956.

Ainmneacha Gaeilge na mBailte Poist

The first research project undertaken by the Placenames Branch was the completion of the research of the names of the postal towns which had been initiated by the Commission. Despite the change of its terms of reference, the Commission continued to involve itself directly in the determination of the Irish versions of the names based on the evidence collected by the professional researchers. The research approach of the Branch was based on the scientific methodology developed by the institute with responsibility for the study of Swedish placenames, now known as the Ortnamnsarkivet. This entailed collecting all the spellings of a name from historical sources and ascertaining its pronunciation in the local community. In determining the choice of the Irish form, the Placenames Commission gave precedence in most cases to the version used by the last speakers of Irish in the locality. Following widespread consultation with the public, the forms recommended by the Commission were published as the official Irish forms in *Ainmneacha Gaeilge na mBailte Poist* in 1969. These versions were given limited legal status under the provisions of the Placenames (Irish Forms) Act 1973 and were subsequently given equal legal status with their English equivalents under the terms of the Official Languages Act 2003.

THE PLACENAMES BRANCH

The Placenames Branch had been established as an integral part of the Ordnance Survey and, following the completion of work on the postal towns, the Branch became incorporated more into the Survey's mapping programme, while the Commission's role became strictly advisory. The Branch was closely involved in the production of the Irish version of the Ordnance Survey's general map of Ireland, *Éire 1:575,000*, which was published in 1970; the map included most of the names listed in *Ainmneacha Gaeilge na mBailte Poist*, along with a significant number of names of major geographical features that had been researched for the purpose. This map, now long out of date and out of print, remains the only official comprehensive Irish-language map of the whole country to be published since the foundation of the state.

From the 1970s the research work of the Placenames Branch was directed towards providing the Irish versions of placenames on the Ordnance Survey's large-scale metric rural maps at the scale of 1: 2,500, which were to replace the original six-inch maps. These maps contained the names of townlands, baronies and electoral divisions, along with a limited number of names of geographical features. The placename research for the maps was undertaken on a county basis.

In the early 1990s, the Ordnance Survey began production of a new national tourist map series at the scale of 1:50,000, to be known as the Discovery Series. On the advice of the Placenames Commission, a decision was made that maps in the series would be bilingual as far as practicable. In actual practice, this meant that only the names of the postal towns and names of significant geographical and archaeological features would be included bilingually. For purposes of uniformity, the Irish versions of townland names were specifically excluded, even in the case of those counties for which they were available. A significant decision was made in relation to the placename forms in Gaeltacht areas, however, in that priority was to be given to Irish versions on the maps covering these; the Irish forms of the townland names that had been determined by the Placenames Branch were to be included, and where space did not allow the inclusion of the two forms of a name, the Irish form would take precedence over the English form.

In the late 1990s a decision was made to restructure the Ordnance Survey and to change its status from that of an office of the Department of Finance to that of a commercial state body to be known as Ordnance Survey Ireland. As part of that reorganization, responsibility for Irish-language placename policy was transferred from the Department for Finance to the Department of Arts, Heritage, Gaeltacht and the Islands which resulted in the Placenames Branch becoming part of the Irish Language Division of that department in 1999 and in responsibility for the Placenames Commission being transferred to the Minister of the Department in 2000. The Branch and the Commission were subsequently transferred to the newly-created Department of Community, Rural and Gaeltacht Affairs in 2002.

With its transfer from the Ordnance Survey, the Placenames Branch's direct input into the Survey's mapping programmes came to an end. Since its establishment, however, the Branch always had associations with outside bodies. Apart from its core work for the Ordnance Survey's various map programmes, the Placenames Branch researched and provided Irish versions of numerous placenames for a variety of bodies on request, including Rannóg an Aistriúcháin (the Government translation service), An Gúm, Coillte (the forestry body), and the Office of Public Works. The greatest demand for Irish placename forms came from Bord Fáilte, which had responsibility for road signage for over thirty-five years. In the early 1990s, the Central Fisheries Board requested the Branch to supply the Irish versions for some five hundred river names for its river signage scheme. Following its transfer from the Ordnance Survey, the Placenames Branch researched and provided the Irish versions of all the electoral divisions in the state, about 3,500 names, at the request of the Central Statistics Office. In 2002, a townland signage scheme was devised by CLÁR, a division of the Department of Agriculture with responsibility for funding disadvantaged rural areas, now part of the Department of Community Rural and Gaeltacht Affairs. The scheme encouraged, and funded, local communities in these areas to display the names of their local townlands on stone signs. Since its initiation the Placenames Branch has researched hundreds of townland names in many areas covered by the scheme.

PUBLICATION

By the late 1980s the Placenames Branch had embarked on a programme of publishing the results of its research in book form in order to make them more accessible to those who had a need for Irish name-forms or those who had a general interest in placenames. The first of its publications, *Gasaitéar na hÉireann/Gazetteer of Ireland* (1989), contained 3,300 of the most widely used placenames in the country in their English and Irish forms along with a certain amount of geographical information. By this period, research had been completed on all administrative names for a number of counties and the names of several of these were published in bilingual list form in the series *Liostaí Logainmneacha*. The first volumes in the series, those for Limerick, Waterford and Louth, were published in 1991, followed by a further three volumes appearing shortly afterwards, Kilkenny (1993), Offaly (1994) and Monaghan (1996). Following a hiatus, the volume for Tipperary was published in 2004. It is intended to continue the series and volumes for Galway, Dublin, Wexford and Cork are planned for 2008-9.

Logainmneacha na hÉireann Imleabhar I: Contae Luimnigh (1990), by Art Ó Maolfabhail, was the first in a planned series of volumes designed to present all the historical evidence for the names along with explanations of their origins. Due to other priorities, the preparation of further volumes was deferred and the second volume, *Logainmneacha na hÉireann Imleabhar II: 'Cill' i logainmneacha Chontae Thiobraid*

Árann, by Pádraig Ó Cearbhaill, did not appear until 2007. Two other volumes, covering the placenames of County Wexford and those of an area in County Cork, are in preparation.

THE OFFICIAL LANGUAGES ACT, 2003
The Placenames (Irish Forms) Act 1973 allowed the Minister to declare by Order, having received and considered the advice of the Placenames Commission, that the equivalent in the Irish language of a placename specified in the Order was such words or words as might be specified in the Order. The Irish words then would have the same meaning and same force and effect as the placename. Only two Orders were made under the 1973 Act, one in 1975 to declare Irish-language versions of the names of postal towns as they had been published in *Ainmneacha Gaeilge na mBailte Poist*, and second in 2001 to amend one of the Irish forms in the 1975 Order.

There was an reluctance to make further Orders under the 1973 legislation which was due in part to the wording of the Placenames Act itself. The problem was that while the 1973 Act allowed definitive Irish-language versions of placenames to be made available for official use, it also meant in legal terms that the placename remained in the English language only. This situation was deemed unacceptable and during the passing of the Official Languages Bill through the Houses of the Oireachtas the Minister for Community, Rural and Gaeltacht decided to incorporate the provisions of the 1973 Act, with fundamental amendments, in the Official Languages Act 2003. Under Part 5 of the 2003 Act, the Minister may by Order declare the Irish-language version of a placename specified in the Order. Once such a statutory order is made in respect of any particular placename in any area outside the Gaeltacht, the effect of the new legislation is that the Irish and the English versions of the placename have the same status and the same legal force and effect.

Where the Minister makes an Order in respect of a Gaeltacht placename, the English version of that placename ceases to have any legal force and effect. While this is without prejudice to any private use and most public use of the English version, the Act provides that the English version may not be used in future in Acts of the Oireachtas or Statutory Instruments, or road and street signs or on Ordnance Survey Maps. The Minister's intention with regard to this amendment was to give equal status to the Irish versions of the country's placenames.

Since 2003, the Minister has made ten Orders under Part 5 of the Act on the advice of the Placenames Commission. The Orders reflect research that has been completed and published on the advice of the Commission down through the years since its establishment in 1946. The orders declare the Irish forms of the names of the provinces and counties, the names of administrative units and other names in counties Limerick, Louth, Waterford, Kilkenny, Offaly, Monaghan and Tipperary, and the names of centres of population and districts in counties not covered by other Orders. The Order covering the names of administrative units and of centres of population and districts in Gaeltacht areas came into force in 2005. A further Order will be made in 2008 to give legal status to the Irish versions of the almost 6,000 non-administrative placenames in Gaeltacht areas shown on the Ordnance Survey maps at the scale of six inches to one mile. Following the making of these orders Irish versions only of Gaeltacht placenames will be used in the definitive large-scale series of maps of the country used by Ordnance Survey and the Land Registry. It is intended that these regulations will be extended in the future to include all maps produced by Ordnance Survey Ireland and other mapping bodies, including maps for tourists.

ON-LINE DATABASE OF PLACENAMES: logainm.ie

The Official Languages Act of 2003 created other demands for authoritative Irish forms of geographical names. Under Part 5 of the Act, the Ordnance Survey Ireland Act 2001 was amended to require OSI 'to depict placenames and ancient features in the national mapping and related records and databases in the Irish language or in the English and Irish languages.' Up until then, all placenames in OSI's database of addresses, GeoDirectory, were in English only, including approximately 35,000 streetnames in cities and towns throughout the state. While the local authorities have responsibility for streetnames in their respective areas, few have reliable lists of the Irish versions of these names. OSI retained the Placenames Branch on contract to supply authoritative Irish versions for all streetnames within the state by the end of 2008, in cooperation with the respective local authorities.

The Act had further consequences in relation to the provision of Irish placename-forms, in that all public bodies are now required to publish certain documents, including annual reports, in Irish and in English, or in Irish only. This means that all placenames occurring in these documents must have official Irish versions. This requirement has led to an exponential increase in the demand for Irish forms of placenames. Servicing this demand had negative ramifications for the core work of the Placenames Branch, the completion of the research of the administrative names on a county basis in particular.

Since its establishment in the Ordnance Survey over sixty years ago, the Placenames Branch has built up a large archive of placename material, including Irish-language versions of the names and the historical evidence for these. This material was held in a number of different formats, however, including handwritten index cards, typed A4 sheets and various types of electronic files, including a placenames database. In order to make this material readily available to those that required it, the Department of Community, Rural and Gaeltacht Affairs engaged the services of Fiontar in Dublin City University on contract to develop a web-based national database of placenames in cooperation with the Placenames Branch. Fiontar had already been responsible for the successful development of the on-line database of Irish-language terminology, Focal.ie, for An Coiste Téarmaíochta in Foras na Gaeilge. Work on the placenames project began in April 2007 and the database will be available on www.logainm.ie before the end of 2008.

The first task for the developers was to redesign the Placenames Branch's existing database as a web-based application. This database contained the names of all administrative units in the country, approximately 68,000 names in total, including the names of all the townlands, parishes and baronies, and electoral divisions, along with related geographical information, including a national grid reference of each townland. The database already contained the Irish versions of approximately 18,000 placenames, including all of those covered by Placenames Orders made under the provisions of Official Languages Act 2003. The next step was to populate the database further with material from the Branch's archives, starting with all the Irish versions of placenames that had been recommended over the previous sixty years. Finally, the historical evidence for the names is being entered into the database, starting with that recorded on the handwritten index-cards and the manually typed A4 sheets. In order to facilitate the process, this material has been scanned electronically and the scanned images have been linked to the appropriate placenames. Finally, all the historical evidence held digitally in Word and Excel files will be added through automated links. By the time it is made available on-line to the public in late 2008, the database will contain over 110,000 names, including 68,000 administrative names, about 6,000 non-administrative names and approximately 35,000 streetnames. The database will eventually include all the non-administrative names listed on the Ordnance Survey's six-inch map series, approximately 30,000 names in total.

Comprehensive historical evidence will be available for about 35,000 administrative names and a limited number of historical references will be available for the remaining administrative names, mainly that contained in the Ordnance Survey Name Books. New historical evidence will be added on a daily basis and it is estimated that by the time the research has been completed on all the townland names that the database will contain up to one million historical references. Explanatory notes on the names will also be included on an ongoing basis.

Over the next five years it is envisaged that the database will provide an audio guide to pronunciation of certain names, including the Irish and English versions of the names listed in *Gasaitéar na hÉireann / Gazetteer of Ireland*, and the Irish versions of placenames in Gaeltacht areas. This facility may be extended in future to include all the names in the database. The database will contain a number of powerful search tools, which will enable users to search for information by full name or part of a name, in both Irish and English forms.

Placenames will be ordered hierarchically according to county, barony, civil parish, electoral division and townland. Each townland and geographical feature name will be referenced according to the national grid and the Ordnance Survey's six-inch map series; the approximate position of these names will be indicated on an outline map of the country. Additional features will be added in future, including facilities to search for historical forms, and to create distribution maps of names according to their constituent elements.

The launch of the national placenames database will provide the Placenames Branch with a powerful tool to progress its research programme. It will also provide the general public and scholars with an immense resource to explore the richness and complexity of Ireland's placenames, a resource unimaginable to the members of the Placenames Commission who set out on the tortuous journey 'to search for the original Irish versions' of our placenames over seventy years ago.

Irish in the Education System

John Harris

Any examination of Irish in the education system in a paper such as this has to be selective. The range of issues relating to curriculum, materials, teaching, teacher education and teacher proficiency at both first and second level is so large that any attempt to be comprehensive would fail. When we consider the relationship of these various in-school topics to larger societal and political issues of language promotion and revitalization, the challenges are greater still. I have chosen to concentrate instead, therefore, on a small number of key strategic issues relating to Irish at primary level. In the course of examining these issues, however, we will also identify some of the implications for Irish in other types of schools and at other educational levels.

The key challenges facing Irish in ordinary mainstream primary schools is that a significant minority of children fail to make worthwhile progress in learning to speak Irish and that there has been a very substantial long-term decline in standards of proficiency over the last two decades or so. The findings come from large-scale comparative national surveys conducted over a seventeen year period (Harris 1984, 1988, 1991; Harris et al 2006; Harris & Murtagh 1988, 1999). These reveal, for example, that there has been a fall in mean Irish Listening score at sixth grade of 12.9 raw score points, almost one standard deviation. At the level of individual objectives, the percentage of pupils who now achieve *high levels of performance* ('mastery') in nearly all aspects of Irish Listening and Speaking has fallen significantly since the mid-1980s. Correspondingly, the percentage of pupils now *failing* has grown significantly.

The change is dramatic. The percentages of sixth-grade pupils attaining mastery of six of the seven Irish Listening objectives which we tested fell significantly. For example, there was a fall of 36.1% and 40.5% respectively in the percentages mastering the *Listening vocabulary* and *General comprehension of speech* objectives. This leaves very small minorities of pupils in ordinary schools (only 5.9% and 7.8% of pupils respectively) who now achieve mastery on these two objectives. Objectives relating to *Understanding the morphology of verbs in listening* and *Understanding the morphology of prepositions in listening* are associated with falls of 24% and 22.1% respectively, with only 2.9% and 11.8% respectively now still mastering these objectives. For two other objectives, the decline in the percentages achieving mastery is 16.6% and 13.1%. Only in the case of *Sound discrimination* is the decline in performance not statistically significant.

For most objectives, the decline in the percentage of pupils in ordinary schools attaining mastery is associated with a moderate increase in the percentage of pupils reaching the lower level of performance defined as 'minimal progress', but a larger increase in the percentages failing. For example, *Listening vocabulary* and *General comprehension of speech* are associated with an increase between 1985 and 2002 of 27.9% and 24.4% respectively in the percentages failing, while increases in the percentages making at least minimal progress are only 8.3% and 16% respectively.

The trend in achievement in Irish Speaking is also consistently downwards. All eight objectives tested show decreases since 1985 in the percentages of pupils achieving high levels of performance (mastery), all but one of which are statistically significant. Some of the decreases are very substantial – from 54.0% to 32.9% (a difference of 20.4%) in the case of *Fluency of oral description* and from 50.3% to 29.9% (a difference of 21.1%) in the case of the *Communication* (second grade) objective. In the case of a number of Irish Speaking objectives (such as *Speaking vocabulary* and *Control of the morphology of verbs in speaking*), the percentage failing now constitutes a majority. The percentage failing *Speaking vocabulary* is 65.9%, while for *Control of the morphology of verbs* it is 76.5%, and for *Control of the syntax of statements* 64.1%.

While these results are obviously a cause for concern, it is important to interpret them correctly and in particular not to overstate their implications. In the first place, it is notable that a majority of sixth-grade pupils in ordinary schools are still making worthwhile progress in relation to certain key aspects of Irish Listening and Irish Speaking, even if their achievements are substantially lower than those of corresponding pupils in the mid 1980s. For example, if we add together the percentages attaining mastery or making minimal progress (i.e. the percentage who do not fail) we find that the total amounts to a majority in the case of key objectives such as *Listening vocabulary*, *General Comprehension of speech*, *Understanding the morphology of verbs*, *Basic Communication* (second grade) and *Fluency of oral description*.

We must also bear in mind that these results concern pupil performance on objectives appropriate to pupils' *present grade level*. The latter phrase is critical. Even though a pupil may fail a particular sixth-grade objective, this does not mean that he or she has made no progress in relation to this aspect of Irish at all. Pupils may well have made some progress, either mastery or minimal, in relation to the *corresponding* speaking or listening objective at a lower grade level.

The greatest cause for concern, of course, is that performance has changed very substantially over the seventeen year period examined and that that decline is sustained across a wide range of Irish listening and speaking objectives. It is hard to avoid the conclusion, therefore, that the results indicate the existence of an educational challenge which has major implications for national aims in relation to the Irish language. They reinforce the view of An Coimisinéir Teanga (2004) expressed in his *Inaugural Report* that 'there is an urgent need for a comprehensive and impartial review of every aspect of the learning and teaching of Irish in the educational system'.

THE DECLINE IN PROFICIENCY AT INDIVIDUAL AND NATIONAL LEVEL
When significant proportions of children fail to make worthwhile progress in learning the language, or fail to benefit academically in more general terms from the years they have spent studying it, there are ramifications at a number of different levels: the personal educational level, including the motivation to continue studying the language at post-primary level; the direct loss to the language revitalization effort in terms of building up proficiency in the general population; and the erosion of the attitudinal base which provides legitimacy for the various state initiatives in promoting the language. In weighing the kind of response needed, therefore, it is necessary to consider the consequences of the decline in proficiency at each of these levels.

Personal educational consequences
The decline in achievement in spoken Irish which we have documented is obviously important from an educational point of view. It is essential, for example, that pupils at a personal level should benefit from studying a subject in which they invest so much time and effort. In this regard, it is notable that our experience of teaching Irish in ordinary mainstream schools here seems to mirror in some respects recent experiences with core programmes in French in Canada. *Canadian Parents for French*, the parents' group that set up the first French-immersion programmes, have now begun to emphasize the need to improve the results produced by *core* French programmes similar to our Irish-as-a-subject programme in ordinary schools. They point out that one of the greatest problems with existing core programmes is that many students feel they are not learning enough of the language to be able to actually use it for communication (Canadian Parents for French, 2004). They argue that the main goal of renewal and development in core language programmes should be to produce worthwhile levels of proficiency in the language in order to maintain pupil motivation. Similarly in Ireland, if we expect pupils to be personally invested in continuing to study Irish at post-primary level, it is crucial that they experience real success in learning Irish along the way. A failure to address the underlying causes of failure, therefore, has the potential in the long-term to undermine what up to now has been a solid national consensus about the place of the language in the education system.

Direct loss in language revitalization terms
The decline in standards of speaking proficiency at primary level described above is also serious from a national language-maintenance or language-revival point of view. The capacity of primary schools to reproduce a basic competence in Irish in each new generation has always been a crucial strategic component of the larger language-maintenance and language-revitalization effort (Harris et al 2007). As has been pointed out before (Harris 1991, 1997; Ó Riagáin & Harris 1993) ordinary schools have a particularly important role in reproducing competence in Irish in each new generation. Because the rate of natural transmission of the language outside Gaeltacht areas is low, the renewal function of ordinary primary schools is central to maintaining existing levels of speaking proficiency in Irish nationally.

There are a number of reasons for the importance of ordinary schools. First, there is the fact that the overwhelming majority of children learn Irish in these schools (rather than in the considerably smaller number of Gaeltacht or Irish-medium schools). Thus, any initiative which enhances, however modestly, the success of such schools has the potential to affect large numbers of pupils and, thereby, make a substantial contribution to the language-revival effort nationally. But the opposite is also true: a decline in achievement in ordinary schools is a matter of great importance to the language because of the number of pupils involved. Second, exposure to Irish at primary level is probably both more intense, and more focused on speech and conversation, than it is at post-primary level. The informal use of Irish for school and class communication, and the teaching of one or more other subjects partly or wholly through Irish, are more common in primary than in post-primary schools. The importance of ordinary core second-language programmes to the achievement of major national linguistic goals is also illustrated by recent Canadian perceptions and actions. The Canadian Government's recent *Action Plan for Official Languages* (Government of Canada 2003) has the ambitious goal of doubling the number of functional bilinguals nationally by the year 2014. In this context, the Plan notes that the demand for immersion education levelled off during the 1990s. While it is proposed to promote immersion, the Plan also recognizes that a radical re-examination of the potential of core programmes and other related initiatives such as intensive French and extended core programmes (Canadian Parents for French 2004) must also now be actively pursued.

Implications for the motivational base which supports state efforts in favour of Irish
Any state of affairs which results in substantial numbers abandoning the study of Irish at either primary or post-primary level – either formally opting out or, for all practical purposes, no longer engaging with the learning process – is a threat to the whole attitudinal basis for the national revitalization enterprise. In the Republic, for example, both individual attitudes to Irish and the strength of public support for various state efforts and institutions designed to maintain and extend the use of Irish *depend crucially* on the proportion of the population

who have had a positive and successful experience of learning Irish themselves. Thus, it is important that the widest possible range of people study the language for long enough (i.e at post-primary as well as primary) to acquire a worthwhile proficiency in the language.

It scarcely needs to be said that the decline in standards of pupil proficiency are also of concern to teachers. The very fact that the great majority of teachers in ordinary schools believe standards have declined (Harris et al 2006) has implications for professional self-esteem and motivation. To the extent that the decline is seen to be due to factors which are outside the power of individual teachers to remedy, the effect over a long period could be considerable. Not surprisingly in this context, data in the Harris et al (2006) study also show a substantial and statistically significant long-term decline in the percentage of teachers who derive satisfaction from teaching Irish.

NEED FOR A COMPREHENSIVE RESPONSE TO THE MULTIPLE CAUSES OF DECLINE
One clear message emerging from the Harris et al series of studies is that *a range* of factors, both inside and outside the school, combine to determine the eventual level of pupil achievement in Irish in ordinary schools. If we do not acknowledge that the decline in proficiency also has multiple causes, our response will be inadequate. Just some of the factors involved are (Harris et al 2006):

1. A lack of a suitable method and materials for teaching Irish over a long period.
2. The very substantial contraction in the core time for Irish.
3. A decline in teaching through Irish outside the Irish lesson proper.
4. A long-standing, general feeling of disillusionment among many primary teachers, a feeling that they were carrying a disproportionate share of society's responsibility for the Irish language.
5. Lack of engagement by parents – the impact on teachers and pupils of the hands-off attitude to the teaching and learning of Irish often adopted by parents (Harris & Murtagh 1999).
6. The growth of all-Irish schools – in itself a very positive development – may have overshadowed the traditional achievements of ordinary schools.

7. The circumstances described in (4) – (6) above have taken a toll on teacher attitude and motivation which in turn have had other indirect consequences. Despite the fact that teacher commitment to Irish is still generally high, there is evidence (Harris et al 2006) of changes in their attitudes, perceptions and practices – less favourable views on Irish in primary school, a reduction in satisfaction in teaching Irish, a conviction that standards have fallen and changes in the amount of teaching through Irish.

8. The lack of sufficient speed and energy in official responsiveness, particularly in relation to emerging problems with methods and materials throughout the 1990s. This may have added to the perception among teachers that the leadership and institutional support traditionally given by the Department of Education and Science (DES) in relation to the language was weakening.

9. This lack of responsiveness, and of policy development, in relation to Irish at primary level may in turn be linked in part to the major structural and institutional changes in education, both inside and outside the DES, which occurred during the 1990s.

There are two major issues in formulating an adequate response to this multiplicity of factors affecting achievement in Irish. The first is that public discourse on the standard of Irish achieved by schools almost invariably focuses exclusively on the question of methods and materials – the very first factor mentioned above. This is not to minimize the contribution of problems with methods and materials to the long-term decline in proficiency in Irish. Neither is it to ignore the fact that, while we have not yet had a major national evaluation, all the indications are that the new teaching approaches and materials (NCCA 1999a, 1999b) are having a positive effect on proficiency.

But we cannot allow this acknowledgement to detract from the importance of the range of *other* educational, sociolinguistic, administrative and planning factors which determine the standard of proficiency produced by a programme. The narrowing of focus to methods and materials leads easily to the unrealistic belief that if we fix problems in these areas, low levels of proficiency will no longer occur.

The reality is that each of the negative factors identified above requires a focused response within an overall plan. In some cases we already have prototype programmes which respond to some of these problems and which could be generalized. For example, a pilot programme to involve parents in their (primary school) children's learning of Irish (Harris & Ó Cathalláin, 1999; Harris & Ní Fhearghail, 2003) has been successful and could be incorporated into a wider plan of action. Other initiatives are discussed below. The phenomenon of narrow focus is accentuated, perhaps, by the fact that politically and administratively it is often easier to fix some of the curricular and materials issues than it is to tackle the research and innovation or policy aspects of the other issues listed above.

The second issue in responding effectively is that worthwhile individual initiatives related to each of the problems mentioned above will have limited real impact without an agreed, explicit plan. What is needed is a long-term exercise in educational and linguistic planning covering not just Irish as a subject, but the wider use of Irish in school and the complex interaction between learning Irish and the supports available in the home and in the community. Ideally, this planning exercise would involve research, development and creative work designed to provide solutions to the challenges presented by the real sociolinguistic situation in which schools operate. It would need to take account both of the educational aspects of the issue and the national aim of promoting bilingualism and the wider use of Irish. Broad-based plans and initiatives of this general kind are currently being implemented in countries such as Wales (Edwards & Pritchard Newcombe 2005) and Canada (Government of Canada 2003).

Such an exercise would be much more effective, of course, if it covered all educational levels. Its effectiveness would be further enhanced if explicit political agreement at a national level was secured for the goals and implementation processes of the plan (as was done in the case of the Government of Canada's *Action Plan for Official Languages*). While the legal and constitutional framework for promoting Irish in the education system already exists, there is always a substantial grey area concerning what is desirable or possible in terms of official initiatives. This makes it difficult for government departments and statutory bodies to always act decisively. The process of deliberating on a national plan, and securing political agreement for it, would bring great clarity and energy to the whole enterprise and would harness support of a very different kind for it.

The main elements of policy development and implementation recommended here would appear to be a matter for the DES: the definition of what needs to be done, scrutiny of the DES's role vis à vis other bodies in relation to Irish, the development of a language education policy for Irish, the assembly of a plan of action relating to the teaching and learning of the language in primary schools and implementation of that plan.

PROMOTING PARTIAL IMMERSION AND CLIL AS A STRATEGIC IMPERATIVE
In the concluding section of this paper, I would like to focus briefly on what I think is the most critical specific problem relating to Irish at primary level requiring a response: the reduced exposure to the language which pupils at primary level now receive compared to two decades ago. Fortunately, this is also a problem to which there is, I believe, an extremely effective solution. Three separate national surveys between 1976 and 1985 showed that the amount of time per week spent on Irish varied from 5.6 to 5.1 hours. In the introduction to *Curaclam na Bunscoile* (NCCA 1999c), however, the core ('minimum') time for Irish as a second language is specified as 3.5 hours. In reality, this was largely a confirmation of a process of contraction which had been taking place for a long time. This does not make its impact any less critical for the level of proficiency in Irish which can be achieved and it has to have been a major factor in the fall in standards in Irish documented in Harris et al (2006). The negative consequences of this reduction in core time for Irish were increased by the fact that during the same period teaching through Irish outside the Irish lesson also declined (Department of Education and Science 1986, 2003; Harris et al 2006).

Time in contact with the language in a school programme has long been known to be a key factor in determining achievement or proficiency in a second language. Other related factors such as intensity (e.g., number of classes per week) and engaged time (time actually used in teaching and learning) are also important (Bloom 1974; Collins, Halter, Lightbown & Spada 1999; Curtain 2000; Johnstone 2002). As Johnstone points out, 'in all countries "time" is an important factor, but in some it is vitally important where there is very little exposure to the target language in society...' (Johnstone 20).

It is important to emphasize that the reduction in core time for Irish, irrespective of how it came about, was a greater loss for Irish than was the corresponding reduction in time for other subjects. This is because the use of Irish does not easily extend beyond the Irish slot without the special effort of the teacher. English reading, writing, and mathematics, for example, extend easily, naturally and by necessity into other areas of the curriculum all the time. So, there is a sense in which these subjects continue to be taught, directly or indirectly, for a great part of the day, outside whatever core slots they may have. Pupils will learn new English vocabulary, for example, in the course of studying a range of other topics; mathematics will be required in the science class, and so on. The consequences of reducing core time for these subjects, therefore, cannot be equated with the consequences for Irish. In many schools, the reduction in core time for Irish will have seriously undermined the only foothold the language had in the curriculum.

Perhaps the single most important initiative needed, therefore, the one which would make the greatest contribution to improving proficiency nationally, is one which would increase the amount of exposure to the language among children in ordinary schools. The most effective way of doing this without taking time from other subjects is to promote, on an *entirely voluntary basis*, a limited but significant programme of teaching through the medium of Irish. This could take two general forms:

1. promoting the teaching of one or two subjects, or parts of subjects, through Irish in ordinary schools – an *extended core programme*.
2. developing *intermediate forms of immersion education*, less ambitious than the full-immersion approach of all-Irish schools but more ambitious than a subject-only or extended programme.

Partial immersion programmes are relatively common elsewhere (see Swain & Johnson 1997) and produce improvements in second language achievement which reflect the additional hours of real communicative contact with the language. One of their key advantages, of course, is that they achieve the additional contact hours without taking time away from other school subjects. These approaches have also now become part of a larger educational movement operating under the general umbrella of *content and language integrated learning* (CLIL) (Marsh 2002) which is actively supported by the Council of Europe's Language Policy Division.

Strategically, therefore, the aim should be to achieve the maximum Irish programme that each school locally, and each set of parents, is willing to implement. Where the teacher's own outlook and motivation make it possible to place a special emphasis on Irish in a particular school, and where local parental attitudes permit it, there should be easy access to the support, structures, training and materials to capitalize on that potential and to deliver that more ambitious programme. There is clearly a considerable amount of unused potential of this kind at present. Results of a survey reported in Harris et al (2006) showed that 24 per cent of parents in schools that presently do not teach any subject through Irish would support the teaching of one or two subjects through Irish.

Considerable planning, materials preparation and teacher training would be necessary, however, to develop real programme options and to harness the potential and goodwill which exists. The DES itself would have to take the initiative in promoting these new partial immersion and CLIL programmes since there is no group similar to Gaelscoileanna specifically promoting and setting up such programmes at present. It would also require a team of Project Leaders to promote the option among teachers and schools and to manage the development of materials. Even if only a minority of children who are currently learning Irish as a core subject in ordinary schools were to participate in an 'extended core' or partial immersion programme of the kind we are proposing, however, the impact on pupil proficiency nationally could be dramatic.

REFERENCES

An Coimisinéir Teanga. 2004. *Inaugural report*. Dublin: An Coimisinéir Teanga.

Bloom, B.S. 1974. 'Time and learning' in *American Psychologist* 29: 682-688.

Canadian Parents for French (CPF). 2004. 'The state of French second-language education in Canada 2004', retrieved June 2005 from www.cpf.ca/english/Resources/FSL2004/2004%20ndex.htm.

Collins, L., R. Halter, P. Lightbown, & N. Spada. 1999. 'Time and the distribution of L2 instruction' in *TESOL Quarterly* 33(4): 655-680.

Commission of the European Communities. 2003. *Promoting language learning and linguistic diversity: An action plan 2004-2006. Communication from the Commission to the Council, the European Parliament, the Economic and Social Committee and the Committee of the Regions.* Brussels. Office for Official Publications of the European Communities.

Curtain, H. 2000. 'Time as a factor in early start programmes' in Moon, J. & M. Nickolov (eds), *Research into teaching English to young learners: International perspectives*. Pécs. University Press.

Department of Education. 1986. *Tuarascáil staitistiúil (Statistical report) 1985/1986*. Dublin. Stationery Office.

Department of Education and Science. 2003. *Tuarascáil staitistiúil (Statistical report) 2002/2003*. Dublin. Stationery Office.

Edwards, V. & L. Pritchard Newcombe. 2005. 'When school is not enough: New initiatives in intergenerational language transmission in Wales' in *The international journal of bilingual education and bilingualism* 8: 298-312.

Government of Canada: Privy Council Office. 2003. 'Action plan for official languages', retrieved June 2005 from www.pcobcp.gc.ca/aia/default.asp?Language=E&Page=ActionPlan.

Harris, J. 1984. *Spoken Irish in primary schools*. Dublin. Institiúid Teangeolaíochta Éireann.

Harris, J. 1988. 'Spoken Irish in the primary school system, in *The international journal of the sociology of language* 70: 69-87.

Harris, J. 1991. 'The contribution of primary schools to the maintenance of Irish' in Kroon, S. & K. Jaspaert (eds), *Ethnic minority languages and education*. Amsterdam. Swets & Zeitlinger.

Harris, J. 1997. 'Speaking proficiency in Irish in primary school children: Educational and sociolinguistic factors' in Wolck, W. & A. De Houwer (eds), *Plurilingual XVIII: Recent studies in contact linguistics*. Brussels. Research Centre on Multilingualism at the Catholic University of Brussels.

Harris, J. 2007. 'Bilingual Education and Bilingualism in Ireland North and South' in *The international journal of bilingual education and bilingualism* 10(4): 359-368.

Harris, J., P. Forde, P. Archer, S. Nic Fhearaile & M. O'Gorman. 2006. *Irish in primary school: Long-term national trends in achievement*. Dublin. Department of Education and Science.

Harris, J. & L. Murtagh. 1988. 'National assessment of Irish-language speaking and listening skills in primary-school children: Research issues in the evaluation of school-based heritage-language programmes' in *Language, culture and curriculum* 1(2): 85-130.

Harris, J. & L. Murtagh. 1999. *Teaching and learning Irish in primary schools.* Dublin. Institiúid Teangeolaíochta Éireann.

Harris, J. & L. Ní Fhearghail. 2003. *Éist liom, labhair liom.* Unpublished report. Dublin. Institiúid Teangeolaíochta Éireann.

Harris, J. & S. Ó Cathalláin. 1999. *A partnership approach to developing parental support for Irish in primary school.* Unpublished report. Dublin. Institiúid Teangeolaíochta Éireann.

Johnstone, R. 2002. *Addressing 'the age factor': Some implications for language policy.* (Guide for the development of language educaton policies in Europe: From linguistic diversity to plurilingual education. Reference study). Strasbourg. Council of Europe.

Marsh, D. 2002. *CLIL (Content and Language Integrated Learning): The European dimension: Actions, trends and foresight potential.* Jyväskylä. University of Jyväskylä.

NCCA. 1991a. (National Council for Curriculum and Assessment). (1999a). *Curaclam na bunscoile: Gaeilge: Teanga.* Dublin. Stationery Office.

NCCA. 1999b. *Curaclam na bunscoile: Gaeilge: Teanga: Treoirlínte do Mhúinteoirí.* Dublin. Stationery Office.

NCCA. 1999c. *Curaclam na bunscoile: Réamhrá. Primary school curriculum: Introduction.* Dublin. Stationery Office.

Ó Riagáin, P. & J. Harris. 1993. 'Ireland: Multilingual policies in Irish first and second level schools' in Ammon, U. et al (eds), *Multilingual concepts in the schools of Europe: Sociolinguistica* 7: 152-161.

Swain, M. & R.K. Johnson. 1997. 'Immersion education: A category within bilingual education' in Johnson, R.K. & M. Swain (eds), *Immersion education: International perspectives.* New York. Cambridge University Press.

Teaching and Learning Irish Today

Anna Ní Ghallachair

INTRODUCTION

Statistics from the 2006 census show that almost 1.66 million people in the Republic of Ireland stated that they were able to speak the first official language of the state in 2006; in percentage terms, this is a slight decline when compared with the 2002 figures, but, in real terms, it probably translates into a slight increase, given the overall increase in the population in the intervening years. The fact is that, rightly or wrongly, much of the burden of language revival and maintenance has been placed on the educational system, and the educational system can take much credit for what, on the face of it, appears to be the relatively healthy state of the Irish language.

One could, of course, take a more pedantic view and query precisely what level of language competence is implied in 'being able to speak Irish'. Does it mean the sort of level promised by some commercial language learning methods which entice prospective learners with advertisements promising that they will 'learn French in three months' or are we talking about the level of fluency described by the Common European Framework of Reference for Languages (2001) as C1: 'can express him/herself fluently and spontaneously, almost effortlessly. Only a conceptually difficult subject can hinder a natural, smooth flow of language'? Or perhaps we should be more exercised by the obvious conclusion that somewhere in the region of three million people in Ireland consider that, having spent up to fourteen years in an educational system where the teaching and learning of Irish were compulsory, they are 'not able to speak the language'. Of course, fairly crude surveys of language practice are notoriously unreliable: in response to one Eurobarometer survey (2000) in advance of the European Year of Languages in 2001, forty per cent of Irish people declared that Irish was their mother tongue, a response that probably demonstrates an emotional affinity with a language which, given the census data, nevertheless somehow seems to elude many of them.

Nevertheless, I believe it is fair to extrapolate from these census data, lacking nuance as they do, that people learning Irish in Ireland have been both very well served and very badly served by the educational system. On the positive side, some of the best speakers and writers of the language today, including many of those working in university Irish departments, are not native speakers and are largely the products of good teaching. On the less positive side, many students complete their Irish-language education with less than desirable outcomes. An Coimisinéir Teanga stated in his inaugural report in March 2005:

> It is estimated that almost 1,500 hours of tuition in the Irish language is provided to school pupils over a period of 13 years, from the first day at primary school to the end of secondary level. This clearly raises the question: is the State getting value for money from this investment, if it is true that so many are going through the educational system without achieving a reasonable command of the language – even in the case of students who succeed in getting a high grade in Irish in their final examinations?

IRISH IN THE SCHOOL SYSTEM

While the census statistics bear out An Coimisinéir's concerns about standards of achievement in the language, we are not convinced that all pupils in the country who remain in school until the Leaving Certificate have had 1,500 hours of Irish teaching. Anecdotal evidence would suggest that some primary school teachers spend less than the required number of hours teaching the language. Indeed, we have heard of primary schools where Irish is not taught, even for a few minutes, every day. This is probably not school policy, but down to the preferences and Irish-language competence of individual teachers. A short essay in *The Irish Times* by a transition year student, Michael Ward (2007), of St Colmcille's Community School in Dublin, would seem to confirm what many already believe:

> Primary-school days pass, and Irish is taught for as little as 15 minutes a day. Then these students go into secondary school, where they are expected to be able to create intelligent sentences so as to argue their opinions about, say, a poem or short story.

Many primary school teachers do, of course, devote the prescribed number of hours (2.5 hours per week for junior and senior infants and 3.5 hours per week for 1st to 6th classes) to the teaching of the language. But the result of this inconsistency of approach is that secondary school teachers are presented with first-year classes of pupils of varying levels of competency in the language and must address the deficits of the weaker pupils, thus limiting the scope for language development in the classroom. There is also anecdotal evidence to suggest that emphasis on Irish in the primary-school classroom can vary from region to region, which may explain patterns of performance in the language in state examinations.

At second level, the emphasis is on examinations. Teachers frequently complain that after the first two years they can no longer afford to teach the language but must teach to the examinations. Pupils are frequently given essays and answers to other questions to learn by heart, which will be regurgitated on the day of the state examination. Nor should either party be criticised for so doing. Teachers in Ireland (and students) are judged almost exclusively on the results obtained at examination. If an examination lends itself to this kind of practice, then it is the examination which is at fault. This practice is also common in the case of foreign-language learning in Ireland. Indeed, much of the foreign-language oral examination can be prepared well in advance of the examination and learned by rote. Enough research has been done in the field of language testing to avoid the current undesirable washback effect of the Leaving Certificate language examinations, allowing for language knowledge to be tested, rather than the ability to learn by rote. In this regard, the increased weighting proposed for the Leaving Certificate oral Irish examination in 2012 will not have the desired positive washback effect on communicative competence unless the examination tasks are modified.

THE LITERATURE VERSUS LANGUAGE DEBATE

There have been many calls for the removal of literature from the Leaving Certificate Irish syllabus. It would seem that the debate has been reduced to the opposition of literature and communication, with the inherent suggestion that it is possible to learn to communicate in the language or gain an insight into Irish literature but not both together. This is not necessarily the case. Irish as a school subject is, and should be, about more than language for communicative purposes. It should be about giving Irish citizens an understanding of their heritage, the Irish world view, both past and present. Applied linguists are now beginning to question the reductionist attitude of those advocating syllabi based exclusively on the communicative approach, particularly as part of the education of the young adult:

> In literature, situations, developments and events are presented in much more detail than is possible in (…) simulation techniques. Therefore, students can respond to much more complex situations and explore and discuss their responses to them, including the style of presentation chosen by the author and his/her reasons for doing so and including the everyday perspective on life, i.e. the embodied form of life of the literary protagonists. (Witte 2006).

Literature is the ideal medium for fostering intercultural understanding, whether between individuals from different countries or, as in this case, from different language backgrounds. Who, after all, would suggest that English literature should not form part of the English Leaving Certificate syllabus? For most Irish citizens, their journey through the educational system at second level will be the only time they will encounter Irish-language literature. Exposing them to only the English-language literature of Ireland would be telling them only part of the story of Ireland. Indeed, literature has been an optional part of the Leaving Certificate foreign-language syllabus for some years now, and with disastrous consequences. Many teachers and pupils alike find the syllabus unsatisfying, and university language departments every year receive scores of students into their first-year classes who have never encountered literature in the target language in their six years of secondary school. Their levels of communicative competence are not noticeably higher as a result, and knowledge of the written language, if anything, appears to have deteriorated. It may not be a coincidence that most university language departments, with the exception of Spanish, which is most frequently taken at beginners' level, have experienced a significant decline in take-up in the corresponding period.

Adult Learners

Until 2005 the provision of Irish-language courses for adults was patchy and ad hoc. In March 2005, the Language Centre at NUI Maynooth introduced an examination and certification system for Irish for adult learners entitled Teastas Eorpach na Gaeilge (TEG), which is currently available at five levels.

The tests are linked to the Common European Framework of Reference for Languages: Learning, Teaching and Assessment (CEFR), a Council of Europe initiative, launched in 2000. The CEFR provides descriptors for six levels: A1, A2, B1, B2, C1 and C2. A1 is for complete beginners and the highest level, C2, is described as 'mastery', denoting the level of language competence held by those using the language professionally. 304 candidates took the TEG examinations in 2007 at five centres, in Maynooth, the three biggest Gaeltachtaí and Charles University, Prague. Examinations will be held at these centres in 2008 and at the Centre Culturel Irlandais (formerly the Irish College), Paris. While the number of candidates has increased threefold in the past year, numbers following the courses are greater still: TEG syllabi are taught in many locations throughout Ireland, and at several universities in Europe and North America. In Ireland, many of those who took TEG examinations did so in the context of the Official Languages Act (2003). Following many requests from teachers, teaching materials for the first two levels, Bonnleibhéal 1 (A1) and Bonnleibhéal 2 (A2), were designed and made available on the TEG website, and materials for Meánleibhéal 1 (B1) and Meánleibhéal 2 (B2) are currently in development.

BEST PRACTICE FROM EUROPE

A development of the CEFR which is under-used but would no doubt prove very beneficial for Transition Year students is the European Language Portfolio (ELP). The ELP is made up of three parts: (1) Language Passport, (2) Language Biography and (3) Language Dossier. The Passport provides an overview of the language competence of the student in terms of the levels of the CEFR. It allows for self-assessment and for assessment by teachers and institutions. The function of the Biography is to encourage the learner to plan his/her learning and to state what s/he can do in the language(s). Finally, the Dossier is used to provide samples of work which illustrate the achievements recorded in the Passport and Biography. An important aspect of the Council of Europe's approach to language learning is the notion of 'partial competences', an attempt to get away from the 'all-or-nothing' approach, and to convince learners that a limited ability in any of the four language skills (reading, writing, listening, speaking) is also worthwhile. The second-level version of the ELP is available in Irish.

ICT AND IRISH

Information technology has opened the way for a number of initiatives which have already proven their worth in the case of other languages. In particular, it has made possible the provision of up-to-date materials at a low cost to both providers and learners. It also allows for access to a much wider audience. One example provided by the Language Centre at NUI Maynooth is *Vifax don Ghaeilge*, a multimedia language learning system whose patent is owned by Professor Michel Perrin of the University of Bordeaux I. Comprehension exercises based on two items of the TG4 news are prepared at three levels each Monday for twenty weeks and made available on the Language Centre website, together with an answer key and scripts of the new items, by 2pm the following day. The news items are available on video file on the website, so that access is not confined to the areas in which TG4 broadcasts. Vifax is used by many learners working alone, secondary schools and most universities in Ireland, as well as by individuals and third-level teaching institutions in North America.

Beo.ie, which is published monthly by Oideas Gael, describes itself as an 'Internet magazine for Irish-speakers in Ireland and worldwide'. While it contains interesting articles on many different subjects likely to engage the serious, advanced reader, it also extends a helping hand to the less proficient speaker by providing instant translation of the more complex phrases and vocabulary which are a feature of this level of Irish. It is a very useful addition to the Irish classroom and for those attempting to improve their knowledge of the language at home.

A number of other websites, which it is not possible to detail here, and which should prove invaluable to the learner and teacher of Irish alike, are appended to this chapter.

TEACHER EDUCATION

No article on the teaching and learning of Irish would be complete without addressing the thorny issue of teacher education. As has already been stated above, there are many excellent teachers of Irish. It is, however, our belief that, on the whole, teachers have been badly served by the educational system. If some primary school teachers choose to devote little time to Irish, it may be because they are not comfortable with the language. The difficulty of Gaelscoileanna in recruiting teachers, with, in some cases, no teachers applying for posts where teaching is carried out exclusively through the medium of Irish, is, by now, well documented.

In the case of post-primary schools, the time has come when we must ask if the traditional BA plus H Dip in Ed is any guarantee of an ability to teach Irish, or any other language for that matter. However much universities might choose to deny it, there is no doubt that a good degree of 'dumbing down' or grade inflation has taken place over the past ten years or so. This was an inevitable consequence of dispensing with the academically more lightweight general degree. The number of first and second honours degrees awarded has increased dramatically in recent times, a development which has been highlighted in research carried out by colleagues at the Institute of Technology, Tralee (O'Grady & Guilfoyle 2007). The concern is that these improved results have not been accompanied by an improvement in standards. Some academics suggest that what has happened, in effect, is that all students are now taking, de facto, general degrees. Whether or not that is the case, many honours graduates emerge from universities without the kinds of language skills necessary to ensure confidence in the language classroom.

University language departments are essentially literature and language departments. Although many now also offer modules in areas such as film studies, history, linguistics, and other related areas, the major emphasis is on literature. And that is as it should be. Traditional language departments are not, and should not be, teacher training units. It is, however, no secret that a majority of language graduates eventually enter the teaching profession. As has already been stated, second-level language syllabi are essentially communicative courses, with the exception of Irish, which does include some literature. Specialized language teacher education courses in the context of the Higher Diploma in Education programmes are confined to a couple of hours a week of language teaching methodology. It is taken for granted by Education Departments that students' language skills are what they should be, having obtained a degree in the language, and no further attention is given to this area.

There is, therefore, a disconnect between the training provided by universities for student teachers and the reality of the classroom in which they will probably spend the next forty years of their professional lives. The challenge, in the case of Irish, is perhaps even greater. Students, graduates and teachers of other languages can always hone their language skills by spending time in the countries of their target languages. Sadly, spending time in the Gaeltacht, which is now bilingual, no longer automatically means immersion in the language, and those wishing to participate in Irish-speaking society must, in many cases, make considerable efforts to do so. But, most pupils, at whatever level, have been exposed to speakers with a high degree of fluency in the language, thanks to TG4 and Raidió na Gaeltachta. And while they may not always be in a position to spot grammatical weakness, most can tell whether the teacher can speak the language or not. A teacher whose level of Irish is not what it should be therefore starts out at a disadvantage in the classroom.

Some informal studies have shown that the most common features shared by schools with the strongest performance in the state examinations were high levels of target-language competence on the part of teachers and use of the target language in the classroom. A language degree, therefore, does not necessarily equip prospective teachers with the necessary language skills to provide this target-language environment for young learners.

Furthermore, in the case of Irish, a minority language being taught to the majority, most of whom are native speakers of English, but some of whom are native speakers of Irish, an awareness on the part of the teacher of the sociolinguistic situation and its implications, would seem a requisite. The particular needs of native speakers of Irish, whether in the Gaeltacht or outside, are addressed neither by teacher education nor by the curriculum.

Undoubtedly, the fact that most BA degrees are two-subject degrees, where the second is not necessarily a language subject, militates against the notion of language specialization.

On the positive side, some of these issues are beginning to be addressed by the sector. The MA in Language Teaching (Irish), offered by NUI Galway appears to be a step in the right direction. Prospective candidates, however, must already hold a teaching qualification to be eligible for the course. The Graduate Diploma in Education (Languages) offered by the University of Limerick, while it does not provide training for teachers of Irish, is another positive development.

Teacher education for those teaching Irish to adult learners has been largely ignored. Many of these teachers of Irish have not had the benefit of formal teacher training. In introducing syllabi for Teastas Eorpach na

Gaeilge, it was felt by the NUI Maynooth team that, in addition to the obvious need for a theoretical and practical knowledge of the issues, it was high time that efforts were undertaken which would lead to a greater professionalization of the sector, something which would eventually benefit all parties involved. In February 2007, the Language Centre at NUIM introduced a part-time course in the teaching of Irish to adults, leading to a NUI Certificate. Applicants must pass an Irish-language test to obtain a place on the course, and lectures and workshops take place on one Saturday a month over ten months. Teaching practice forms an integral part of the course.

TRANSLATION

A welcome development in recent years has been the introduction of postgraduate courses in translation. Some of these are courses in translation studies and therefore are not intended to produce professional translators. However, a rather obvious outcome of good translation courses is the increased level of knowledge of both the source language (usually English) and the target language (usually Irish), which has a beneficial impact on language maintenance.

One such professional qualification offered by NUI Maynooth is a Higher Diploma in Translation, a two-year, part-time, on-line postgraduate course in translation. The course was designed to meet the need for translators, arising from the introduction of the Official Languages Act, 2003, and the designation of Irish as an official and working language of the EU in 2007. Students are required to come on campus only three times in the first year, once to take an entrance examination in Irish and English, once for a weekend workshop, and once for the end-of-year examination. In the second year, there is also one workshop and the final examination. The course is in its second year, with twenty-six students in the first year and thirteen in the second year. So far, just under half of applicants have been successful in gaining places on the course. Currently, students are based all over the island of Ireland, in Spain, Germany and Belgium. The first cohort will graduate in June 2008.

The MSc in Translation offered by the Galway-Mayo Institute of Technology in association with Europus Teo. and Údarás na Gaeltachta, where students undertake work placements in Gaeltacht-based companies, is another interesting model.

Conclusion

Irish is both very well taught and very badly taught. Until relatively recently, criticism of any area relating to the Irish language was perceived as criticism of the language itself and was thought to endanger its position within the educational system, and even within the state. Today, however, attitudes to the Irish language, in Ireland, are, on the whole, positive. It is the wish of most parents in the country that their children learn Irish at school and that they learn it well. This places a particular responsibility on those of us charged with the delivery of Irish-language education at whatever level: we must provide the best possible syllabus, taught as competently as possible and assessed in the fairest way possible. There is much that we can learn from research in applied linguistics and language education models elsewhere, particularly on the continent of Europe. A review of language teacher education, in particular, should be a priority.

The Book of Invasions (An Leabhar Gabhála), a mythical account of the history of Ireland, tells us that the Irish language is made up of the best elements of all of the languages of the Tower of Babel (Ahlqvist 1982); a fitting metaphor, perhaps, for a future language education policy.

Appendix of relevant websites

(My thanks to Éamann Ó hÉigeartaigh of the Language Centre, NUI Maynooth for this list)

Acmhainn http://www.acmhainn.ie/
Before You Know It http://www.byki.com/fls/iris/irish
Beo http://www.beo.ie/index.php
Blas http://www.bbc.co.uk/northernireland/blas/
An Chrannóg – Foclóir http://www.crannog.ie/focloir.htm
An Chrannóg – Seanfhocail http://www.crannog.ie/mam.htm
CRAMLAP http://www.cramlap.org
Cumann na Matamaitice, Coláiste na Tríonóide http://www.maths.tcd.ie/gaeilge/gaelic.html
Daltaí na Gaeilge http://www.daltai.com/home.htm
Focal.ie http://www.focal.ie/Home.aspx
An Foclóir Beag http://www.csis.ul.ie/focloir/
Gaeilge.ie http://www.gaeilge.ie/
Gaelic-L Dictionary http://www.smo.uhi.ac.uk/~smacsuib/focloir/gaelic-l/index.html
Gaelport http://www.gaelport.com/
Gaeltalk http://www.gaeltalk.net/index1.html
Irish Dictionary on-line http://www.englishirishdictionary.com/dictionary
Tobar http://www.tobar.ie/

An Tobar (Foclóir) http://www.smo.uhi.ac.uk/~smacsuib/bng/tobar/
Teastas Eorpach na Gaeilge http://www.teg.ie/
Turas teanga http://www.rte.ie/tv/turasteanga/learning_irish.html
Vicipéid http://ga.wikipedia.org/wiki/Pr%C3%ADomhleathanach
Vifax http://www.nuim.ie/language/vifax.shtml

REFERENCES

Ahlqvist, A. 1982. *The early Irish linguist.* Helsinki. *Commentationes humanarum literarum* 73: 47. (My thanks to Dr Muireann Ní Bhrolcháin, Scoil na Gaeilge, NUI Maynooth for this reference).

Central Statistics Office. 2007. *Census 2006. Volume 9, The Irish language.* Dublin. Stationery Office.

Council of Europe, Modern Languages Division. 2001. *Common European Framework of Reference for Languages: Learning, teaching, assessment.* Cambridge: CUP.

Eurobarometer. 2000. *Report 52.* Available at: http://europa.eu.int/comm/dg10/epo/ (accessed 5 October 2007)

European Language Portfolio, Language Policy Division, Council of Europe. Available at: http://www.coe.int/T/DG4/Portfolio/?L=E&M=/main_pages/levels.html (accessed 1 October 2007)

Ó Cuirreáin, S. 2005. *Inaugural Report,* Gaillimh, p.7. Available at: http://www.coimisineir.ie/downloads/Tuarascail_Tionscnaimh_2004.pdf (accessed 1 October 2007)

O'Grady, M., & B. Guilfoyle. 2007. 'Evidence of grade Inflation 1994-2004 in the Institute of Technology Sector in Ireland'. [Network for Irish Educational Standards: Paper 1.] Available at: http://www.stopgradeinflation.ie/Grade_Inflation_in_Institutes_of_Technology.pdf (accessed 25 September 2007)

Ward, M. 2007. 'My TY,' in *The Irish Times,* 3 October.

Witte, A. 2007. 'Mediating cultural context in the foreign language classroom,' in Gallagher, A. & M. Ó Laoire (eds), *Language education in Ireland: current practice and future needs.* Maynooth: IRAAL.

Modern Irish Scholarship at Home and Abroad

Aidan Doyle

Unlike many more widely spoken languages, Irish as an academic subject is studied mainly in Ireland. Furthermore, because of the state's recognition of Irish as the first official language on a par with English, university courses are taught exclusively through the medium of this language. University teachers for the most part have a personal commitment to the revival of Irish, and at least in the Republic of Ireland, postgraduate research is always conducted in this language in modern Irish departments. Those scholars who are committed to the language revival write and deliver papers in Irish as often as possible. As the number of people who know the language well enough to participate in academic discussion is tiny, this inevitably means that many publications and conferences in Irish fail to reach a wider audience. There are, however, a number of people who as well as looking after the Irish-speaking market, also write in English in the hope of stimulating debate among the broader academic community.

Few native speakers of Celtic languages study them at postgraduate level, and even fewer become full-time academics. Irish is no exception to this. Generally speaking, teachers and lecturers have a high competence in the language, but this is a far cry from the competence of a native speaker. What one may call the academic style of Irish has been developed mainly by non-native writers, and inevitably bears the hallmarks of their native language, English.

Outside of Ireland, in those places where the Irish language is studied, precedence is often given to old and middle Irish rather than the modern language. As a result, few foreign students master the language well enough to engage in serious research. Even if they come to Ireland to study, the policy of conducting undergraduate courses only in Irish seriously impedes their chances of acquainting themselves with the language in a comprehensive manner. The handful of scholars working on modern Irish outside the country often find themselves in a position of isolation compared to their colleagues working on early Irish. Thus, international conferences like the *International Congress of Celtic Studies* tend to be dominated by contributions on such subjects as historical linguistics or medieval literature, with only a small number of papers on, for example, contemporary writing in Irish. A further complication is that a writer or lecturer dealing with modern Irish cannot assume familiarity on the part of an international audience with either the language or literature, and is forced to spend a great deal of time providing background information that is not deemed necessary for early Irish. Not surprisingly, foreign journals like *Zeitschrift für celtische Philologie*, while officially welcoming contributions on any subject, in practice accept more articles on early than on modern Irish.

Because of the divergence between home and abroad, I will deal with the two academic communities separately below.

SCHOLARSHIP IN IRELAND

From the beginning of the academic study of Irish in the nineteenth century, we can detect the presence of a strong philological tradition, which regarded the study of modern Irish in much the same way as it did the study of Classics or early Irish. Adherents of this approach saw as their primary concern the editing and publishing of manuscript material, the collection of dialect materials, the compilation of dictionaries, and the study of the history of Irish since 1200. For the most part, it used English as the language of academic discourse, even if many individual scholars, such as Brian Ó Cuív or Osborn Bergin, had a personal commitment to the revival of Irish. This tradition is maintained to the present day in the School of Celtic Studies in the Dublin Institute for Advanced Studies, which was established to foster the full-time academic study of Irish, and whose annual meeting, *An Tionól*, provides a forum for people working in this field. At the universities, the philological approach is very much in evidence, as can be seen, for instance, in the fact that the edition of a manuscript from the period 1200-1900, or the collection of dialect material, are still regarded as the standard routes to obtaining a doctoral degree. The annual journals *Éigse* and *Ériu*, and *Celtica*, which appears irregularly, accept articles on early modern Irish and historical and dialectal linguistics, and occasionally on late Irish material. Editions of individual manuscripts and dialectal studies are published by the School of Celtic Studies, by the publishing house An Clóchomhar in the series *Imleabhair Thaighde*, and by the Irish Texts Society.

While much valuable work continues to be done in this area, it is fair to say that philology has made but little contribution to the literary interpretation of the contents of the manuscripts being edited. With the founding of the new Irish state in 1922 and the reorganization of the study of Irish that accompanied the political change, a new generation of scholars came into being who saw literary criticism as their primary concern. This new generation also tended to have a strong commitment to the revival of Irish, and hence wrote mainly in this language. The leading adherent of this approach was Seán Ó Tuama, professor of Irish at Cork from the 1940s to the 1990s. Another influential figure in placing contemporary literature on university courses in the post-war era was Tomás de Bhaldraithe, professor of Irish at UCD. Both of these inspired a number of younger scholars to follow in their footsteps, many of whom are still active in the field These academics work on the interpretation of classics of medieval and late Irish literature, works like *Dánta Grádha*, or *Cúirt an Mheán Oíche*, using the tools of twentieth-century criticism. They are also very much concerned with promoting and studying contemporary writing, regardless of whether it is written in dialect by native speakers, or in the standardized Irish used by many urban learners.

If we compare the state of literary studies in Irish today with the situation fifty years ago, we can appreciate the vast progress which has been made in this area. Despite this, however, there is still no academic journal for modern literary criticism in Irish, which is a serious disadvantage to practioners of this discipline. The monthly review *Comhar* (1942 - 2007) published occasional articles in this area, and another important outlet is the series *Léachtaí Cholm Cille*, published by Maynooth University. With respect to books, the situation is better, with An Clóchomhar, An Gúm, Coiscéim, Cló Iar-Chonnachta and Cois Life, publishing between them a reasonable number of literary studies every year. In recent years, literary scholars have played an important role in making Irish-language material available to English-speaking audiences through translation, and in writing articles for reference works on the literatures of Ireland. The fruits of their labours can be found in such publications as the *Field Day Anthology of Irish Writing*, or the *Cambridge History of Irish Literature*.

As far as language studies are concerned, the most important new development that can be discerned in the post-independence period is in the area of sociolinguistics, particularly in the field of language-planning. As a result, whatever linguistic activity there is tends to be in such areas as bilingualism, code-switching, language death, and attitudes towards Irish among the general populace, while there is a dearth of theoretical studies of the grammatical structure of the language, of the sort one finds for most other European languages. One body which did much to offset this neglect was *Institiúid Teangeolaíochta Éireann* (The Linguistics Institute of Ireland), set up in 1967. For many years researchers employed by this institution produced valuable studies concerning the applied linguistics of Irish, and also produced a journal, *Teangeolas*, in which they published the results of their research. Unfortunately, this institution was closed down in 2006. A new sign of hope is the holding since 1997 of an annual conference, *Teangeolaíocht na Gaeilge*, which welcomes contributions on any area of language studies connected with Irish or Scots Gaelic. This conference is held in a different venue in Ireland or Scotland every year and attracts a rich and varied range of papers from scholars in the field.

Summing up, the main strength of Irish scholarship in Ireland is its rigorous insistence on the primacy of philological study. This reliance on textual evidence manifests itself even in the area of literary criticism. Its weakness is its conservatism, its reluctance to utlilize recent tools of academic enquiry, and at times, its total opposition to anything or anyone who has not been sanctioned by tradition. The question of the linguistic medium for academic research, Irish versus English, is a vexed one. One might argue that this is irrelevant, that what matters is the actual content, but in the case of a lesser-used language, the issue is not so simple. First, by writing in Irish one of necessity limits one's potential audience. Second, the huge advances made in such areas as linguistics and literary theory in the last fifty years are not reflected in Irish-language scholarship for purely practical reasons: hardly any of the material is translated into Irish, and hence the technical tools are not available for conducting the relevant scientific discourse in this language. This isolationism has a serious impact on the quality of research. It is not being suggested that one should yield to every passing academic fad merely to keep up with the latest fashion, but one cannot simply ignore all contemporary intellectual developments out of a sense of loyalty to tradition. To be fair, a number of Irish scholars are aware of this problem and try to incorporate recent changes into their work. An important element of the writings of such academics is the coining of new terms and the elaboration of an appropriate academic style. Much has been done in this area in recent years with respect to literary criticism, but this was not unproblematic. Nic Eoin (2000) described the difficulties faced for many years by colleagues and students working without an authorized, published list of such terms. Last year, however, the group of experts which had been compiling a list of literary and critical terms for a number of years under the auspices of An Coiste Téarmaíochta in Foras na Gaeilge published a subject-dictionary in this area of discourse (An Gúm 2007).

The question of the language of scholarship is directly related to that of the language of instruction at third-level institutions. Students enter university with no more than a vague grasp of the rules of Irish, and usually leave without having improved their language skills significantly. Despite this, they are required to take various courses through the medium of Irish, often without any support in the form of textbooks and other teaching aids. Not surprisingly, many of them fail to benefit from the various modules offered in such areas as literature and philology.

Until the teaching of the language itself is improved, this situation is unlikely to change. In my opinion, the greatest challenge facing Irish academic teachers is the compilation of a modern language course such as is available for other foreign languages. Here I have in mind not yet another 'teach-yourself' course, but something much more comprehensive, covering intermediate and advanced levels as well, and containing a wide array of imaginative and challenging exercises and tasks. For this kind of course to be developed and accepted, a change of heart is required on the part of the academic community. For one thing, it would mean officially acknowledging that the teaching of Irish has failed across the whole educational system. In other words, Irish would be treated as a foreign language like French or German, and the fiction could no longer be maintained that people have the same competence in Irish as in English, and that one could rely on students to pick it up without consciously learning it. Second, it would necessitate Irish departments cutting the umbilical cord which binds them to the Gaeltacht culture of bygone years. The usual practice in foreign-language teaching is to expose the students initially to a standardized form and pronunciation. Most modern Irish departments insist on students learning the dialect of the nearest Gaeltacht, even though the pronunciation and grammar of the dialects differ considerably from what the students are exposed to at school. Not only that, but many of the dialect texts are written in a semi-phonetic orthography, and numerous forms encountered in the texts are not to be found in the largest Irish-English dictionary available, Ó Dónaill (1977). This approach has demonstrably failed, and it is high time to abandon it for a more imaginative one. Of course, this can only be done if Irish society as a whole acknowledges certain unpalatable truths about our educational system and the teaching of our first official language.

This still leaves the question of the medium of instruction for those parts of university programmes not directly related to language-learning. As things stand, it is hard to defend the policy of lecturing through the medium of Irish, considering the lack of teaching aids and books mentioned above. The obvious alternative would be to lecture through the native language of lecturers and students alike, i.e. English. This, of course, would necessitate the abandonment of the revival of Irish, a cause which seems to be more important for some academics than the quality of the education they provide. It is certain that there would be strong opposition to the introduction of English-medium courses. Nevertheless, it seems that sooner or later this issue will have to be addressed, if the study of Irish is to continue.

SCHOLARSHIP ABROAD
In North America and Great Britain, and in a few other English-speaking countries like Australia, modern Irish is mainly taught as part of programmes in Irish studies, a discipline that encompasses literature in English and Irish, history, and various other subjects related to Irish culture. Given the fact that teaching aids for learning Irish as a foreign language are comparatively primitive, the achievements of the language teachers are impressive, but most students do not progress

far enough to be able to undertake original research on source material. Inevitably, their study of Irish literature is based on translations, which only represent a small part of the total corpus, and which often fail to convey the full flavour of their originals. There are exceptions to this trend, such as the Irish Studies Institute of the University of Notre Dame, where the language component is an integral part of the programme. Apart from this, universities like Glasgow or Harvard, where there are full degree courses in Celtic Studies, allow their students to pursue the study of modern Irish at an advanced level, and a number of these students go on to engage in research in this area. The Celtic Studies Association of North America has an annual meeting which welcomes contributions on all aspects of the modern language. As far as research is concerned, the most important activity of scholars in North America and Britain concerns the Irish-speaking diaspora in these places, particularly that of the nineteenth century. The most important journals for Irish scholars in North America and Britain are the *CSANA Yearbook* and *Proceedings of the Harvard Celtic Colloquium*.

On the continent of Europe, Irish is studied at a number of universities, usually as part of an English department or a department of linguistics. As stated earlier, the emphasis tends to be on early Irish, but many institutions offer courses in modern Irish as well. There are two exceptions to this trend: in Lublin, Poland, the contemporary language is the main object of study in the Celtic programme, and in Königswinter, Germany, the *Studienhaus für keltische Sprachen und Kulturen* offers courses in modern Irish at an advanced level. As far as research is concerned, the philological tradition is represented by the edition of texts, usually from the early modern Irish period, and by historical and dialectal linguistics, with the latter being particularly strong in Holland, Germany, and Scandinavia. The most important journal for philological publications is *Zeitschrift für celtische Philologie*, published in Germany. Some scholars of modern Irish also translate contemporary literature into their native languages.

In 2006 the Minister for Community, Rural and Gaeltacht Affairs, Éamon Ó Cuív, announced a fund of some €300,000 to support the teaching of the Irish language in third level institutions abroad where it formed part of the academic programme. It is still too early to assess the impact of this fund, but it appears an imaginative initiative with much potential if it can be developed into a long-term integrated policy on the study of Irish at third level both at home and abroad.

As can be seen, in general there is considerably less academic activity abroad than at home, for reasons mentioned in the introduction. There is one exception to this, namely, in the area of synchronic linguistics. Both in North America and on the continent of Europe, a number of linguists have taken an interest in modern Irish, particularly its phonology and syntax. In the last twenty years a number of important studies have appeared which have greatly enhanced our understanding of the grammatical structure of this language. The *Celtic Linguistics Conference*, which takes place every three to four years, provides a forum for linguists investigating theoretical issues relating to Irish. The results of linguistic research are made available in the leading linguistic journals, like *Linguistic Inquiry*, *Lingua*, and *Natural Language and Linguistic Theory*, and also in a specialist publication, the *Journal of Celtic Linguistics*.

The overall number of scholars working on Irish outside the country is much smaller than the community at home, and it must be borne in mind that the majority usually have other teaching and research duties unrelated to this subject. This is a disadvantage, in that they are not able to give as much time and energy to their research on Irish as their counterparts in Ireland. On the other hand it can benefit their work, since these scholars bring to their investigation of Irish an expertise in other fields which enables them to offer new prespectives on the material under examination. There is considerable interest among foreign postgraduates in Celtic languages, an interest which many departments of early Irish in this country have responded to by providing teaching and supervision for such students. By failing to develop English-medium courses, modern Irish departments deprive themselves of many potential postgraduate students of a high intellectual calibre.

CONCLUSION

From 1920 until the present day Irish scholarship has operated on more or less the same principles. It is characterized first and foremost by a respect for tradition, for the achievements of the scholars who laid the foundations for the discipline in the first half of the twentieth century. It is also marked by a strong commitment to the revival of the Irish language. Not infrequently, Irish scholars also subscribe to a particular view of history which views language not as a neutral entity, common to all human beings, but as a reflection of the psyche of a particular ethnic group, something which makes it different from other nations. In short, the overall approach is imbued with the spirit of nineteenth century romanticism. On this view of things, scholarship is not primarily about the scientific analysis of the linguistic and literary legacy of modern Irish, but rather serves to bolster the identity of the Irish nation as defined by the ideologues of the late nineteenth and early twentieth century.

The merit of the approach outlined in the previous paragraph is that it makes students and researchers aware of their ancestral heritage, and can inspire them to explore this for themselves, thus enhancing their sense of identity. The disadvantage is that it is directed solely at what are perceived as the main inheritors of the tradition, and hence excludes other groups. For example, while much research has been done on Catholic writings of the seventeenth century aimed at countering the effects of the Reformation, comparatively little has been written about the Protestant translations of the *Bible* and the *Book of Common Prayer* in the same period. Once again, there have been attempts made by individuals in recent times to offer a more inclusive version of the Irish-language heritage, but the overall impression is still one of exclusivity, based on a particular group identity.

With the ethnic composition of Ireland changing at breakneck pace in recent years, the old approach to the study of Irish seems less and less viable. In ten years time a new generation of students will be entering our universities, many of whom will be the children of immigrants, with no historical allegiance to the Irish language. Their command of and interest in the language will depend on factors like the quality of education they receive at school, not on their ethnic origin. Whether or not these Irish citizens will participate in the study of Irish, either as students or researchers, depends very much on the direction that Irish scholarship takes in the next decade. There are exciting possibilities opening up for the discipline, but in order to exploit them, a new, more forward-looking attitude on the part of the academic community is required.

REFERENCES

An Gúm. 2007. *Foclóir litríochta agus critice / Dictionary of literature and criticism.* Dublin.

Bourke, A. et al. 2002. *The Field Day anthology of Irish writing*, IV-V. Cork. Cork University Press.

Deane, S. et al. 1991. *The Field Day anthology of Irish writing*, I-III. Derry. Field Day.

Kelleher, M. & P. O'Leary. 2006. *The Cambridge history of Irish literature.* Cambridge. CUP.

Nic Eoin, M. 2000. 'Téarmaí liteartha agus critice na Gaeilge: forbairt agus dúshláin' in *Aimsir Óg*: 349-359.

Ó Dónaill, N. 1977. *Foclóir Gaeilge-Béarla.* Baile Átha Cliath. Oifig an tSoláthair.

Current Attitudes to Irish

Ciarán Mac Murchaidh

INTRODUCTION

It may be said that there are almost as many attitudes towards the Irish
language on this island as there are people to hold them. Very few
topics currently engender such debate, reasoned or otherwise, as the
subject of the Irish language and its role in modern-day Ireland. As
Ireland continues to absorb large numbers of foreign nationals, many of
whom are settling down here with families of young children, the issue
of the relevance of the Irish language in an increasingly multicultural
and multilingual society is being questioned more rigorously on a daily
basis, as many of those coming into the country have very limited
English. The question of Irish being a compulsory subject for all Irish
students in primary and post-primary schools continues to be a point of
debate and the Fine Gael political party has already made it clear that
if elected to government in the future, it will abolish the requirement
of so-called compulsory Irish in post-primary schools. Other issues
such as the recruitment of people who were educated as teachers in
institutions outside the state for service in primary schools, the role
of the language in the Civil Service, the rights of the minority to have
access to public services through the medium of Irish, to name but a
few, are also coming to the fore.

It is hoped, within this short essay, to address the impact that this public
debate and these many strongly held views are having on the question
of current attitudes to Irish and its future well-being in general. For ease
of structure and reference, it is proposed to deal with certain themes
which are frequently debated among government officials, public
figures, journalists, educationalists and the public at large. It is intended
to draw on a range of letters and articles published over the last five or
six years in one of the main Irish daily newspapers, *The Irish Times*
(IT). Among the themes which will be considered here are education
and 'compulsory' Irish, Irish-medium education or *gaelscolaíocht* and

the prospects for the future of the language. It is hoped that a review of a cross-section of the letters written by members of the public, as well as those directly involved in the Irish-language movement may help to shed light on where the debate on Irish is as we approach the end of the first decade of the twenty-first century.

EDUCATION

When a debate is begun about the Irish language it takes very little time for the conversation to veer towards education and the arguments surrounding the pros and cons of 'compulsory Irish' This hoary old chestnut raises its head with unceasing regularity and this will continue to be the case until the lobby promoting the abolition of the compulsory status of the language achieves its goal. The debate comes to the fore in each generation and was an issue of contention even in the early years of the state. Diarmuid Ferriter comments in his chapter on the period 1923-1932 that:

> The real obstacle to the Irish-language policy was the failure of adults to make the language a part of their daily lives, which had much to do with the grim and stern manner in which the issue was presented. The determination to impose compulsion in the schools did little to whet the appetite. Rather than presenting it as an enjoyable part of the native culture, a hectoring approach was adopted by governments. (2004: 351)

Representing views uncannily close to the sentiments expressed here was a feature by Declan Kiberd in *The Irish Times* of 7 November, 2006 entitled 'Make Irish a gift, not a threat', which provoked a raft of letters to the paper in response. Kiberd's basic thesis was that few of the policies for promoting the study of the language had succeeded and that a newly-published report showed that more and more students were opting out of its study. He stated that:

> Contemporary Irish writing is brilliant and the syllabus texts bang up-to-date, but it all seems to make no difference. The speed and rigour with which people mastered English in the nineteenth century contrasts utterly with their failure to remaster Irish in the twentieth, despite massive support from the state... Irish declined only when large numbers decided no longer to use it.

Kiberd's proposal was not new – to remove the element of compulsion and that if only, say, 20 per cent '... studied the language for love, [they] might make the sort of commitment to it that could prove of wider value to the community. Then Irish might be seen as a gift rather than a threat by the next generation.' This, however, assumes that the Irish public wish to make the necessary commitment to that ideal and past evidence does not augur well for the future. Gabriel Rosenstock robustly challenged Kiberd's view that the 20 per cent of students who might choose Irish would become 'torchbearers for future generations' and wondered if there were any international studies to suggest that such a move might be successful. He suggested that to make the claim 'that only 20 per cent of our youth is capable of "getting it" sounds a little pessimistic to me' (IT 08.11.2006). This exchange simply illustrates what has been and will continue to be a central feature of this debate. There are large numbers of people who feel passionately that the language should be promoted as widely as possible and there are also those who echo the view held by another letter-writer that 'many of us are unwilling to bury the stinking corpse' of the language (IT 21.07.2006).

The discussion rages among adults of all ages and among teenagers, too, who are at the very heart of the school system. Junior Certificate student, Eoin Daly, captured one extreme of the argument very well when he stated 'For 11 years I have been forced by the state to learn a language which I will neither need or want to speak during my lifetime – a situation which is not only impractical, but wrong… The Irish language will further decline unless the learning of it becomes an optional privilege, not a compulsory duty' (IT 25.08.2001).

Many feel that this view is indicative of the attitude of our young school-pupils. General impressions are not always accurate, however, as was indicated by the results of a telephone poll of voters conducted between 15 and 24 November 2005 by TNS MRBI on behalf of Fine Gael (IT 01.12.2005). The poll was taken immediately after Fine Gael proposed in a policy document that compulsory Irish should be dropped from the Leaving Certificate. Sixty-two per cent of those polled expressed the belief that Irish should become a subject of choice after the Junior Certificate. Thirty-four per cent believed that it should remain compulsory and 4 per cent expressed no opinion. The break-down of the statistics proved even more interesting, however, as the table below shows. The most surprising result contained in the poll was the very high perecntage of people in the 18-34 age-group who stated that they thought that Irish should remain compulsory at second level. The gender-based statistics are also interesting in that there was a significant difference between the views of male and female respondents.

Agree that compulsory status for Irish should be maintained:	
Age-group	%
18-24	52
25-34	37
35-54	30
55-64	25
Over 65	30

Agree that Irish should:		
	Male respondents	Female respondents
Remain compulsory	28%	40%
Be a subject of choice	68%	57%
No opinion	4%	3%

In the 'Teen Times' feature in *The Irish Times* of 21 February 2006 entitled 'Flogging a dead language,' 16 year-old school student, Naomi Elster, stated:

> Ireland is not bilingual, and if it ever will be, the second language will be Chinese or Polish, not Gaeilge… In fact I don't think that Irish is alive any more… Nothing irritates me more than all of these great government initiatives to keep Irish alive… Today's teenagers have enough to worry about – we do more subjects in our final exams than most other countries in Europe. So foisting the responsibility for upholding a decayed language on us simply isn't fair.

Most commentators would assume this to be the general attitude regarding Irish prevalent among young students today. The figures quoted above, especially those relating to the two younger age-groups, give the lie to this assumption. Elster's piece provoked a strong response from other young people. Another Dublin 16 year-old, Aoife Crowley, responded with a strongly pragmatic approach to the matter:

> I found her assertion that the language is a burden to learn was in total contrast to my own experience. If you put in the time and effort it will reward you greatly… Her description of Irish as a dead language is ludicrous… If Irish is dead, then how do I hear it every day on the radio, watch Irish-language TV shows and speak it in school? (IT 24.02.2006)

A letter from a male correspondent, Aonghus Ó hAlmhain, again challenged the notion of Irish being a dead language:

This is news to me, and to the many others who speak Irish every day. Certainly, all of us also speak English. In fact many of us speak a third, and sometimes a fourth language. Not everybody can be raised bilingually in Ireland. But everybody in Ireland has access to Irish at the touch of a radio button or a TV remote control... We would be foolish to jettison this advantage. Being fluent in Irish does not hinder fluency in English.' (IT 23.02.2006)

It is not only students who sometimes feel anger at the compulsory nature of the Irish-language requirement. Some teachers vent their annoyance about the central role the language plays in the day-to-day work of the classroom as well as the recruitment procedure itself. Teachers trained outside the state, for example, are required to sit the *Scrúdú Cáilíochta Gaeilge* (SCG) when they wish to take up service in schools. Failing this Irish-language qualification means that they cannot be recognized as fully-qualified teachers in this state. In 2003 only a third of those who sat the examination managed to pass it (IT 08.03.2004). A branch of the Irish National Teachers' Organisation in Northern Ireland received unanimous support for its motion from delegates attending its Northern conference who called for a review of the requirement. They claimed that it particularly disadvantages teachers trained in Northern Ireland, some of whom would like to teach in the Republic, but who were not afforded the opportunity of learning Irish while in school north of the border. Others take the view that the Department of Education and Science allows teachers up to five years to gain the necessary skills involved and that they are not, therefore, being unduly discriminated against.

These attitudes to Irish are illustrative of the wider polarization of the public at large with respect to the future of the language. From the foundation of the state, the argument has raged combatively from one side to the other. The language is an object of passion, it seems, for most people and the same ideological battles are fought out again and again from one generation to the next. While most commentators would readily acknowledge that the Gaeltacht areas continue to be under pressure from all manner of threats, very few would deny the phenomenal increase in the numbers of people living outside these areas who are fluent in Irish. This is in no small part due to the role being played in the promotion of the language by classes and by gaelscoileanna (Irish-medium schools). Ironically, too, the school system, which has been blamed for so many of the ills besetting the Irish language, is still the main reason why significant numbers of our population have a knowledge of the language, in degrees varying from basic familiarity to complete fluency. This fact is very frequently ignored in the heated exchanges which regularly take place in the public domain.

GAELSCOLAÍOCHT

While financial or educational considerations sometimes adversely influence how the public views the Irish language, the growth of gaelscoileanna in Ireland generally attracts positive comment. Most Irish people understand the philosophy behind these schools and see them as one of the more successful enterprises in the promotion of the language as a living entity outside the gaeltachtaí. Even those who have not had direct contact with gaelscoileanna are aware of how they contribute to the promotion of a supportive public attitude towards Irish.

There are now 170 gaelscoileanna (primary schools) and 43 gaelcholáistí (post-primary schools) throughout the island of Ireland. Almost 28,000 children at primary level in the state are attending Irish-medium schools outside Gaeltacht areas. This represents an increase of about 10 per cent within the last ten years. The debate about the reason for these increased figures is intense. David McWilliams recently described it as a symptom of the Celtic Tiger economy: 'The revival of gaelscoileanna, traditional music and Celtic mythology could not have happened without the Brown Thomas charge card' (McWilliams 2005: 228). He develops his thesis by suggesting that the economic factor is related to class considerations and he indirectly intimates what many feel is the case, that an Irish-medium education is not pursued in order to evidence a commitment to the language but to gain access to something more utilitarian: 'The aim of the HiCos [Hibernian Cosmopolitans] is not to turn themselves into gaeilgeoirí but to get the best for their family. As with everything they do, gaelscoileanna allows them to pick the best bit from what the Hibernian menu has to offer and move on. It is an economic free lunch, spiced with the virtue of authenticity' (McWilliams 2005: 236). It would appear difficult to refute such suggestions when the evidence shows that gaelscoileanna rank highly in university feeder-school lists. Six of them appeared in the top twenty-five in 2006 (IT 17.04.2007). McWilliams' comments may be believed by many in the country to be unequivocally correct but other evidence refutes the 'middle-class, elitist' tags which are often ascribed to gaelscoileanna.

Growth in number of Irish-medium schools outside the Gaeltacht 1972-2006

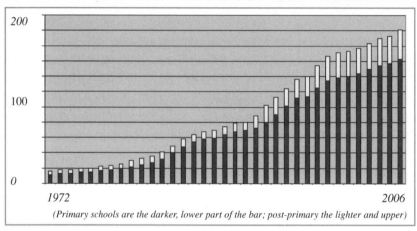

(Primary schools are the darker, lower part of the bar; post-primary the lighter and upper)

The facts themselves prove that the range of social groups represented in gaelscoileanna is wide and varied, a point argued by Nóra Ní Loingsigh of Gaelscoileanna who stated: 'We, like Mr McWilliams, believe that gaelscoileanna are both Hibernian and cosmopolitan, but we reject the thesis that they are merely "the school of choice for the sophisticated elite in Dublin's southside suburbia"... Irish-medium education is available to all: Irish children and children of other nationalities (many of whom attend both primary and post-primary Irish-medium schools), and "gnáthdhaoine" from all social classes and backgrounds' (IT 15.12.2005). These views were strongly supported by Breandán Mac Cormaic, chairman of An Chomhairle um Oideachas Gaeltachta agus Gaelscolaíochta (the Council for Gaeltacht Education and Gaelscoileanna):

> ... it is worth pointing out that while there are two all-Irish schools in upper-class Ranelagh there are three in Tallaght, two in Clondalkin, two in Cabra, two in Ballymun and one, newly set-up in September, in Finglas... Indeed the salient sociological fact and one of the strengths of the gaelscoileanna movement is that it is rooted in every social class and is present in all parts of the country: urban and rural working class, middle class and upper class. (IT 16.12.2005)

Gaelscoileanna have been inordinately successful for a number of reasons. The first is the fact that the school provides a natural environment in which the children develop their level of skill in the language at a steady pace and which nurtures and sustains the target language. Even children from backgrounds where neither parent can speak the language begin to develop fluency in Irish very quickly. Much of this has to do with the 'total immersion' approach used in gaelscoileanna. International research has consistently shown that second language immersion-education improves children's general linguistic skills to a degree not always attained in first-language schools. It has also been established that children attending second language-medium schools generally have an ability in reading and writing the first language equal to those who attend schools where the first language is the medium of instruction. As most gaelscoileanna start from humble beginnings, parental involvement and support is crucial and essential from the earliest days of the life of the school. A feature of gaelscoileanna has been the continued involvement of parents and supporters of each school right through its various stages of development. This provides parents with a strong sense of ownership and involvement in the school itself and, hence, in their children's education. Other schools do not necessarily have this level of parental participation. The inclusive nature of gaelscoileanna is another key aspect of this type of education. Dónall Ó Conaill, the chief executive of An Foras Pátrúnachta, the group which is charged with patronage of over fifty gaelscoileanna throughout the country, has stated quite succinctly the core of the gaelscoileanna philosophy: 'This is a grass-roots, demand-led movement and anyone who wants to be part of it is welcome' (IT 17.04.2007).

THE FUTURE

In his exploration of the Ireland of the 1970s in his book *The Transformation of Ireland 1900-2000*, Diarmuid Ferriter wrote:

> Attitudes to the Irish language continued to reveal a gulf between theory and practice, even fifty or sixty years after independence. Declan Kiberd pointed out that a 1975 government report showed that three quarters of the people still believed it essential to Irish identity, but less than one quarter believed it would still be thriving in the twenty-first century. There was a new trend favouring Irish-language schools in the cities and an Irish-language TV station, but Irish-speakers were now ironically, if with a degree of success, making their case on the basis of minority rights (Ferriter 2004: 753-4).

It is interesting to note that despite all the odds, Irish is still thriving as
we come towards the end of the first decade of the twenty-first century
and that Irish-language speakers have gained significant benefits and
protections for the language through the pursuit of these protections
under minority rights legislation.

The debate continues to rage year after year among those who have
the greatest vested interest in seeing the language either die or prosper.
What is most pertinent to the discussion is that while these groups
thrash out their differences, Colossus-like, on the national stage, others
go quietly about the business of beginning to learn Irish, improving
their intermediate knowledge of it or perfecting their use of it not only
here in Ireland but across the world. The language is also attracting
considerable interest from immigrants and foreign nationals and proof
of this interest is borne out by the work of the group, iMeasc, which
seeks to provide opportunities and encouragement to foreigners to
learn the language. A letter to *The Irish Times* from a number of people
involved in iMeasc eloquently stated the raison d'être for their group:

> As members of a group of Irish-speaking immigrants to Ireland, iMeasc, we wish
> to strongly dispute the insinuation in *The Irish Times*' editorial of June 20th that
> English, to the exclusion of Irish, will be the sole language of choice for immigrants
> to Ireland... Lest our efforts be tiresomely and patronisingly dismissed as 'trying to
> be more Irish than the Irish,' iMeasc was formed directly out of deep concerns as
> to where repeated attempts in the national media to use immigrants as a weapon
> against the Irish language, and on a lesser level, native Irish culture, could lead.
> (IT 26.07.2006)

This response clearly indicates that while the native Irish quite often
engage with the language debate at a superficial level others, some
of whom have come from multilingual backgrounds, can explore the
issues with greater insight and awareness. Anna Heussaff's essay, 'The
Irish for Multicultural,' in *Who Needs Irish?*, also helps to explain why
increasing numbers of foreign nationals are investing time in learning
Irish. The interest of people outside of Ireland in the language is no
new phenomenon, either, as some universities in the US have long had
dedicated Departments of Celtic Studies (in Harvard, for example).
The University of Notre Dame went one step further in recent years
and endowed a Chair and Department of Irish Language and Literature
in 2004. Some 120 students were enrolled on various undergraduate
courses there during that first year. American students of all kinds of
backgrounds are involved in such courses and Irish graduates can avail

of teaching opportunities in Notre Dame and elsewhere, which lends a new meaning to the expression, 'the Irish diaspora'.

Two articles in *The Irish Times* in early 2007 further illustrated this commitment to learning and promoting the Irish language as a valuable cultural resource. One piece was entitled 'First Gaeltacht abroad planned for Canada' (IT 23.01.2007) and the second, longer feature concerned the same story, 'Irish at home in Canada' (IT 17.02.2007). Some of these people are second- or third-generation Irish but others are people who simply have developed an interest in the language and have set themselves the task of learning it. In this case they have gone even further than this by buying a sixty-acre piece of land which they intend to develop as a facility for Irish-speakers. 'We want a place people can come to all year round and speak Irish. At first, there will be no one living there on a full-time basis, however, that could all change in the future,' stated Aralt Mac Giolla Chainnigh, a leading member of Cumann na Gaeltachta in Kingston, Canada.

One might contrast this with some of the issues facing Gaeltacht areas in Ireland in recent years. Supports for these areas, which are designed as a means of protecting their distinctive linguistic mores and cultural traditions, are increasingly being challenged as discriminatory against those who wish to choose to live anywhere or use the language of their birth, regardless of what impact that may have on the delicate linguistic balance in many Gaeltachtaí in Ireland. During 2004, for example, Galway County Council imposed Irish-language conditions on developers who intended building housing developments in Gaeltacht areas (IT 02.12.2004). This decision was challenged by the developers in the courts and An Bord Pleanála itself questioned the extension of the language condition to Gaeltacht areas where the language has become significantly weakened. Similarly, An Bord Pleanála controversially overturned a decision by Kerry County Council to allow a developer to build a holiday home development in the west Kerry Gaeltacht village of Baile na nGall on the basis that the Council had granted permission for the development without asking for a linguistic impact assessment (IT 21.09.2005). Issues concerning the Gaeltachtaí are dealt with more fully elsewhere in this book but it is worth stating that language planning and development planning will be crucial in preserving the distinctive cultural and linguistic identity of the Gaeltachtaí.

The Language Commissioner, Seán Ó Cuirreáin, while addressing the Board of Údarás na Gaeltachta in Galway in December 2005, stated that the next decade would be a 'make or break' period for Irish. Although he claimed that the death of the language had been predicted continuously since the Battle of Kinsale, he stated that the last native speaker 'has not yet been born'. He also commented that planning for the future of the language needed to be based on 'substance rather than symbolism' and pointed out that children from more than ninety linguistic backgrounds were born in Dublin hospitals during 2000. Commenting on the need for all sectors of the community to become involved in the promotion of the language he also warned that '… no amount of legislation or no one Act can of its own save the language' (IT 16.12.2005).

A vibrant, informed and robust discourse concerning the future of the language is carried on in the various Irish-language media. The series of pamphlets in Irish, published regularly by Irish-language publisher Coiscéim since 2002 (*An Aimsir Óg: Paimfléid*), is a case in point. These pamphlets, addressing a range of aspects concerning the language, provides the kind of intellectual stimulation for the debate called for by Michael Cronin in his book, *Irish in the New Century* (2005). In fact Cronin also states that the discourse must take place in the English-language media so that everyone is aware of what precisely is at stake: '[Irish] must look to the immediate marshalling of explicative and aesthetic arguments in the English language because it is ironically but understandably in English that the fate of Irish will be decided' (Cronin 2005: 45). It is a cold fact of life that a substantial core of people who most need to be more fully informed about the language question can only be reached through English.

The arguments surrounding the current status of Irish in the education system in Ireland, its position in public life and the use of public money by government to fund initiatives to help the preservation and promotion of the language will continue to be hotly argued. The issue is by no means simple. What is needed as Irish enters the 'new age', as Michael Cronin puts it, is a fresh means of addressing the issues in a way which avoids the adversarial debates of the past. The cycle of claim and counter-claim will have to be broken if we are to make progress in exploring the most effective way of preserving and celebrating a key element of our rich cultural heritage.

REFERENCES

Cronin, M. 2005. *An Ghaeilge san aois nua / Irish in the new century.* Dublin. Cois Life.

Ferriter, D. 2004. *The transformation of Ireland 1900-2000.* London. Profile.

McCloskey, J. 2001. *Guthanna in éag: An mairfidh an Ghaeilge beo? / Voices silenced: Has Irish a future?* Dublin. Cois Life.

Mac Murchaidh, C. (ed). 2004. *Who needs Irish?: Reflections on the importance of the Irish language today.* Dublin. Veritas.

McWilliams, D. 2005. *The Pope's children: Ireland's new elite.* Dublin. Gill & Macmillan.

The Global Diaspora and the 'New' Irish (Language)

Brian Ó Conchubhair

INTRODUCTION

The extent of Irish emigration in the modern era is extraordinary. As many as ten million people have emigrated from Ireland since 1700 and consequently, it may be argued, that mass emigration is the defining characteristic of modern Irish history. The figures, while well known, are sobering: in 1890, 40 per cent of all people born in Ireland lived abroad and 66 per cent of all emigrants (one quarter of all Irish-born people) lived in the United States. The crucial event that caused the Irish to flock abroad was the mid-nineteenth-century famine. This singular event in nineteenth-century European history combined with industrialization, urbanization, and educational policy to realize what Seán de Fréine (1984: 84) terms 'a millennial or utopian movement' where native Irish-speakers abandoned their language with a haste and endeavour that was as spectacular as the rate of emigration.

Equally spectacular is the economic success described as the 'Celtic Tiger' and the ensuing rapid transformation of Irish culture and society. As Ireland embraces globalization and practises open-market economics, immigration, since 1996, has replaced emigration. The Celtic Tiger economy, seen as a cultural remedy for the Famine, subsequent emigration and its trans-generations traumatic impact on Irish enterprise, confidence and creativity, has 'reinvented' Ireland. This reinvention, however, calls for a denial of the past, offers negative portrayals of the past at every opportunity and demands deeper global integration and immediacy between domestic policy and international contexts. The embrace of globalization in the early 1990s laid the foundation for the Celtic Tiger economy and the subsequent rise in immigration.

This essay examines the impact of globalization, migration, transnationalism and transculturalism on the Irish language in Ireland and globally. The first part considers the impact of recent immigration on Irish, the response of various groups to the social and cultural reconstitution of Ireland's sociolinguistic and cultural environment and considers the portrayal and role of Irish in this emerging immigration discourse. The latter section charts efforts by the Irish diaspora in the United States, Canada, Australia and England to foster, preserve and enjoy the Irish language and how the global technological revolution and globalization has transformed the nature and practices of the off-shore Irish-language networks.

THE NEW IRISH (LANGUAGE)

Yu Ming is ainm dom (2003), a short film directed by Daniel O'Hara, centres on a young Chinese man intent on emigrating to Ireland. In preparation Yu Ming studies and masters Ireland's first official language, Irish. Once fluent, he flies to Dublin where he flounders linguistically. In a youth hostel staffed by non-nationals who do not speak Irish, he experiences a series of cultural difficulties involving accommodation, food and cutlery. Finally he enters a bar seeking work. The barman, failing to recognize Irish and misunderstanding *obair* for a brand of beer, ironically offers him a Guinness, explaining 'it's Irish.' An older man recognizing that Yu Ming is speaking Irish, initiates an Irish-language conversation and explains the paradoxical nature of Irish sociolinguistic behaviour. Despite bilingual signage, explains the older man, '… ní labhraítear í … ach i gcúpla ceantar in Éirinn.' The film closes with a mini-bus of tourists travelling a scenic costal road before arriving in a Gaeltacht pub, where they are greeted by Yu Ming in Irish, who was found employment and a home among an Irish-speaking community.

What was whimsical in 2003 is in 2007 a national issue. The recent and dramatic increase in immigration has radically changed the immigration debate in Ireland. The utopian image of an integrated Ireland where immigrants become *Hiberniores Hibernis ipsis* expired in 2004. *Yu Ming* captures the anti-racist optimism which emerged in Ireland and how '… in many ways 1997 represented the high-water mark of anti-racist optimism in Ireland' (Lentin & McVeigh 2006: 2-3). But that moment of optimism, captured in *Yu Ming is ainm dom*, passed in 2004: 'This end of optimism,' they write 'was symbolized through the enacting of an increasingly draconian immigration regime – culminating in the Citizenship Referendum and the Immigration Act 2004.' *Yu Ming is ainm dom*, therefore, appeared at a particular moment in Irish cultural history where immigrants were welcome and were perceived as neither an economic nor cultural threat.

Immigration is now the dominant social concern in the Republic of Ireland. The immigrant population increased by 53 per cent between 2002 and 2006 and foreign-born residents accounted for 14 per cent of the population in 2006 compared with 10 per cent in 2002. In the twelve months prior to April 2006, 86,900 immigrants entered the State, 22,900 (26 per cent) of which were Polish and 6,100 (7 per cent) were Lithuanian. Controversial commentator Kevin Myers warns of dire consequences: 'Immigration is now not merely the dominant feature of Irish life, it is the greatest threat to the existence of the Irish nation as a coherent, and cohesive whole. No country has ever accepted, never mind assimilated, the volumes of foreigners now present in this state' (Myers 2007). Whereas media attention focuses on Nigerians, Chinese and Poles, United Kingdom nationals represent the largest ethnic minority residing in Ireland. 112,548 United Kingdom nationals reside in the Irish State (2.7 per cent of population), considerably more than the 63,276 Polish nationals (1.5 per cent). Yet while the UK nationals are highly dispersed and predominantly scattered throughout rural areas or along the south and west of the country, in particular rural areas of Cork, Kerry, Leitrim, Roscommon and Donegal, other immigrant groups are more concentrated. Immigrants comprise more than 25 per cent of the population of large areas of Dublin, including most of the city centre and parts of Blanchardstown, Clondalkin and Tallaght. Of the 52,345 'Asian/Asian-Irish' population in the Republic, 30,624 (58.5 per cent) reside in Dublin; 47.7 per cent of 'Black/Black-Irish' ethnicity also live in Dublin. Analysing the 2006 census figures in *The Irish Times*, former Taoiseach and respected academic Garret Fitzgerald (2007) estimated that between 2002 and 2006:

> The number of Asians here had also more than doubled to 45,000, and the number of Africans had risen by three-quarters to 35,000. The number of people from western European countries had risen by one-half, but the number with British nationality had grown by only one-tenth. A key feature of both eastern and western European immigrants was that very few of them - fewer than one in 10 - were children, and only a tiny number were retired people. This contrasts sharply with our indigenous population, one-third of whom fall into these two dependant categories. Thus the burden these European immigrants impose on our educational system is a relatively light one. Nevertheless, when the other immigrant groups are

also taken into account, by April last year the total number of immigrant children under 15 exceeded 50,000. It is true that 20,000 of these came from Britain or other English-speaking counties, many of them the children of returning immigrants, but that still left us with 30,000 children who must have language problems.

Current Government policy rejects multiculturalism in favour of integration which is to be achieved by providing additional English-language instruction for pupils in the educational system and classes for adults via the Vocational Educational Committees – through which structure adult education programmes are delivered. The knowledge that many immigrants are highly skilled university graduates, but lacking English-language skills drives this policy – but behind it is the fear of consecutive generations of immigrants concentrated in urban enclaves with poor English and limited opportunities. Such conditions would, most likely, lead to social tensions and unrest. The acquisition of language-skills is, therefore, paramount to social integration and equal opportunities, and the first step is to address the language needs of children, but this in itself is problematic, as Fitzgerald warns:

> If such children form too large a proportion of the number in a particular school this could cause problems. First of all this may make integration more difficult, for if the immigrant children form too large a proportion of the pupils, they may stick together, thus isolating themselves. Moreover too large a proportion of children with limited English in the same class may make it difficult for both Irish and immigrant children to make progress with their education.

Once again the educational system, and teachers in particular, are charged with implementing the government's cultural and linguistic agenda. Given the poor track-record of teaching additional languages in Ireland since the foundation of the Free State, and the current high level of functional illiteracy, the wisdom of this strategy is debatable. Should the integration project fail, and a third ethnic generation emerge in Ireland with poor English-language skills, who will shoulder the blame - English, its grammar, the policy of compulsion? There is no dispute that successful delivery of English-language communicative skills is essential for social integration and economic advancement. The acquisition of English by all Irish citizens has long been recognized and regularly endorsed by Irish-language organizations and advocates. In *Facts About Irish* (1970: 41) scholar, language activist and author Seán Ó Tuama wrote:

> No matter how well the Irish revival advances, everyone in Ireland should know English, since it is a world language. A special point should be made not alone of teaching all non-*Gaeltacht* people good colloquial Irish, but of teaching all *Gaeltacht* people good colloquial English.

Yet while most, if not all, are agreed on integration, there is little consensus as regards what immigrants are to be integrated into or the contribution they may offer. Irish identity(-ies) and its constituent parts are contested, debated and contentious. Other than supplying English-language teachers, there is little debate over what composes Irish identity or the parameters of Irish identities.

Nor is Ireland alone in this dilemma. Stuart Hall in *New Left Review* (1995) believes 'the issue of cultural identity as a political quest now constitutes one of the most serious problems as we go into the twenty-first century.' Linguists and cultural theorists recognize the existence of various forms of *english* practised across the globe. Post-colonialists distinguish between:

> The 'standard British' English inherited from the empire and the english which the language has become in post-colonial countries. Though British imperialism resulted in the spread of a language, English, across the globe, the english of Jamaicans is not the english of Canadians, Maoris, or Kenyans. We need to distinguish between what is proposed as a standard code, English (the language of the erstwhile imperial centre), and the linguistic code, english, which has been transformed and subverted into several distinct varieties throughout the world. (Ashcroft et al 1989: 8)

But there is little discussion as to what form of global *english* will be on offer in Ireland – RP (received pronunciation), Estuary, Hiberno-English, Dublinese, Dart-accent english, english with a Navan drawl, a Cork lilt or a Belfast twang? Government policy appears to be solely focused on the economy and has adopted a *laissez-faire* attitude toward culture and heritage. Cultural transmission has been outsourced to voluntary groups: GAA, Comhaltas Ceoltóirí Éireann, and others - if it is important to the people, the public will assume responsibility for it. The government may fund cultural and sporting organizations, but there ends their involvement. This economic driven attitude conceives of government as the successful management of the economy and dismisses the administration, cultivation and development of culture as tangential (Kirby 2006: 7-14). In this worldview Saint Patrick's Day is an opportunity to showcase Irish economic progress, not to embrace the Irish diaspora, celebrate culture and express religious beliefs. Consequently, Irish and Irish-language literature becomes less the bedrock of an Irish identity and more an issue of human rights safe-guarded by the constitution, the courts and more recently The Official Languages Act 2003. An Taoiseach, Bertie Ahern, in a speech to the National Economic and Social Council (2006), touched on integration of immigrants and declared:

> While it is no easy task to state clearly what it means to be Irish today, there are certain aspects of our community and Republic which, I believe, deserve respect and understanding from those who have come among us. That extends, clearly, to the rule of law and the institutions and practices of constitutional democracy. It includes the characteristic features of community life in Ireland, our traditions of mutual support and family solidarity. It includes our distinctive cultural traditions, including the unique place of the Irish language, Irish literature, music and folklore, and our religious and spiritual sense.

Additionally, proposed legislation, due to be published in early 2008, will require immigrants seeking Irish citizenship to demonstrate 'reasonable competence' when communicating in English or Irish in addition to being of 'good character' and pledging fidelity to the state (O'Brien and Mac Cormaic, 17 December 2007). This inclusion of Irish was derided in an *Irish Times* editorial (18 December 2007) which suggested that 'Perhaps, Minister, it would be appropriate to suggest that those aspiring citizens who opt to demonstrate their linguistic capacity only in Irish could be required to live in the Gaeltacht.'

Despite An Taoiseach's speech and inclusion of Irish as a characteristic tradition, recent Government statements and, more pointedly, policy and actions, suggest otherwise. In response to increased immigration there appears to be a redefining of Irish identity and an agenda to marginalize the Irish language under the guise of integration and anti-racism measures. Just as 'national security' became an unquestionable rationale underpinning any action in post 9/11 America, any questioning of anti-racism/pro-integration policies in Ireland risks castigation as racist. Whereas objections in the United States were labelled unpatriotic, in Ireland protestations are dismissed as cultural apartheid.

Despite the Irish government's 2006 *Statement on the Irish Language* and An Taoiseach's speech, Irish-language advocates are alarmed by the notion evident in certain pronouncements that the language may be jettisoned from Irish identity in order to achieve integration. Irish, it appears, has no role to play in the lithe and vacuous entity – Irish identity – as envisioned by certain commentators into which the new ethnic communities are to be integrated. Official contempt for Irish and Irish-speakers existed prior to the Celtic Tiger as detailed by Máirtín Ó Murchú in *Ag Dul ó Chion: Cás na Gaeilge 1952-2002* (2002), but the arrival of significant numbers of immigrants has allowed a manipulation of integration policies that further threaten Irish and cause anxiety as identified by *Lá Nua*'s editorial marking the opening of the 2007 *Oireachtas* Festival (*Lá Nua*, 01.11.2007). The combination of the fragility of Irish as a communal language, the perceived threat posed by rival languages and the manipulation of fear and uncertainty born from the emergence of competing language communities, all lead to new and increased concern among Irish-language activists and the population in general. This anxiety stems in no small part from the conscious efforts by groups opposed to the Irish language to avail of the changing configuration of Irish society to promote an anti-Irish agenda.

An Post's recent policy change is illustrative in this regard. When challenged why the Irish mail service had ceased to deliver letters in Dublin marked *Baile Átha Cliath*, An Post justified the abandonment of this long-established practice on the grounds of the number of immigrants employed in the sorting office and the inability of automated machines to deal with the Irish-language version of Dublin (Ó Liatháin 2007). Similarly, efforts to undermine teaching through Irish in An Daingean (Dingle) were initially framed as discrimination against Anastasia Lyamina, a Russian-born student, now living in the area. The need to ensure English-language literacy among the immigrant community has prompted an attack by the Department of Education and Science on highly successful language-immersion practices in *gaelscoileanna* (Irish-medium schools) despite these policies adhering to international best practice and producing high levels of literacy in English and Irish.

The Labour Party supported the recent removal of the Irish-language examination for barristers, claiming that 'it reflects the zealotry of a by-gone age, rather than the needs of an inclusive, pluralist Ireland and the needs of a modern and competitive legal system' (O'Brien, October 2007). Indeed the paradoxical position taken by commentators on the new language issue reveals the schizophrenic nature of linguistic debate in Ireland. Eilis O'Hanlon writing in *The Sunday Independent* (2007) calls for compulsory English: 'Being able to speak English, however, is a different matter. That is something on which there can be no compromise. ... there can never be true equality between those who speak the language of the country in which they live and those who do not.' There also lurks a suspicion that Irish may be sacrificed in the interest of integration, an aspect alluded to by Brenda Power in *The Sunday Times*:

> But what, precisely, are the elements of our national identity that need changing in order to allow immigrants to integrate more successfully? What outmoded and oppressive notions will we have to abandon to make sure that our country isn't pockmarked with no-go ghettos in a decade's time? Will, for example, the old-fashioned concept of teaching Irish language and history to children in Irish schools have to be abandoned so that the Poles don't feel left out?

From the perspective of Irish-language advocates, the crisis caused by an inability to facilitate immigrants' needs and entitlements is being manipulated to deconstruct the language revival project. The speed with which governmental offices, state bodies, the private sector and privately-owned newspapers embraced multilingualism and ran pages in various languages was noted with no little sense of scepticism by Irish-speakers given the reluctance and open hostility of the same organizations toward Irish in the past (Mac Síomóin 2006: 50).

The abandonment of the Irish-language entry requirement for trainee officers of An Garda Síochána in contrast to the controversy surrounding the refusal to permit a Sikh officer wear a turban as part of the regular uniform reveals the ease with which Irish may be jettisoned in the cause of integration. The requirement to hold a qualification in both Irish and English in the Leaving Certificate or equivalent was replaced by a prerequisite to hold a qualification in two languages, one of which must be Irish or English. Ironically the re-modified language requirement for entry into An Garda Síochána may prove a blueprint for the future as it not only embraces multilingualism but also allows for Irish-language instruction for trainee officers as the Minister for Justice explained: 'All Garda recruits will be required to achieve an appropriate standard in Irish before becoming full members of the Force, and basic training in Irish will be given to recruits who have no qualification in the language'

(McDowell 2005). The Minister for Social Integration, Conor Lenihan has subsequently called for a 'relaxation' of the Irish-language requirement for entry into the Civil Service similar to that enacted in the case of An Garda Síochána (O'Brien, August 2007) but noticeably without any bilingual provision.

Addressing the potential clash between existing affirmative-action policies for Irish-language promotion and the successful integration of new immigrants, columnist John Waters (2006) finds hope in two distinct developments: *iMeasc* and the gaelscoileanna movement. Addressing discrimination in Ireland, he states:

> Much media comment in recent years has centred on the idea that, in order to be 'welcoming' to immigrants, we must put aside elements of the surviving indigenous culture that may create 'discrimination' against outsiders. This is an utterly spurious idea, based not on openness towards outsiders but our hatred of ourselves.

According to Waters 'By its very existence, *iMeasc* confronts one of the central tenets of our ideology of modernity: that 'progress' ineluctably means the standing-down or dilution of native cultural values.' Formed by Alex Hijmans, Ariel Killick and Tony Pratschke, *iMeasc* combats the perception that immigrants are a threat to the Irish language and contests '... repeated attempts in the national media to use immigrants as a weapon against the Irish language, and on a lesser level, native Irish culture, ... [Ó Muirí 2005]. Founder Killick states '*Tá daoine in Éirinn a bhfuil ríméad ar fad orthu mar gheall ar inimirceoirí bheith tagtha chun na tíre seo mar breathnaíonn siad orainn mar dheis le fáil réidh leis an nGaeilge – ar mhaithe linn, mar dhea.*' (There are people in Ireland who are delighted that immigrants have come to this country as they consider us an opportunity to do away with the Irish language – for our benefit, as if!) According to *iMeasc*, immigrants should not be perceived as a threat to the indigenous culture and they work 'extremely hard in their diverse contributions to Irish-language life and culture in Ireland and deserve not to be dismissed as bizarre and slightly amusing, but on the whole irrelevant, aberrations, but taken seriously as a growing reality within modern Ireland' (Killick 2005).

Lobbying for state-funded Irish classes for immigrant children living in Gaeltacht areas or close to gaelscoileanna, *iMeasc* collates and distributes trilingual phrasebooks (Polish-Irish-English, etc) and also organizes activities such as belly-dancing, yoga and African drumming through the medium of Irish. *iMeasc* aims 'to encourage immigrants to learn Irish and to use Irish in order to interact with that part of Irish culture as a means for better integrating themselves, their children and their identity within society and as a means to integrate into Irish society in a healthy, peaceful, sustainable way in the long term' (Killick 2006). In a similar vein Marcin Ostasz, a Pole living in Ireland since 1998, argues in an interview with Caitríona Nic Giolla Bhríde (2006) that:

> learning Irish served as an important part of my naturalisation into Irish society despite many people not considering it part of their identity: it became obvious to me that Irish speakers in Ireland constitute a sort of cultural or social group and I started to aspire to understand them. One can learn so much about that culture in that way and also understand why Irish society is the way it is.

If Irish is to thrive in the newly configured cultural and linguistic landscape, iMeasc has the potential to offer a valuable contribution and to act as a counterbalance to those who seek to promote an anti-Irish agenda in the media and in civic discourse. Waters' second cause of optimism is the gaelscoileanna movement – the success story of the Irish-language movement, and the great hope for the future. Recently tarnished as a 'circling of ethnic wagons in a multicultural storm' by critics who attribute their recent enrolment boom to parents' desire to avoid contact with immigrant children. Louise Holden (2007) remonstrates that:

> The latest Central Statistics Office figures reveal that one in 10 people in Ireland is a non-national. Predictably, this ratio is not reflected in the *gaelscoileanna* yet. Out of almost 27,649 students in primary Irish-medium schools in the 26 counties, only 108 do not speak English as their first language. At post-primary level, there are 40 non-English speakers in a student body of 6,881.

The appeal and benefits of gaelscoileanna, however, were apparent long before the current crisis and advocates counter that these demographics are rapidly changing and their schools accept:

> All kids from all backgrounds. We absolutely reject the suggestion that we are exclusive. We have schools in Ballymun in Dublin, South Hill in Limerick and in every county in Ireland. Not one of our schools, at primary or secondary level, is fee-paying. We accept every child, regardless of his or her cultural or social background. It's mischievous to suggest that we are cherry-picking. (Holden 2007)

The 2006 census reveals that the number of Irish-speakers (1.66 million) increased by 90,000 since 2002, but declined slightly in percentage terms from 42.8% (2002) to 41.9% (2006). Over one million of those either never spoke the language or spoke it less than once a week. The number of people who speak Irish in the Gaeltacht also declined from 72.6% (2002) to 70.8% (2006). Suggestions in newspapers, however, that 99% of immigrants care little for the Irish language seem wide of the mark. Of the 412,511 non-Irish nationals recorded in the 2006 census, 35,646 (8.9%) reported themselves as Irish-speakers (see Volume 9, Table 40). Regardless of how pure their *blas* or the frequency with which they speak the language – daily, weekly, monthly – the fact that they bothered to reply, and to reply in the affirmative, speaks volumes. The number of Irish-speakers in the State when broken down by ethnicity reveals the following results: White Irish, 1,602,807 (46.6%); Irish Travellers, 2,872 (15%); Any Other White background, 21,964 (7.8%); Black or Black Irish African 4,755 (14%); Any Other Black background 614 (19.4%); Asian/Asian-Irish-Chinese, 1,376 (8.8%); Any other Asian background, 2,856 (8.7%); Other including mixed background 6,965 (16.4%); and Not Stated 7,043 (26.8%). The 2006 census returns regarding 'place of birth' in relation to Irish-language ability shows a surprising number of non-nationals, in particular Americans, Africans and Germans who claim ability to speak Irish.

Place of Birth	% who can speak Irish	Number
Ireland	46.8%	1,546,005
England and Wales	28.4%	57,086
Northern Ireland	23.9%	11,617
Scotland	21.0%	3,489
USA	38.3%	9,155
Other Countries	18.9%	4,215
Africa	12.5%	5,114
Germany	12.4%	1,427
Other European Countries	10.5%	2,768
France	8.3%	748
Asia	7.4%	3,926
Other EU	3.9%	5,432

The emergence of a minority multi-ethnic Irish-speaking cohort within Ireland can only have positive effects for Irish language culture and literature. Language is an ever changing phenomenon, as is quickly established by comparing the Irish of Séathrún Céitinn's devotional tracts to Pádraig Ua Duinnín's novel and plays, to Máirtín Ó Cadhain's short stories and novels to Cathal Ó Searcaigh's homo-erotic verse to the multi-level register heard on TG4's soap-opera *Ros na Rún*. Poet Gearóid Mac Lochlainn has mined the bilingual experience to rich effect in his recent works and the emergence of a trilingual Irish poet mixing Irish, English and Polish/Chinese/Nigerian will be an exciting and innovative moment in the life of the oldest vernacular literature in Europe. Irish-language writing has explored the idea of the 'other' in the past and engaged with issues of race and racism in work as diverse as Tarlach Ó hUid's *An Bealach Chun a' Bhearnais* (1949), a long-time stable feature of the Intermediate Certificate Examination; Micheál Ó Siochfhradha's exploration of racism and xenophobia in the short story 'Troid na mBó Maol' (1953); Máire Mhac an tSaoi's poem to her Ghanaian son 'Codladh an Ghaiscígh' (1973); and Alan Titley's novel of African politics and post-colonialism *Méirscrí na Treibhe* (1978); *Ros na Rún* has featured Séamus Ó Feithcheallaigh as a black Irish-speaking law student; Seán Óg Ó hAilpín, born in Fiji, has delivered an Irish-language address on the steps of the Hogan Stand having led Cork's hurlers to victory in the All-Ireland final. As Mícheál Ó Muircheartaigh put it 'his father's from Fermanagh, his mother's from Fiji, neither an Irish-language stronghold.'

Debates and controversies surrounding Irish in Ireland have traditionally been defined by a simple binary opposition of traditional/modern, antiquity/progress, Irish/English, loyalty/betrayal, native/foreign. The emergence, albeit sudden and dramatic, of significant numbers of alternative languages, and a marked increase in the number of bilingual and polylingual people, be they Irish-born or not, render the monolingual English-speaker the oddity and brings Ireland into line with the rest of the world where bilingualism is the norm. The response of Irish-language organizations to the challenges posed by the changing context in coming generations will be key. How will Irish be marketed to the new immigrants and their children? What new strategies will emerge to replace the binary opposites? Commentators in Ireland tend to bask in the non-emergence of a mainstream anti-immigrant lobby such as the National Front in England. Yet such bodies did not emerge in England until 1967 when recession threatened the economy. The impact that a severe economic recession in Ireland would exert on social relations would alter debate and presumptions dramatically. What is imperative in such an event is that no political group or organization be allowed to hijack the language movement and deploy it as a weapon to promote xenophobia or racial hatred.

Anna Heussaff, author of *Vortex* (2006) and *Bás Tobann* (2004), declares 'The future is full of possibilities of diversity and enrichment for all of us, but becoming multicultural isn't just about change in English-speaking Ireland. It's also about recent immigrants' attitudes and responses to Irish and about Irish speakers' reactions' (Heussaff 2004: 109). If nothing else, the demographic change and resultant multilingual society will render Irish-speakers less exotic, less disdained and less embarrassed of speaking in public. To return to Heussaff 'When I speak Irish to my young son on today's Dublin bus, I no longer feel I'm stared at, because these days we're surrounded by people speaking Latvian, Russian, French, Portuguese. Being different, in whatever way, is a more comfortable experience when lots of other people are different too' (Heussaff 2004: 112).

Irish as a communal language faces the same difficulties as it did prior to the rise in immigration, but is buoyed by the increase in prestige brought about by TG4 and the glamorization of Irish. The prophets of doom and gloom that view the new immigrants and their linguistic ability and richness as a threat predict dire consequences. Such warnings echo many of the sensationalist sentiments expressed in John A. O'Brien's volume *The Vanishing Irish* (1953) with declarations and rhetorical questions such as 'Ireland falling into decay, denuded of her youth, likely to fall in increasing measure into the hands of foreigners, gobbling up farm after farm?' And graphs demonstrating the 'World's Lowest Marriage rate and Highest Emigration Rate bring Ireland to Near Extinction' and 'The Tragic Decline in Number of Irish Children – A Catastrophe Unparalleled in Any Nation.' Similarly the demise of the Irish language has been long foretold. In the face of competition and reassessment of identity and cultural touchstones, Irish may undergo a revival of interest as people seek a specific cultural identity in response to globalization and mass consumer culture. The old arguments conceived during the 1880-1922 revival period are neither applicable nor practical. A new strategy is called for that sees Irish-language organizations working in tandem with other similarly minded groups, as suggested by Helen Ó Murchú in *Dúshlán agus Treo d'Eagraíochtaí na Gaeilge* (2003). Whether the future lies in a return to the revival spirit as espoused by Peadar Kirby in *Pobal, Féinmheas, Teanga: Todhchaí d'Éirinn* (2006) or a 'réabhlóid' as proposed by Tomás Mac Síomóin (2006), the new multicultural, multilingual Ireland offers an opportunity to reaffirm the centrality of Irish, Irish-language literature and culture to any reconfigured definition of Irish identity and to share, exchange and explore two thousand years of heritage with the most recent of many arrivals on the island.

THE GLOBALIZED IRISH-LANGUAGE DIASPORA

Globalization emerges from and creates a world that is increasingly interconnected economically, culturally and politically. According to Roland Roberston (1992) globalization 'refers both to the compression of the world and the intensification of consciousness of the world as a whole' (Guinness 2003: 2). Irish is not immune to globalization. The twin paradoxical effects of globalization: homogenization of consumer patterns and population behaviour across the globe, and a demand for local 'authentic' products and experience, which create culturally-specific opportunities impact Irish in diverse ways. Shell's bullying of a Gaeltacht community in Mayo illustrates its negative potential while Toyota and Coca-Cola's sponsorship of Irish-language endeavours, and increased employment for handcraft industries in Gaeltacht communities, exemplifies its positive potential. Often considered as threatening cultural and linguistic diversity, globalization nevertheless may benefit not only local communities in developing nations but also less commonly taught languages.

Globalization's benefit is keenly felt in the greater access to language and language resources for the Irish-language diaspora. Advances in technology, associated with globalization, shrink the world and make TG4 archives, Raidió na Gaeltachta, RTÉ, Raidió na Life, and BLAS (BBC, Northern Ireland) and print media such as *Lá Nua*, Tuarascáil (*The Irish Times*), *Comhar, Feasta,* and *Beo,* available to the international Irish-language community and language learners regardless of their location or time zone. Websites such as Cló Mhaigh Eo, Cois Life and Cló Iar-Chonnacht keep readers abreast of the latest publications and allow for instant purchase. www.gaelport.com keeps those with internet access current with Irish-related issues in mainstream print media. Irish-language blogs have become a key component in this global conversation that remains obscured from mainstream commentators. Such blogs include:

hilaryny.blogspot.com

gaeilgepanu.blogs.ie

miseaine.blogs.ie

www.cainteoir.com

dorasoscailte.blogspot.com

imeall.blogspot.com

chetwyndedowns.blogspot.com

caomhach.blogspot.com

aonghus.blogspot.com

gaeilgefaoithalamh.blogs.ie

The convergence of technologies has unquestionably been English-language orientated and further underscores American-English as the premier global language of trade, commerce, finance and profit. It has, nevertheless, transformed the experience of Irish-speakers abroad. To consider Irish-speakers in any particular nation-state in isolation at the beginning of the twenty-first century is to ignore the transnational, transcultural, global reality of modern Irish. The global communication revolution allows Irish-speakers to participate in the virtual hyper-Gaeltacht any where, any time which results in Irish being available, spoken, read and written twenty-four seven, worldwide. Regardless of the time zone, someone somewhere is downloading, updating, pod-casting in Irish. The Irish-language communication network, rather than a local organic community, is now a global phenomenon which is no longer restricted to Irish-based and Irish-born. The following is a brief overview of traditional Irish-language networks in the United States, Canada, Australia and England.

The United States of America

When precisely Irish was first spoken in America is unknown. Discounting Saint Brendan who, manuscripts allege, first 'discovered'

America, Irish, presumably, was initially spoken in the 'new world' by early settlers. The execution of Anne Glover as a suspected witch in South Boston in 1688 is, however, well documented and provides an early recorded instance of Irish in the colonies. The Famine undoubtedly brought large numbers of Irish-speakers to America. Historian Kevin Kenny indicates that 'it is estimated that between one-quarter and one-third of American-bound emigrants (from Ireland) during the famine were Irish-speakers. Half of all the famine emigrants came from the two provinces of Connacht and Munster, where at least half the population still spoke Irish as late as 1851' (Kenny 2000: 99), and post-famine emigration 'made the language more common in many Irish-American neighbourhoods than it had been earlier in the nineteenth century, often provoking cultural conflict between the newcomers and the established community (Kenny 2000: 138). Kenneth Nilsen (1990, 1996, 1997) has published significant articles detailing the existence and survival of Irish-language communities and networks in New York and Portland. Stiofán Ó hAnnracháin's *Go Meiriceá Siar: Na Gaeil agus Meiriceá* (1979) is an indispensable collection of essays on Irish-speakers and their literary production in the United States and essential reading for anyone concerned with Irish-America or the Irish diaspora. Similarly Thomas Ihde's *The Irish Language in the United States: An Historical, Sociolinguistic and Applied Linguistic Survey (1994)* is requisite reading, as is Nancy Stenson's seminal essay 'Speaking Irish in America: language and identity' (2001).

Irish is currently offered at the Centre for Celtic Studies at the University of Wisconsin, Milwaukee; New York University; Lehman College at the City University of New York who also offer language courses on-line; University of Minnesota; Harvard University; Boston College; University of Notre Dame; University of California, Berkeley; New College, California; University of Saint Thomas; University of California, Fordham University; University of Montana; and University of Pennsylvania. The growth in community and out-reach programmes based in universities such as Yale, support Ihde's claim that 'the greatest expansion in Irish-language teaching seems to be taking place in continuing education programmes at two-year colleges' (Ihde 1996: 186). The establishment of the O'Donnell Endowed Chair in Irish Language and Literature, currently occupied by Breandán Ó

Buachalla, and the foundation of the first department of Irish language and literature at the University of Notre Dame is an important landmark for Irish in the United States. In her study of foreign language enrolment in United States institutes in higher education in 2002, E.B. Welles calculates that Irish was taught at thirteen institutes with an enrolment of 705 students (Welles 2004: 7-26). This is an increase from the 326 studying in 1998, 133 in 1995 and 121 in 1990. If anecdotal evidence conveys any elements of truth then the next survey due to be collected in 2007 and published in 2008 will reveal a surge in the number of registrations in Irish courses. While these numbers may appear low, Irish, nevertheless, outperforms many including: Turkish, Croatian, Bulgarian, Czech, Dutch, Finnish and Slovakian in terms of student enrolment in institutes of higher learning in the United States.

Daltaí na Gaeilge, founded by Ethel Brogan in 1981, is the leading Irish voluntary organization in the United States. Boasting classes in every state, *Daltaí na Gaeilge* organizes weekend immersion courses several times throughout the year, principally Jamison, PA; Esopus, New York; and Long Beach, New Jersey. The website www.daltai.com acts not only as an information site for teachers and students throughout the United States and Canada, but serves as an active chat-room in English and Irish where members exchange opinions on the language, its grammar, and current events. Launched in 1996, *An Doras* www.gael-image.com/doras is an on-line journal offering an American perspective on Irish-language culture and politics. American Irish-speakers are also well served by New York-based Hilary Mhic Shuibhne's blog which received the 2007 *Irish Blog Award* for use of the Irish language. Seamus Blake's successful Irish-language radio programme, *Míle Fáilte* broadcast on WFUV, Fordham University in the Bronx, NY, began as a ten-minute slot in 1989, now airs weekly on Saturday mornings from 8:00-9:00 a.m. New York, given its confluence of universities and substantial Irish community is arguably the most active American city in Irish-language terms. *The Irish Echo* publishes a weekly Irish-language column, written by Elaine Ní Bhraonáin, entitled 'An Tíogar Ceilteach' detailing a single woman's social adventures in Manhattan. *Páistí na Gaeilge* www.paistilegaeilge.com provides Irish-language classes for children and is popular with parents intent on returning to Ireland. A monthly newsletter, published by

Páistí na Gaeilge provides advice on raising children bilingually and interviews with Irish-speakers raised through the medium of Irish.

The 2006 U.S. census recorded 25,870 Irish-language speakers residing in the country. Of these 4,775 (18.45%) resided in New York state with other substantial numbers located in Massachusetts, 3,275 (12.65%) and California, 3,123 (12.07%). Illinois boasts 1,849 Irish-speakers (7.14%), while there are also more than one thousand Irish-speakers in Pennsylvania, (1,354) (5.23%) and Florida, (1,315) (5.08%). South Dakota and Idaho have the lowest number of Irish-speakers with a mere 15 (0.05%) and 20 respectively (0.07%).

A difficulty and common complaint among language-learning networks across the globe is the challenge of locating and retaining suitable and qualified language instructors. In this regard two recent developments are of particular importance – the Foreign Language Teaching Assistants Program administered by the Fulbright Commission and *Ciste na Gaeilge* funded by the Department of Community, Rural and Gaeltacht Affairs. The Fulbright programme selects young Irish graduates and places them in colleges and universities in the United States for an academic year where they teach Irish-language classes, organize language clubs and enhance the Irish-language opportunities for students. While the Fulbright programme focuses on the United States, *Ciste na Gaeilge* subvents Irish-language instruction worldwide and has benefited several universities and groups in the United States in hiring language instructors and providing languages courses.

Canada
Brought to Canada by Irish immigrants, the Irish language survived as a community-based language in *Talamh an Éisc* / Newfoundland until the mid-twentieth century. It has now all but died out and Irish in Canada is currently maintained by immigrants and learners. Irish is offered in several universities including: Saint Francis Xavier University, Antigonish, Nova Scotia; Saint Mary's University, Halifax; Concordia University, Montreal; Saint Michael's College, University of Toronto and the University of Ottawa. In the voluntary sector there are active language classes in Ottawa, Montréal, Toronto and Kingston. Similar to the United States, activities take the form of weekly classes and bi-annual immersion weekends. Ottawa boasts a weekly language class that produces plays and organizes an annual immersion weekend.

In addition this group edited a volume of memoirs and short prose texts in Irish in 2005 entitled *Nuair a bhí mé óg: Stories from the Coffey Circle*.

The most exciting development in Canada is the new Gaeltacht project near Kingston in South-East Ontario, on the US border and approximately 250km northeast of Toronto. Under the guidance of Cumann na Gaeltachta, founded in 1995, and driven by Aralt Mac Giolla Chainnigh the site was officially opened on 14 June 2007. Purchased at a cost of $60,000 they intend to develop this sixty-acre site as a permanent base for various Irish cultural and language groups in Canada. When complete the site will house a cultural centre for Irish language and culture, accommodation for one hundred people, a playing field and an outdoor amphitheatre, as well as providing a permanent base and lasting legacy.

Australia
Little is known of the introduction of Irish to Australia or New Zealand other than to presume that early convicts brought the language when the first fleets sailed into Botany Bay in 1788. Little evidence other than anecdotal is available on Irish in Australia, but such evidence indicates it existed, was spoken and considered a secret language to be feared and distrusted by authorities. Australia offers an alternative perspective to America where Irish is not strongly represented in universities despite the presence of a widespread interest in Irish Studies. Consequently enthusiasts are endeavouring that Irish become an official subject in the Victorian secondary school curriculum as has happened at Kilbreda Catholic Secondary College in Mentone.

Despite the activities of the Albert Dryer Branch of Conradh na Gaeilge in Sydney in the 1920s, Catholicism, rather than language, served as the primary ethnic marker for Irish-Australians. Interest in language and language-based culture peaked in the 1980s when a government policy of multiculturalism led Irish-Australians to seek distinctive ethnic markers. The 2001 Australian census showed 826 respondents claiming Irish-language ability, an increase of 5.9 per cent on the 782 recorded for 1996. Most of the Irish-speakers are concentrated in Melbourne and Sydney, but classes are available in Victoria, South Australia, New South Wales, Queensland and Canberra. *Daonscoil*

Victoria, first convened as a summer school in 1995, now meets several times a year and there is also a *Scoil Gheimhridh* (Winter School) in Sydney since 2002 which combines classes in Irish and Scots-Gaelic. A fortnightly Irish-language programme on SBS – Special Broadcast Service – broadcast from Melbourne featuring Irish-speakers as guest hosts began in the 1980s and included: Louis de Paor, Mossie Scanlon, Eileen and Vincent Loughnane, David Lucy, Áine Szymanski, Eamonn Naughton, Colin Ryan, Jean Tongs, Ted Ryan, Cathal Keating, Vincent O'Gorman and Nora Finucane as presenters. This programme has since regrettably lapsed. The vacuum left by the programme's demise has in some part been filled by an electronic newsletter *An Lúibín* edited and written by Colin G. Ryan and distributed in, and beyond, Australia.

As in many other diasporic communities, Irish-speakers are scattered and fragmented throughout the landmass and classes are difficult to organize and coordinate. The Irish Language Association of Australia, formed in 1992 to promote the Irish language, coordinates classes and activities through its website and newsletters. The decline in recent years of Irish immigrants to Australia limits the number of teachers available to those wishing to (re)learn Irish. As in the United States and Canada, the role of Oideas Gael in supplying guest lecturers and specialist teachers for yearly gatherings and immersion courses is essential. It provides an invaluable focus for students and links the diaspora to contemporary Irish-language based culture and encourages foreign-based language enthusiasts to visit Ireland, the Gaeltacht and participate in language/heritage courses in the Irish-speaking areas in particular.

England
Both England and Ireland, and English and Irish share a long mutual history of interaction and fascination. Yet, for all we know of the history of English in Ireland, we know remarkably little about the history of Irish in England. Irish-speakers have migrated to the neighbouring island since the beginning of time and English ports were often the first stop for Irish-speaking famine victims. In the post-famine era the areas of St. Stephen and Vauxhall in North Liverpool appear to have been Irish-speaking enclaves; Cardinal Manning reports that Irish was not uncommon in London and Irish-speaking priests were required in Bradford and York (Nic Craith 1997: 174-7).

The Guardian newspaper reports that language teaching in general is in decline in British universities '... languages are becoming an elite subject, studied by middle-class students and offered by only the top universities' (Bawden 2007). While Irish – Old or Modern – is offered at several universities including: Aberdeen, Aberystwyth, Edinburgh, Glasgow and Liverpool, this is hardly reflective of the size of the Irish population in Britain. Given the precipitous decline in language departments and courses in British universities in the past ten years, the 2007 announcement of a new Irish-language course at Cambridge University is both noteworthy and symbolic. Funded by the Department of Community, Rural and Gaeltacht Affairs, Cambridge University now offers Irish classes at beginner, intermediate and advanced levels as well as informal Irish conversation sessions for enthusiasts and claims to be the only English university to teach both modern and medieval Irish.

Similar to other countries, estimates regarding the number of Irish-speakers and instructors vary widely and are unreliable, but Leyland suggests approximately thirty Irish-language teachers in Britain as a 'reasonable estimate' (Leyland 1996: 150). Nic Craith (1997: 171) further contends:

> Though Irish migrants are principally concentrated in London and the West Midlands, Irish-speaking communities can be found throughout the three countries of Scotland, England and Wales. While many of these groups emerged as a consequence of the migration of Irish-speakers from Ireland, others have been formed by language enthusiasts of Irish descent.

England boasts numerous Irish-language classes most of which are an 'ad hoc, uncoordinated network of evening classes' (Leyland 1996: 148). Conradh na Gaeilge which was active in England from its foundation in 1893, now has branches in Liverpool, Manchester, Wolverhampton, Coventry, Birmingham, Worcester, London and Ipswich (Nic Craith 1997: 179). Coláiste na nGael acts as an umbrella organization, co-ordinating classes and promoting the study of Ireland's history, politics and culture via its website www.irishlanguagebritain.com and biannual publication *Iris na Gaeilge*. Providing information and articles in English and Irish, the publication informs members about classes and events in various locations including: Camden Town, Chelmsford, Shropshire, Derbyshire, Litchfield, Milton Keynes, Coventry, Leighon-Sea, St. Albans, Guernsey, Winchester, Durham, Twickenham, Cromford and Basingstoke. In addition there is an annual Irish-language film festival in the Tricycle Cinema in Kilburn, London.

While the experience of Irish in Britain mirrors many of the difficulties experienced by Irish-language practitioners in other countries – lack of teachers, inadequate resources, dispersed community, lack of appropriate materials (Leyland 1996: 160-4) – it also suffers particular disadvantages. Learners and speakers of Irish encounter difficulties in Britain due to the perceived links between the language, the nationalist movement and the IRA's former bombing campaign in English cities. Gribben also documents the reluctance of Irish-speakers to use their language publicly in England in the 1960s and 1970s (Gribben 1995: 9). Irish has no official status within the United Kingdom and recent efforts to pass a Language Act in the North of Ireland met with vitriolic reaction from Unionists (Moriarty 2007). Nevertheless Nic Craith concludes that: 'Irish-language learners appear to come from a diverse range of socio-economic and socio-cultural backgrounds … there is demonstrable demand in the North-West of England for Irish-language classes and more support for people who have already learned some Irish and wish to progress' (Nic Craith 1997: 184).

CONCLUSION

Attention to Irish and Irish-language culture is popular and continues to grow abroad. Such interest, it appears, stems from three diverse groups: Irish emigrants seeking to relearn and recover the Irish they once learned in school; second-, third-, fourth-generation Irish interested in exploring their ancestral heritage and culture; and individuals with no ancestral ties to Ireland but attracted by the language or prompted by academic interests. One thesis proposed in the United States to account for the popularity of Irish-language courses is Hansen's third-generation theory (Bender & Kagiwada 1968: 360). First propounded in 1938, this thesis in summary argues that what the immigrant's son wishes to forget, the immigrant's grandson wishes to remember. As second-generation immigrants endeavour to integrate into the host community, they abandon any and all cultural indicators that mark them as 'other'. Conversely, the third generation, now secure in their identity and sense of belonging in the host community, seek to embrace the culture of the original immigrants which the second generation renounced.

Alternatively, Leyland in considering the North-West of England suggests that 'Irish learners in Britain, whilst differentially motivated, are self-consciously seeking to collectively assert both linguistic and cultural diversity' (Leyland 1996: 168), and argues that 'learning Irish in Britain can be regarded as a tangible expression of ethnic identity and culture ... and it can be suggested that this experience is accompanied by feelings such as a greater sense of belonging to, or being part of a geographical/national territory and/or solidarity with a culturally distinct social/ethnic grouping' (Leyland 1996: 171). Whether as a response to a homogenized global culture, a search for an ethnic identity, an embrace of ancestral heritage or as an academic exercise, interest in Irish continues to be an international phenomenon. For a multiplicity of reasons there exists, dispersed and scattered throughout the world, a not insignificant number of people with a keen interest in the Irish language who volunteer time, effort and energy to the language as learners, teachers and facilitators. Among the many challenges facing Irish at the beginning of the twenty-first century is the task of organizing and utilizing this resource for the benefit of the language and delivering the materials and information they require to further promote their obvious interest in Irish and to channel it into effective meaningful action.

REFERENCES

(NOTE: Works of creative literature cited above with dates are not included.)

Ahern, B. 2006. Speech by the Taoiseach at the launch of the NESC Report, *Migration policy* and the IOM Report, *Managing migration in Ireland*. 22 September.

Ashcroft, B., G. Griffiths & H. Tiffin (eds). 1989. *The Empire Writes Back*. London. Routledge.

Bawden, A. 2007. 'Chattering Classes' in *The Guardian*, (Education). 13 March.

Bender, E. & G. Kagiwada. 1968. 'Hansen's Law of "Third-Generation Return" and the study of American religio-ethnic groups', *Phylon* 29(4): 360-70.

Clarke, D. 2003. 'An embarrassment of riches' in *The Irish Times*. 16 July.

Central Statistics Office. 2007. *Census 2006 Volume 9, Irish Language*. Dublin. Stationery Office.

de Fréine, S. 1969. *The great silence*. Cork. Mercier.

Fitzgerald, G. 2007. 'Census belies inflated view of immigrant level' in *The Irish Times*. 7 April.

Gribben, P. 1995. 'Delighted at pioneering language scheme' in *The Irish Post*. 22

July.

Guinness, P. 2003. *Globalisation*. London. Hodder & Stoughton.

Hall, S. 1995. 'Negotiating Caribbean identities' in *New Left Review* 209: 3-14.

Heussaff, A. 2004. 'The Irish for multicultural' in Mac Murchaidh, C. (ed), *Who needs Irish?: Reflections on the importance of the Irish language today*. Dublin. Veritas.

Holden, L. 2007. 'The rise of the gaelscoil – is this the new playground of the elite?' in *The Irish Times*. 17 April.

Ihde, T. 1996. 'A hundred years: Irish language courses in American colleges' in *Éire-Ireland* 30(4).

Ihde, T. 1994. *The Irish language in the United States: An historical, sociolinguistic and applied linguistic survey*. Westport, CT. Bergin & Garvey.

Kenny, K. 2000. *The American Irish: A history*. Harlow. Pearson Education.

Killick, A. 2005. 'The Official Languages Act' in *The Irish Times*. 24 June.

Killick, A. 2006. 'Immigrants and the Irish language – 2005 and onwards' in Ó Murchú, H. (ed), *Reflections: Irish language communities in action*. Baile Átha Cliath. Glór na nGael.

Kirby, P. 2006. *Pobal, féinmheas, teanga: todhchaí d'Éirinn*. Baile Átha Cliath. Coiscéim.

Lentin, R. & R. McVeigh. 2006, *After optimism?: Ireland, racism and globalisation*. Dublin. Metro Éireann Publications.

Leyland, J. 1996. 'Irish language learners in North-West England' in Nic Craith, M. (ed), *Watching one's tongue: Issues in language planning*. Liverpool. Liverpool UP.

Mac Cormaic, R. 2007. 'Signs of new vitality in how film and drama treat immigrants' in *The Irish Times*. 23 May.

Mac Síomóin, T. 2006. *Ó Mhársa go Magla: Straitéis nua don Ghaeilge*. Baile Átha Cliath. Coiscéim.

McDowell, M. 2005. Address by Michael McDowell, T.D., Minister for Justice, Equality and Law Reform, to an information seminar for ethnic communities on Garda recruitment. National Consultative Council on Racial and Interculturalism (NCCRI). 6 October.

McKeon, B. 2005. 'Of Joyce, Auden and mother' in *The Irish Times*. 9 July.

Moriarty, G. 2007. 'Irish language debate turns heated' in *The Irish Times*. 10 October.

Nic Craith, M. & J. Leyland. 1997. 'The Irish language in Britain: A case study of North West England' in *Language, culture and curriculum* 30(3): 171-185.

Myers, K. 2007. 'The problem isn't racism, it's the tidal wave of immigrants' in *The Irish Independent*. 5 September.

Nic Giolla Bhríde, C. 2006. 'Gaeilge goes global' in *The Irish Times*. 5 July.

Nilsen, K.E. 1996. 'The Irish language in New York, 1850-1900' in Bayor, R.H. & T.J. Meagher (eds), *The New York Irish*. Baltimore. Johns Hopkins UP.

Nilsen, K.E. 1997. 'The Irish language in nineteenth century New York City' in García, O. & J.A. Fishman (eds), *The multilingual apple: Languages in New York City*. New York. Mouton de Gruyter.

Nilsen, K.E. 1990. 'Thinking of Monday: Irish speakers of Portland, Maine' in *Éire-Ireland: A Journal of Irish Studies* 25(1): 6-19.

Ó hAnnracháin, S. (ed). 1979. *Go Meiriceá siar: Na Gaeil agus Meiriceá*. Baile Átha Cliath. An Clóchomhar.

O'Brien, J.A. 1953. *The vanishing Irish*. New York. McGraw-Hill.

O'Brien, C. August 2007. 'Call to increase foreign nationals in Civil Service' in *The Irish Times*. 13 August.

O'Brien, C. October 2007. 'Irish exam for lawyers opposed' in *The Irish Times*. 22 October.

O'Brien, C. & R. Mac Cormaic. 2007. 'Citizenship to involve language test' in *The Irish Times*. 17 December.

O'Hanlon, E. 2007. 'Linguistic double standards do exist in immigrant integration' in *The Sunday Independent*. 26 August.

Ó Liatháin, C. 2007. 'Díothú "Baile Átha Cliath" ag An Post'. in *Lá Nua*. 10 May.

Ó Muirí, P. 2005. 'Rachaidh mé síos *iMeasc* na ndaoine ...' in *The Irish Times*. 6 July.

Ó Murchú, H. 2003. *Dúshlán agus treo d'eagraíochtaí na Gaeilge*. Baile Átha Cliath. Coiscéim.

Ó Murchú, M. 2002. *Ag dul ó chion: Cás na Gaeilge 1952-2002*. Baile Átha Cliath. Coiscéim.

Ó Tuama, S. 1970. *Facts about Irish*. Corcaigh. An Comhar Poiblí.

Power, Brenda. 2006. "Immigrants need to adapt, not us' in *The Sunday Times* [Irish edition]. 1 October.

Roberston, R. 1992. *Globalisation*. London. Sage.

Rialtas na hÉireann. 2006. *Ráiteas i leith na Gaeilge / Statement on the Irish Language*.

Waters, J. 2006. 'New Irish may save language' in *The Irish Times*. 26 June.

Welles, E.B. 2004. 'Foreign language enrolments in United States institutes of higher education, Fall 2002' in *The association of departments of foreign languages bulletin* 35(1-2): 7-26.

Irish and the Legislative Perspective

Pádraig Ó Laighin

Legislative protection for the Irish language has never been stronger. Constitutional provisions and a language law are in place, and Irish is an official and a working language of the institutions of the European Union, with all of the dynamic changes that that entails. The language is supported by a government department, the Department of Community, Rural, and Gaeltacht Affairs; the Gaeltacht has its own regional development authority, Údarás na Gaeltachta; and a cross-border agency, Foras na Gaeilge, has responsibility for the promotion of Irish throughout the island. The government of Ireland has committed itself to the development of a twenty-year strategy whose aim is to promote bilingualism in Irish and English. There is movement towards legislative protection for Irish in Northern Ireland. The main institutions of society are having to acknowledge the fact that there are two significant language communities in Ireland, with much overlap between them.

While the overall view can readily be defined in positive terms, the pursuit of language rights and the implementation of language policies are problematic concerns in many countries, and Ireland is no exception. Language legislation only arises where two or more languages come into contact, and constructing the rules to govern that contact brings diverse ideological and economic interests into play. The intention here is to look at the legislative measures which are in force in relation to Irish.

THE CONSTITUTIONS OF 1922 AND 1937

In keeping with the position of the elected representatives who established an Irish parliament in Dublin in 1919, and of those who fought for political independence, Article 4 of the Constitution of the Irish Free State in 1922 declared Irish to be the national language, with English being 'equally recognised as an official language'. Making Irish the national language, encompassing a resolve to use that language for official and administrative purposes and to counteract the effects of colonization on its status, was a deliberate act of nation-building. The same Article permitted Parliament to make special provisions 'for districts or areas in which only one language is in general use'. This was generally taken to refer to the use of Irish in Gaeltacht areas, or to English in parts of the six north-eastern counties following the possible re-integration of the national territory. Other articles ensured that the Irish and English texts of Acts were to be published simultaneously, and to be equally authoritative.

The *Constitution of Saorstát Éireann* was replaced by *Bunreacht na hÉireann (Constitution of Ireland)* in 1937. Article 8 of the new Constitution declares Irish, as the national language, to be the first official language; English is 'recognised as a second official language'. Section 3 of the Article permits provision to be made by law for the exclusive use of Irish or English for official purposes 'either throughout the state or in any part thereof'. The status of Irish as the national language had been strengthened, and the status of English reduced. The wording of the third section had been altered to permit special provisions to be applied throughout the state or in any part of it, rather than in specifically unilingual areas. The text of the Constitution is in both official languages, and in case of conflict between the two versions, the national language prevails. In a modification of the earlier position, the 1937 Constitution holds the signed texts of Acts to be conclusive evidence of the provisions of the law.

The language articles in both constitutions were expressed as declarations rather than as rights per se. In the absence of explicit constitutional rights or legislative provisions, individuals attempted to establish their linguistic entitlements through the courts. The overall trend in judgements has been towards a greater acknowledgement of the linguistic rights of Irish-speakers, a broadening of the constitutional bases of linguistic rights to include equality issues, and a greater clarification of and insistence on the duties of the state to protect and vindicate those rights. By and large, the principles which arose from these proceedings have been transposed into secondary language legislation, which will be discussed later.

In a case decided in 1963, the Supreme Court held that Article 8.3 of the Constitution meant that either of the official languages could be used for official purposes unless provision had been made by law requiring that a specific language be used (*Attorney General v Coyne and Wallace*, 101 ILTR 17, 1967). This judgement was tantamount to giving the state the right to choose which language it would use in official transactions. A serious decline in the provision of services through Irish followed, and in 1979 the state ceased, for the first time since 1922, the practice of publishing Acts of the legislature in Irish and English simultaneously. Though the courts affirmed from time to time the right of citizens to obtain specific documents in Irish, they consistently failed to formulate a general principle of state duty in this regard. A Supreme Court decision in 2001, qualified – at least – the earlier interpretation, and remedied to some extent the deficits in interpreting the scope of the constitutional provisions (*Ó Beoláin v Breitheamh na Cúirte Dúiche Mary Fahy agus Eile*, [2001] 2 IR 279). The Court directed the state to publish all Acts of the Oireachtas in Irish, and an official translation of the *District Court Rules 1997*, without delay. The majority judgements held that the delay of over twenty years in publishing Irish translations of laws enacted in English was neither justifiable nor reasonable. They excoriated the state for what they considered to be a blatant disregard of mandatory requirements over an extended period, and broadened their criticisms to include the general failure to provide Irish versions of all necessary forms and documents. The Supreme Court was asserting that, in practical terms, the state, which is expressly committed to bilingualism, is required to facilitate the use of either language for official purposes, without discrimination against Irish-speakers.

THE OFFICIAL LANGUAGES ACT 2003

Secondary language legislation may be viewed as falling into two main types. The first type is legislation designed to ensure the delivery of official services in one or more official languages, creating duties for the state, and the corollary of rights, more frequently implied than described as such, for the citizen. The second type is legislation which is primarily rights based, and which is usually more comprehensive in scope and applicability. The Canadian *Official Languages Act*, the *Welsh Language Act 1993*, and the Irish *Official Languages Act 2003*, belong to the first type, duty based, and Québec's language legislation, *Charte de la langue française*, to the second. While a greater emphasis on rights might be expected in a country with a written constitution,

Irish governments at the beginning of the twenty-first century showed a political preference for duty-based legislation, especially in areas of social and economic policy. Value differences concerning the provision of services were seen to be more properly a matter for resolution through political process than a question of rights to be arbitrated by the courts.

The substantive provisions of the *Official Languages Act 2003* deal with the Oireachtas and the courts, public bodies, the establishment of an office of Coimisinéir (commissioner) of the official languages, and place-names. The Act – in providing for the exclusive use of English for official purposes under certain conditions, and in requiring public bodies to meet particular Irish-language requirements in Gaeltacht areas – is a law of the type envisaged by Article 8.3 of the Constitution. However, other provisions of the Act ensure that the constitutional imperative which requires the state to establish and maintain Irish as the national language is not diminished as a result in the long run.

The primary objective of the Act is to ensure the better availability of public services through the medium of Irish, and the intention is to achieve this primarily through a statutory planning framework involving 'schemes' – renewable three-year plans prepared upon request by public bodies, and approved by the Minister. Public bodies for the purposes of the Act are those categorized or listed in a Schedule, and they include government departments and offices, local governments, and various state agencies, boards, and companies, including, for example, universities and radio and television stations. About 650 public bodies come under the aegis of the legislation, the actual number being subject to change from time to time by regulation.

The schemes framework is cumbersome, given the number of public bodies involved, and the fact that each scheme is unique. By the beginning of October 2007, schemes covering over a hundred public bodies had commenced. To date, few of these bodies, with the exception of the Department centrally concerned and the office of the Coimisinéir, have taken anything resembling a proactive approach in informing the public about the availability of services through Irish. The schemes create legal duties for public bodies, but not individual or collective rights to service through the medium of Irish. There is no provision in the Act to permit citizens to take action in the courts if services promised in the schemes are not provided.

Besides the schemes, there are two critical measures in the Act which require public bodies to use Irish officially. The legislation establishes the unrestricted right of persons who communicate with public bodies in writing or by electronic mail in an official language to receive a reply in the same language. Furthermore, public bodies furnishing information to the general public or to particular groupings are required to do so in Irish or bilingually. These duties are in effect in the case of all public bodies, and are unrelated to whether or not schemes are in place. A third critical measure enables the Minister to make regulations which impose duties on public bodies in relation to the use of the official languages in oral announcements, stationery, signage, and advertisements. Equalizing the status of the official languages in these contexts, or giving pre-eminence to Irish, would undoubtedly benefit the Irish-language community. Signage is especially important in the creation of a linguistic landscape which would be conducive to the use and promotion of Irish. No regulations have yet been made under this section, although draft regulations were published in 2006.

The legislation provides that members of the Oireachtas are entitled to use either of the official languages in parliamentary proceedings, and the right is also extended to all persons appearing in similar circumstances. These sections are significant in that they are the only ones in the Act in which rights being conferred are explicitly identified as such. A further section which states that one of the functions of the Coimisinéir shall be to provide assistance to the public 'regarding their rights under this Act,' does imply that other provisions can also be interpreted as creating rights. Reports of legislative debates and proceedings are to be published in each of the official languages, except that individual contributions are to be given in the language in which they were delivered. In line with the Supreme Court decision on the matter, the simultaneous publication of Acts in both languages is required.

Persons may use either of the official languages in pleading or court documents, without being placed at a disadvantage because of their choice of language. Courts are required to provide facilities for interpretation of proceedings if necessary. Significantly, the state is required to use the language chosen by the other party in civil proceedings, though no individual can be compelled to give evidence in a particular official language.

What is conspicuously absent from the provisions on the administration of justice is any attempt to require that judges appointed to Gaeltacht areas be competent to hear cases in Irish without the assistance of an interpreter. It is also significant that the legislation is silent on the state's obligations in relation to choice of language in criminal proceedings. Allowing for Irish in a system which traces its roots to British courts has not been easy, even if the trend is favourable. The 1737 *Act that all Proceedings in Courts of justice within this Kingdom shall be in the English Language* proscribed the use of all languages other than English in Irish courts: this Act was repealed by the Oireachtas in 1962.

The Act provides for the appointment of a Commissioner of official languages, to be known as An Coimisinéir Teanga, whose functions are to ensure the implementation of the legislation by public bodies, to investigate complaints in that regard, to provide advice to public bodies regarding their obligations, and to citizens regarding their rights, and also to investigate complaints of non-compliance in relation to the language provisions of any other law. The ultimate sanction available to the Coimisinéir is to report adverse findings concerning a public body to each House of the Oireachtas. When such a report has been made to the Oireachtas, the Minister may arrange for compensation for those adversely affected. An Coimisinéir Teanga, appointed in 2004, has furnished three annual reports to date which detail the impressive work of the office in fulfilling its mandate. The third report shows that the office dealt with 611 new cases during the year 2006.

The final part of the Act makes provision for official place-names in Gaeltacht areas to be in Irish only, and to give equal legal status to the Irish and English versions in other parts of the country.

OTHER LEGISLATIVE MEASURES
While language legislation per se is the main focus of this chapter, other laws which included language provisions, or created language bodies, have been critical to the maintenance and promotion of Irish since the foundation of the southern state. Space permits only a cursory summary in this regard.

The pivotal role played by education in language policy is evident in the *Education Act, 1998*, which requires everyone involved in its implementation to promote a greater use of Irish at school and in the community. Supporting the use of Irish in Gaeltacht areas is set as an objective, as is responding to the choices of parents in relation to the language and cultural needs of the students. An advisory body, An Chomhairle um Oideachas Gaeltachta agus Gaelscolaíochta, has been established under the Act to support Irish-medium schooling. *The Universities Act, 1997* requires universities 'to promote the official languages of the State, with special regard to the preservation, promotion and use of the Irish language'.

Údarás na Gaeltachta was established by the *Údarás na Gaeltachta Act, 1979*, to further the economic, social, and cultural development of the Gaeltacht, with special emphasis on the 'preservation and extension of the use of the Irish language as the principal medium of communication' there. Foras na Gaeilge, established under the terms of the *Belfast Agreement* of 1998, has a broad mandate to promote Irish throughout the island of Ireland, through facilitating its use, advising governmental administrations and public bodies, undertaking supportive projects, conducting research, developing dictionaries and terminology, grant-aiding various language organizations, and supporting Irish-medium education and the teaching of Irish.

Provisions to encourage the use of Irish are included in the *Local Government Act, 2001*. Under the *Planning and Development Act, 2000*, relevant area development plans must include objectives for 'the protection of the linguistic and cultural heritage of the Gaeltacht including the promotion of Irish as the community language'.

INTERNATIONAL COMMITMENTS

Ireland has not signed the *European Charter for Regional or Minority Languages*. In respect of Irish, this is a perfectly reasonable position, since Article 1 of the Charter defines 'regional or minority languages' as languages which are, among other things, 'different from the official language(s) of that State'. The downside of this situation is that the Council of Europe's control mechanism – designed to monitor compliance with a view to recommending improvements in legislation, policy, and practices – is not available.

Ireland has ratified the *Framework Convention for the Protection of National Minorities*. While noting that this convention is not considered to apply to persons speaking Irish, the Advisory Committee in an opinion on Ireland, published in 2006, took the 'opportunity to welcome the positive measures taken in respect of this language, spoken by a minority of the population, in various fields, ranging from the media to education.' (ACFC/OP/II(2006)007, Council of Europe)

LEGISLATION IN NORTHERN IRELAND

For a long period after the establishment of the northern state, the Irish language had no official status there, and was explicitly excluded from the public arena. The 1737 act prohibiting the use of languages other than English in courts was presumed to be still in effect, and the *Public Health and Local Government (Miscellaneous Provisions) Act (Northern Ireland) 1949* required that street-name signs erected by local authorities should be in English only. The latter Act was modified by the *Local Government (Miscellaneous Provisions) Order 1995* which permitted a language other than English to be added to the signs. The last decade has seen the political landscape of the area transformed, with important language provisions put in place and envisaged.

Participants in the Multi-Party Agreement – the political component of the *Belfast Agreement* of 1998 – committed themselves to recognizing 'the importance of respect, understanding and tolerance in relation to linguistic diversity', including the Irish language and other languages. Irish is singled out for special treatment in a further paragraph which details the resolve of the British government to 'take resolute action to promote the language', promising among other things to encourage Irish-medium education and to explore ways of extending the availability of Irish-language television.

The British-Irish Agreement – the international component of the *Belfast Agreement* – was followed by parallel enactments in both jurisdictions in 1999 which, inter alia, established Foras na Gaeilge as the Irish-language agency of the North/South language body. Also arising out of the political rapprochement, the *Education (Northern Ireland) Order 1998* places a duty on the Department of Education to encourage and facilitate the development of Irish-medium education. In pursuit of this objective, the Department established a promotional body, Comhairle na Gaelscolaíochta, in 2000. On the issue of broadcasting, the British government established an Irish-language Broadcast fund in 2005, and, in the same year, the British Irish Intergovernmental Conference authorized the broadcast of the Irish-language television station, TG4, in Northern Ireland.

The British government made a commitment in the *St Andrews Agreement* of 2006 to 'introduce an Irish-language Act reflecting on the experience of Wales and Ireland and work with the incoming Executive to enhance and protect the development of the Irish language'.

In pursuit of this objective, the Department of Culture, Arts and Leisure published its *Consultation Paper on Proposed Irish language Act for Northern Ireland,* in December 2006 which sought views on the nature and content of possible Irish-language legislation. They reported that they had received 668 substantive responses to the consultation paper, and that the vast majority of those were in favour of introducing rights-based legislation. Instead of proceeding on that basis, they embarked on a further consultation, seeking views on proposed draft clauses by early June 2007. In the interim, in what was viewed as a backdown from a specific promise of an Irish-language act, the British government transferred responsibility for these matters to the Northern Ireland Executive Committee: the *Northern Ireland (St Andrews Agreement) Act 2006* required it 'to adopt a strategy setting out how it proposes to enhance and protect the development of the Irish language.'

The draft legislation proposed by the Department is centred on language schemes, based on the view that 'a progressive approach to minority language legislation can enable the communities involved to develop increased understanding of the cultural, educational and social benefits that may be gained through the promotion of an indigenous language'. An Irish-language Commissioner would be appointed. Irish could be permitted in courts, but disallowed 'in the interests of justice'. There is no reference to making Irish an official language, or to its use in the Assembly or in local government, or to its use in education or broadcasting. The second round of consultation resulted in the region of 11,000 written submissions. There is no assurance that the Assembly will adopt a language act along the lines proposed.

A signatory to the *Framework Convention for the Protection of National Minorities*, Britain was advised by the Council of Europe in 2002 that there was scope for further protection, 'notably concerning the use of Irish.' (ResCMN(2002)9, Council of Europe). Britain ratified the *European Charter for Regional and Minority Languages* in 2001, and made Irish subject to general protection, and to specific protections in various domains including education, judicial authority, public administration, and the media. Despite the advances made, the Council of Europe, having considered the evaluation report of the Committee of Experts, found it necessary to recommend in 2007 that the British authorities 'develop a comprehensive Irish-language policy, including measures to meet the increasing demand for Irish-medium education', and that they increase support for the printed media in Irish. (RecChL(2007)2, Council of Europe).

THE EUROPEAN UNION

In the negotiations leading to Ireland's accession to the European Communities in 1973, the Irish government sought an exceptional status for Irish. They asked that Irish be designated an official language, with this entailing only the translation of the founding Treaties and the accession Treaty. The existing member states, especially France, expressed strong opposition to any provision which would reduce the status of one official language vis-à-vis the others. They were not prepared to accept any modification of the existing language regime, embodied in *Council Regulation No 1/1958*, and are reported to have been astonished that Ireland would seek to exclude its national and first official language from that Regulation. The Irish government persisted, and the outcome was that authentic texts of the Treaties would be available in Irish, but that the language would not become an official or a working language of the Communities.

Ten new countries, bringing with them nine new official languages, were due to be admitted to membership of the EU during Ireland's Presidency in the first half of 2004. This political context was viewed as a favourable opportunity for collective action. A dynamic social movement developed which had as its goal the achievement of status for Irish as an official and working language of the European Union under *Regulation No 1*. The demand for change came from the ground up, and the generation of strategic support from the top down was actively pursued. The campaign was multifaceted, with national and international dimensions. In the end, the Irish government announced in July 2004 that it intended to seek official status for Irish. Once that decision was made, the government acted diligently in pursuit of what had become a national goal.

Acting unanimously in Council, in accordance with Treaty requirements, the Foreign Ministers of all twenty-five member states adopted a Regulation on 13 June 2005 which made Irish an official language of the EU. (*Council Regulation (EC) No 920/2005*). This status took effect on 1 January 2007. Since then, with the accession of Bulgaria and Romania, two further languages have been added. Article 1 of *Council Regulation No 1/1958* now reads as follows:

> The official languages and the working languages of the institutions of the European Union shall be Bulgarian, Czech, Danish, Dutch, English, Estonian, Finnish, French, German, Greek, Hungarian, Irish, Italian, Latvian, Lithuanian, Maltese, Polish, Portuguese, Romanian, Slovak, Slovenian, Spanish and Swedish.

This Article enshrines the fundamental principle of equality of these languages. From a linguistic perspective, it can be said that when Irish became an official and a working language, Ireland became a full member of the European Union.

The Treaties constitute the primary legislation of the EU, comparable to constitutional law at the national level. Article 314 of the *Treaty establishing the European Community* (EC Treaty) lists the languages in which the Treaty is drawn up, and states the basic principle that the texts in each of these languages are equally authentic, or have equal legal validity. The *Treaty on European Union*, the second of the fundamental treaties, has a similar provision. In theory, no single language is considered to be the source language, with the others seen as translations. The same principle applies to secondary legislation, ensuring that a high level of expertise is required in producing the various language versions. As we have seen, Irish became an authentic or a Treaty language on Ireland's accession. Article 21 of the EC Treaty provides that every citizen has the right to write to the institutions of the Union in any one of the Treaty languages, and to receive a reply in the same language.

Secondary legislation in the EU comprises a variety of instruments, especially Regulations, Directives, and Decisions. Of these, Regulations alone are directly applicable in all member states, without further action. *Regulation No 1/1958*, the basic legislation governing the languages of the institutions other than the Court of Justice, was the first Regulation to be adopted by the Council of Ministers in 1958. This Regulation, apart from the addition of languages upon accession of new member states, and of Irish in 2005, has remained unchanged ever since. Among other things, the legislation provides that Regulations, other documents of general application, and the Official Journal, be published in all of the official languages. The Court of Justice designated Irish an official language in 1973.

The new status of Irish has major implications for the viability and strength of the language and for its potential to continue to enrich the cultural heritage of Europe. The symbolic ramifications in terms of language acquisition and intergenerational transmission, the development of the language itself in new translation and interpretation contexts, and the newly acquired practical advantages for Irish citizens in securing employment and in the acknowledgement of their linguistic capital, all point to a more secure future for the Irish-language community.

Official status has direct consequences in employment. As a general rule, a good knowledge of one official language, and a satisfactory knowledge of a second, is a condition of employment for all EU positions. Irish may now be listed by candidates in fulfillment of this general condition. In the languages sector, competitions have been held for Irish-language proof-readers, translators, and secretaries, and all have attracted large numbers of applicants. The institutions also employ Irish-language interpreters and lawyer-linguists.

Members have the right to speak in the European Parliament in Irish. A transitional arrangement is in place which permits restrictions in the case of languages where interpreters are not available in sufficient numbers (A6-0391/2006, European Parliament). There is currently a shortage of qualified Irish-language conference interpreters. The onus is on the Irish government to ensure that qualified interpreters are available for employment. To date the government has sent small numbers of people to London for training. In light of the support systems available for participation in a European postgraduate conference interpreting programme, it would seem appropriate that the government, in collaboration with the universities, should arrange for the delivery of this training in at least one university in Ireland.

The Regulation which made Irish an official language of the EU introduced a temporary derogation limiting the amount of legislation which must be translated. The derogation deals exclusively with legislative acts, and for a period of five years requires the drafting and publication in Irish of only those Regulations adopted jointly by Parliament and Council. This represents a small but growing proportion of the acts. In contrast with legislative procedures in Ireland, the Presidents of these institutions cannot sign legislation until authentic versions are available in all of the official languages, including Irish.

When *Lingua* and other similar programmes were introduced, Ireland had to engage in specific negotiations in order to have Irish admitted. Now all cultural and educational programmes are available as of right, from the outset, to Irish-speakers and the Irish-language community. Specific measures such as Comenius, Leonardo da Vinci, and the 2003 *Action plan for language learning and linguistic diversity* are included. More recently, the 2006 *Action programme in the field of lifelong learning* includes funding for diverse language-learning initiatives, including teaching materials, teacher-training courses, and multilateral networks (2006 L327, Official Journal). Finally, the ambitious *Seventh Framework Programme (2007–2013)* provides wide-ranging opportunities for research activities designed to promote shared understanding and respect for Europe's linguistic and cultural identity and heritage (2006 L412, Official Journal).

Work is under way in translating the *Europa* website to Irish. Progress has been slow to date, with the level reached substantially below that which prevailed in the case of other languages upon their admission as official languages. Some institutions have suggested that their work in this area is voluntary because of the Irish derogation. This claim is without a secure basis in law. The provision of the website in all of the official languages derives ultimately from the equality principle inherent in Article 1 of *Regulation No 1/1958*, which is unaffected by the derogation in respect of legislative acts. Apart from timetable differences, the derogation for Maltese, in *Council Regulation (EC) No 930/2004*, was expressed in precisely the same words as the derogation for Irish, yet none of the institutions sought to delay the full implementation of *Regulation No 1/1958* in respect of Maltese on that basis. Vigilance on the part of the Irish government is necessary in various aspects of implementation, and specifically in relation to budgeting. For clarity, and in keeping with their broader constitutional obligations, it might be expected that the government will insist on ending the derogation when the review of its operation is undertaken before the end of 2010. In the meantime they will need to address translation and interpretation issues, and, as a gesture of goodwill, the translation of key sections of the *acquis communautaire* – community law – not yet available in Irish could be undertaken.

Within the broad structures of Irish and European language legislation, beneficial policies in relation to Irish can be devised and implemented. Language change is the art of the possible.

Glossary of Terms

Bord na Gaeilge: the statutory body established in 1978 to promote the Irish language. It was later subsumed into Foras na Gaeilge (see below).

(An) Caighdeán (Oifigiúil): the official, standardized form of the Irish language.

Department of Community, Rural and Gaeltacht Affairs: the Government Department with overall responsibility for the Gaeltacht and the Irish language.

Foras na Gaeilge: the agency established under the British-Irish Agreement Act, 1999, to promote the Irish language on an all-island basis.

Gaeltacht: a region (or, collectively, the regions) in which Irish is the everyday language. The plural is 'Gaeltachtaí'.

gaelcholáiste: an Irish-medium post-primary school. The plural is 'gaelcholáistí'.

gaelscoil(eanna): Irish-medium school(s), where the Irish language is the medium of instruction. Often used generically of Irish-medium education at primary and post-primary level, although a post-primary school is more accurately called a 'gaelcholáiste'. 'Gaelscoileanna' (with initial capital) is the name of the non-governmental organization which promotes Irish-medium education at primary and post-primary level.

Oireachtas: '(Houses of) the Oireachtas' refers to both houses of the Irish 'parliament' or legislature. Thus the state's legislation is referred to as 'Acts of the Oireachtas'. 'Oireachtas' is also the word used (sometimes 'Oireachtas na Gaeilge') to refer to the annual cultural festival for the Irish language.

TG4: the Irish-medium television channel established in 1996 and originally called 'Teilifís na Gaeilge' (often shortened to 'TnaG').

Údarás na Gaeltachta: the statutory body established in 1979 as the regional authority responsible for the economic, social and cultural development of the Gaeltacht.

Index of Proper Names

Due to their frequency, references to the Irish language or to the Gaeltacht are not included in this index. Titles of publications are in italics; titles of poems are in quotation marks.

Visit our on-line bookshop: www.coislife.ie